Penguin Books
Symbols of Australia

Mimmo Cozzolino and G. Fysh Rutherford

Mimmo Cozzolino was born at Herculaneum, Italy, in 1949. At the age of 11 he migrated to Australia with his parents.
He holds a Diploma in Graphic Design from Prahran CAE and co-founded All Australian Graffiti – an illustration and design studio. With them, he created *The Kevin Pappas Tear Out Postcard Book* (published by Penguin Books Australia).
Before working on *Symbols of Australia* full time, he lectured in design at Preston Institute of Technology. The recent birth of his daughter, Olivia, completed the migrant progression from old country to new.
Mimmo is currently freelancing as a graphic designer.

G. Fysh Rutherford (christened Graeme) was born at Kew, Melbourne, in 1947. In 1971 he entered advertising after writing the satirical comic strip 'Iron Outlaw' for *Nation Review*.
He assisted Mimmo and All Australian Graffiti on a number of projects including *The Kevin Pappas Tear Out Postcard Book*.
Fysh is currently employed as a creative group head at a Melbourne advertising agency.

Cover illustration by Geoff Cook

SYMBOLS of AUSTRALIA

EDITED AND WRITTEN BY MIMMO COZZOLINO WITH G. FYSH RUTHERFORD

Introduced by Geoffrey Blainey and Phillip Adams

Penguin Books Australia Ltd,
P.O. Box 257, Ringwood 3134, Victoria, Australia
Penguin Books Ltd,
Harmondsworth, Middlesex, England
Penguin Books,
625 Madison Avenue, New York, N.Y. 10022, U.S.A.
Penguin Books Canada Ltd,
2801 John Street, Markham, Ontario, Canada
Penguin Books (N.Z.) Ltd,
182-190 Wairau Road, Auckland 10, New Zealand

First published in 1980
This edition reprinted 1980
Simultaneously published by Cozbook, Melbourne

Designed by Mimmo Cozzolino

Cover illustration by Geoff Cook

Set in Century Old Style by The Dova Type Shop, Melbourne

Made and printed in Australia by
Hedges and Bell Pty Ltd, Maryborough, Victoria

CIP

Cozzolino, Mimmo.
Symbols of Australia.

Simultaneously published, Melbourne:
Cozbook.
ISBN 0 14 070094 3

I. Trade-marks - Australia - History.
I. Rutherford, G. Fysh, joint author.
II. Title.

602'.7

Australian Penguin symbol.
First applied to Australian
titles in 1963.

Dedicated to all the Australian artists
whose work created this book,
and to Olivia

Unsurpassed Australian Made.
G. Wolf. Clothing; 1915.

ACKNOWLEDGEMENTS

This book would not have been possible without the help, understanding and encouragement of many people.

I owe my deepest thanks to Chiara and Michele, my mother and father, for having had the courage and foresight to migrate to Australia, and to Sue, my wife, without whose understanding and help, I would not have been able to finish the book.

To Fysh Rutherford, who co-edited and co-wrote this book, I also owe my deep thanks. He brought rationality where there wasn't any and always worked hard to improve the book.

Thanks to Carmine, my brother, for carefully printing all the bromides for the original catalogue and, later, for the book.

To Sandra Blood, who typed the manuscript with care and speed, and to Grant Shallard who assembled the artwork with meticulousness and patience; to Martin Simons, the project photographer, and to my former studio associates Con Aslanis, Geoff Cook, Neil Curtis, Izy Marmur and Meg Williams, who, together with Ross Goode, David Hughes and Annette Whitlock sensivitely retouched many of the trademarks; to Trevor Flett and Flett Henderson & Arnold for their production and design advice: thanks!

Special thanks are also due to Elizabeth Nathan, research officer, Australian Archives, Canberra; to Ross Gibbs, State Library of Victoria; to Kieran O'Dowd of the Melbourne Patents, Trademarks and Designs Sub-office, and all the other staff from the forementioned organizations.

The following people and/or organizations have helped me in a multitude of ways – thanks to each and every one of you: Peter Abbott, Felton Grimwade & Bickford Pty Ltd; Phillip Adams; Rod Amos, CBA Bank; Helen Anastasiou; George Armstrong, Carlton Football Club; J. M. Armstrong, The Local Government Association of Queensland and all member Councils; Australian National Gallery; Melvie M. Banks, Master Ladies Hairdressers' Hairworkers' and Cosmeticians' Association of Victoria; M. Barberis, Nicholas Pty Ltd; David and Jantie Barnes; Elizabeth Barry; Richard Beck; A. V. T. Benner, Bank of New South Wales; Dr Lorraine Bennett, Life. Be in it co-ordinator, Department of Youth Sport and Recreation, Victoria; Garth Beveridge, P.B.L. Marketing Pty Ltd; Elizabeth Birk, Kiwi International Company Pty Ltd; Geoffrey Blainey; J. L. Bragg, Davis Gelatine (Australia) Pty Ltd; Michael Browning, the XII Commonwealth Games Australia (1982) Foundation Limited; Gavin Buchanan, Michelin; E. Bryden-Brown, Taronga Zoo; Stewart Byfield; Ken Campbell, Federal Council, Master Hairdressers of Australia; Ken Cato, Cato Hibberd Design Pty Ltd; David Catterns, The Australian Copyright Council; Anthony Chan; Andrew Clarke; G.J. Coles and Coy Ltd; Annette Constable, Traders Pty Ltd; Lawton W. Cooke, Sidney Cooke Ltd; Des Cooper, Victorian Dairy Industry Authority; Gordon Cooper, Keep Australia Beautiful Council; Marie Coote; Heather Cox; Tony Cozzolino; Paul Craft, Paraphernalia; F. W. Cramer, Samuel Taylor; George Crompton, Victorian Beer Label Collectors' Society; R. W. Davidson, Reserve Bank of Australia; Philip Davin; George Derham; Christina de Water; Rosanna Di Risio; Richard Doggett, Richmond Football Club; Keith Dunstan; Hank Ebes; Hugh Edwards; Stewart Edwards; Jan Elliott; Garry Emery; Malcom Enright; Bill Faulkner, Ross Faulkner Pty Ltd; Jules Feldmann, St Kilda Football Club; Len Gallaway, Selex Decal Pty Ltd; Geelong Football Club; Roger Gibbons, Bryant & May; Lindsay Graham; S. D. Gramp, G. Gramp & Sons Ltd; Alan Grant; Ian Green; W. E. Green (Weg); Betty Greenhatch; Syd Guglielmino; John Gunn, Qantas Airways Limited; Bronny and Tim Handfield; Margaret Harrington, Carlton & United Breweries Ltd; G. Hoffman, The Northern Territory Local Government Association; J. Holko, Herbert Adams Pty Ltd; Fred S. Holt, Australia and New Zealand Banking Group Limited; Elizabeth Honey; Honours Secretariat, Department of Administrative Services, Commonwealth of Australia; John Hooker; Jenny Hopwood, Rentokil Australia Ltd; D. J. Horsnell, Rowntree Hoadley Ltd; Christine Hughes; J. M. Hullick, Local Government Association of South Australia Incorporated; Huveneers Pty Ltd; B. R. Johnson, Municipal Association of Tasmania; C. W. Jones, Commonwealth Banking Corporation; Peter Jones, Arnott's Biscuits Pty Ltd; Shirley Jones; T. L. Jones, Pelaco Ltd; Frank Kenealy; Kutt Skinner Bennett Advertising Pty Ltd; Barry Larkham, New South Wales Rugby League; Sue Lebasi, Fisheries and Wildlife Division, Ministry for Conservation, Victoria; David Lester; Vane Lindesay; John Long; R. Longhurst, John Oxley Library; W. R. Lord, The Royal Aero Club of New South Wales; J. H. Love, State Library of South Australia; R. McConnell, Essendon Football Club; Jim McCoy, Peters Ice Cream; Chris Mack, Victorian Football League Properties; Jim McKay, Rosella Foods Pty Ltd; R. W. McKinnon, J.C. Hutton Pty Ltd; John and Shirley McLaren; Ann McLean; Kate McLoughlin, National Film Archive, National Library of Australia; Colin Macmillan, Rowntree Hoadley Ltd; Eric Maguire; Mandalis Taverna; Les Mason; A. M. Martin, F.H. Faulding & Co Ltd; E. J. Matuschka, Dalgety Australia Ltd; Gary Max and Kevin Merrigan, Carlton & United Breweries Ltd; N. T. G. Miles, Local Government Association of N.S.W., Shires Association of N.S.W.; Mitchell Library; Lyn Morrison, Olympic Consolidated Industries Ltd; J. H. Moser, Lever & Kitchen Pty Ltd; Ann Munari; Helen and Peter Murphy; The Myer Emporium; Neil Newnham, The Herald and Weekly Times Limited; Frank Nichol, Acme Studio; Robina Norton; H. W. Nunn, Public Record Office, Victoria; M. O'Connor, The National Bank of Australasia Ltd; Terry Oliver; Vicky Palmerston; Bill Patey, State Savings Bank of Victoria; Ian Pawsey, Municipal Association of Victoria; E. W. Peatt, Mac's Cyder Pty Ltd; David Peel, Melbourne Football Club; H. W. Powell; J. Pullar, Nutting & Young; Philip Quirk; Jim Rae; M. Reynolds; Wayne Rhodes; Max Ripper; T. J. P. Roberts, Rosella Foods Pty Ltd; Ann Robinson; G. P. Russell, Confederation of Australian Industry; A. E. Ryan, Repco Limited; Vi and Ron Rutherford; Brian Sadgrove; Stuart Sayers; Cal Salton, Bond's Wear; Paul Shaw; Pat Sheddick, Australian Match Cover Collectors Society, Melbourne; Syd Sherrin, T. W. Sherrin; Ken G. Schultz, The Returned Services League of Australia; B. J. Simpson, Amalgamated Wireless (Australasia) Ltd; N. S. Snow, Australian Dairy Corporation; South Melbourne Football Club; St John Lawrence Burrows; Richard Statham; K. J. Stevenson, Speedo Knitting Mills Pty. Ltd; Alex Stitt, Al et Al Pty Ltd; Frank Strahan, University Archivist, Melbourne; W. P. Stretton, Cinesound Productions Pty Limited; Bill Surenne; Alex Szman; Bruce Taylor, H.C. Sleigh Ltd; John Thompson; John P. Thompson, Trans-Australia Airlines; Richard Tipping; Bill Troedel, Ark Offset Printers Pty Ltd; Warwick Turner, Swan Hill Pioneer Settlement Authority; Dennis Veal; Renato Vecchies; Eric Victor-Perdraut; Victorian Railways; Murray Walker; David Wanless, Hawthorn Football Club; Tony Ward; Ian Watson; P. R. Wayman, Arnott-Brockhoff-Guest Pty Ltd; Jack Wheat, A.W. Allen Ltd; Ken Wilkes; Peter Williams, Kraft Foods Ltd; Geoff Wilson, *Butter Fat and Solids*; R. Woods, Bushells Pty Ltd; Clare Worthington; Kevin Zervos; Frank Ziino.

Finally, I thank anyone whom I may have unintentionally omitted.

M.C.

CONTENTS

Introduction 9
Behind the label by Geoffrey Blainey 11
Beneath the lino by Phillip Adams 13
Notes on the text 15

Book I: REFLECTIONS 17

1. ALL UNDER ONE ROOF 19
   The map 20
   The States 24
   The landmarks 25
   The name 26
2. AUSTRALIANS FIRST 27
   Coats of arms 28
   The Southern Cross 30
   The Anzacs 31
3. DINKUM BONZA COO-EE 33
   Coo-ee 34
   Local language 35
   Registered ideas 36
   The blokes 37
   Part of the lingo 38
   Puns 39
   Parwill – the pun that didn't work 44
4. FAMOUS SINCE CAPTAIN COOK 45
   'Abo Brand' 46
   The boomerang 48
   A White Australia 49
   Jolly niggerboys 50
5. NATIVE COMPANIONS – FAUNA 51
   Koalas 52
   Kangaroos 54
   Possums and platypuses 57
   Dingoes, wombats and new breeds 58
6. NATIVE COMPANIONS – AVIFAUNA 59
   Kookaburras 60
   Emus 62
   Lyrebirds, magpies and cockatoos 63
7. NATIVE COMPANIONS – FLORA 64
   Black boys, wattles and waratahs 64
   Gums 65

Book II: OBSERVATIONS 67

8. DON'T WORRY 69
   About the sheep 70
   About the pests 71
   About the rabbit plague 72
   About cures and manures 74
   About the chooks 76
   All around the farm 77
   About the prickly pear 78
9. THE HALF BACK 79
   On glue 80
   On industry 81
   On paint 85
   On transport 86
   On lubricants and fuels 88
   On Qantas 90
   On TAA 91
   On banking 92
   On stencils 93
10. EXPORT QUALITY 95
    Roller flour 95
    Butter marks 97
11. EATMORE 99
    Tea and coffee 100
    Biscuits 103
    Drinks and cordials 105
    Wine 108

From a post card back printed by Donald Taylor Collotype Coy Ltd, Adelaide; 1905.

CONTENTS

Beer 109
Flour 111
Dough 114
Cereal and macaroni 115
General foods 116
Salt and seafood 117
Pork 118
Nothing to argue about 119
Dairy and poultry produce 120
Rosella – the Saucy Bird 121
Sauce, pickles and soup 122
Jam, jelly and honey 123
Fruit 124
Ice cream 125
Lollies 126
Nuts 128

12. THEY FIT 129
Hats and umbrellas 130
Boots and shoes 131
All over 133

13. MARSOAPIAL VIEWS 137
Of cleaning and candles 138
Of toiletries 141
Of polishes 142
Of boot and shoe polish 143
Of insecticides 145
Of pest control 146
Of matches 147
Of sewing and stewing 149
All around the house 150

14. BE IN IT 151
Toys and sports gear 152
Footy gear 153
Footy 154
Rugby 156
Music 157
Movies 158
Reading 159
Smoking 161

15. CUR-EM-QUICK 163
For anything 164
For foot care 169
For tooth decay 170

APPENDIXES
I Local Government seals and shields 171
II Foreign marks using Australian symbolism 172
III Multi-nationals before it was a dirty word 174
IV Foreign thoughts 176
V Being there 178

Index 180

THE SEARCH CONTINUES . . . 190
CALL FOR ENTRIES 192

Boomerang Taxi Service Co., Brisbane; 1945.

INTRODUCTION

Trademarks are a symbol of a culture. They are a country's distilled history. The marks in this book were selected to show, among other things, the more obvious symbols of Australia over one hundred years.

What, for me, started out to be a fairly straightforward design project, turned into an historical revelation. The discovery was a very personal experience. It was also an affirmation of a set of symbols which, as a migrant, I had slowly built up as representing intrinsic Australia – some profound, others less so, but all of them initially foreign to someone coming from a different culture.

They say that converts speak the loudest. As a convert to Australia, I, subconsciously perhaps, felt a need to demonstrate to myself and to others that I was assimilating well into my new culture. Through trademarks, I had found a simple way to prove it.

To my generation, migrant or native, the same search for affirmation of who we are and where we are going as a nation, has been visibly occurring since the early seventies, when the spell of the Menzies Era was broken by Whitlam. Even migrants received a new deal: they did not have to assimilate anymore; they could now quietly integrate!

As well as being a source of reference, of visual delights, and, to my generation, a record of quaint slices of life from the past, I hope that the symbols in this book may also, by linking us with this past, give us confidence in our search for independence, and faith to determine our own future.

Mimmo Cozzolino
Melbourne

Burns, Philp & Co. Ltd, Brisbane.
Clothing; 1917.

BEHIND THE LABEL
by Geoffrey Blainey.

A lost Australia has been found in the last fifteen or twenty years. Folk songs and slang, old buildings, bottles and bedsteads, old Australian paintings and films and books have been appreciated afresh. And in this book Mimmo Cozzolino shows us, for the first time, how Australian trademarks were a mirror of people's dreams, ambitions, and daily life.

Just as the Commonwealth designed its own coat of arms and flag, so thousands of firms designed their own slogans and symbols – in short their trademarks. The rise of the trademark was mainly the result of the industrial revolution and the widening range of products made in factories. Trademarks were also multiplied by a change which has barely reached the history books – the packaging revolution. Whereas in 1850 many households in Australia made soap, candles, clothes, medicines, jam, bread and butter in their own kitchen, in 1900 the factories increasingly made these goods, selling them under distinctive brands and trademarks. In 1850 a general store sold most of its goods straight from the packing cases, vats, chests and barrels and then transferred them to the customers' baskets, bags, containers and billies, but more and more goods in 1900 were sold in individual bottles, tins, jars and other labelled containers.

As the standard of living increased, people could afford to buy a wider variety of products. Bicycles and sewing machines and other innovations entered the market: being almost identical they needed a trademark to show that they were not. Literacy increased, and advertising became an industry. In the era before radio and film, the printed word and the painted picture dominated advertising; and the typical trademark combined the two.

Trademarks were not widely used until the second half of the nineteenth century. In 1862 an English law made the fraudulent forging of a trademark a criminal offence. Between the 1860s and the 1880s the various Australian parliaments enacted their first laws to register trademarks, thus curbing those backyard manufacturers who had found it profitable to copy the labels of well-known products. In Melbourne as late as 1874 a maker of perfumes and soaps issued large advertisements warning the public that his labels were being copied by competitors. 'Beware of imitations' was a warning often made by makers of popular products. The registering and protecting of trademarks was a simple answer to these commercial pirates, and from the old public registers come most of the trademarks reproduced in this book.

The trademarks reflect changing customs and attitudes, ways of leisure and ways of work. A century ago the average Australian drank more tea than did the average citizen of any other country, and tea was widely advertised in many brands. The words of 'Waltzing Matilda' were first popularised in the advertisements for a brand known as 'Billy Tea'. Country people travelling in the train to Melbourne saw the city coming closer because every mile a coloured enamelled plate announced that it was so many miles to the home of Griffiths' Tea. Boots were a strong source of trademarks because most men walked long distances in the course of a week and did work which demanded strong boots. As boots and shoes were expensive, boot polish was vital and gave rise to some of the best known trademarks. Indeed at one time 'Nugget', the trademark for one brand of shoe polish, became the common word for shoe polish in many parts of Australia.

These commercial signs captured the excitement of great events. Gold rushes still fired the imagination of Australians, and so gold-mining terms were popular in commercial trademarks. Words such as 'digger' and 'nugget' were used again and again. Allen's the confectioner made 'Gold Nuggets', and a rival made 'Old Gold' chocolate. A digger panning for gold was the trademark of a large Bendigo maker of jams and pickles. Overseas firms trading in Australia in the era between 1900 and 1914 liked to use gold in their trademarks, and an American tobacco was called 'Welcome Nugget' and an Austrian brand of matches was called 'The Nugget of the Southern Seas'.

The word 'Australia' did not appear on many trademarks until the eve of the creation of the Commonwealth. After 1901 a map of Australia appeared on dozens of trademarks. One early trademark embodying a map of Australia was registered by a Melbourne

The Nugget Polish Co. Ltd, Melbourne.
Leather polish; 1909.

photographer. Facing that difficulty which a host of commercial artists would later face – do we include Tasmania or save a little space – he found his own spectacular solution. In his trademark he moved Tasmania two thousand miles to the west where it could be neatly moored just off the south-west corner of the continent. One hopes that the photographs he took were truer to life.

The new Commonwealth gave birth to scores of trademarks on which stood native animals – even the dingo had his day. The First World War was almost as fertile for new trademarks. The word 'digger' acquired a new meaning. Appeals to patriotism filled tins and boxes. 'Our Wounded Hero Brand' went so far as to depict a one-legged digger. In 1915, the year of Anzac, that trademark was so blatant that it was rejected by the government. In the same year thousands of Australian soldiers camped near the pyramids before sailing from Egypt to Gallipoli. Accordingly a Goulburn manufacturer called his brand of shoes 'Pyramid Girl'. One wonders whether the women of Goulburn, sensing what the pyramid girls were doing in Australian tents, boycotted the shoes.

Curiously, there are few appeals to sex in the trademarks in this book. At first glance the trademark of Parson's Starch, registered in 1903, hints at restrained sex appeal. It shows a woman wearing a white ground-rustling dress, beneath which peeps the tip of one shoe. But she is called 'A White Australian' – an appeal to race rather than sex in that decade when the White Australia policy was shaped. Women shoppers must have bought most of the white starch which was used daily for stiffening clothes; and a starch advertisement was unlikely to have been designed in the hope of titillating men.

Many of the trademarks have a simplicity which borders on the naive. A brand of shoe-polish was called 'Sparkling Wine'. An eye medicament of the 1920s was registered as 'Mallee Eye Drops'. In the era when many people spoke in rhyming slang the simple play on words was central to some trademarks. In the early 1920s, after the visit to Australia of the Prince of Wales, the Swan Brewery in Perth registered the trademark of one beer as the 'Prince of WA ALES'. In the 1930s the trademark of one medical potion, known as Kure-ettes, showed two clergymen – obviously curates. Although simple plays on words were relatively common, trick spelling (e.g. 'rite' instead of 'right') seems to have been uncommon in trademarks until recent times. It may well be that in the last century, when illiteracy was a serious problem, trick spelling was deemed a serious offence, for it could easily mislead adults who were painfully learning how to spell. Furthermore, at a time when so many adults could not spell correctly, trick spelling was more likely to be interpreted as evidence that the owner of the trademark was illiterate rather than clever.

The trademark is valuable as a barometer of nationalism. While much has been written about early nationalism in the labour movement, less has been written about the nationalism of merchants, shopkeepers and factory owners. And yet both kinds of nationalism were important, and it may well be that the nationalism of the marketplace was far more influential in the 1890s and early 1900s. One source of this influence was the trademark, which thrived in the mass media – the daily newspaper, shop window, tobacco tin, and the billboard. We forget that the billboards on railway stations and city streets were mass media in the era before radio and television, and that these advertising hoardings were the shrines of the trademark. Indeed commercial awareness of the value of these insignia influenced the new Commonwealth's own insignia. In the national competition for an Australian flag in 1901, most of the prize-money came from the magazine *The Review of Reviews* and from Havelock Tobacco. The Southern Cross which appeared on the new flag had already appeared in many well-known trademarks.

This first book on Australian trademarks displays imagination, flair, and a feel for the past. Mimmo Cozzolino would not dream of calling himself a historian; but he is.

Geoffrey Blainey
University of Melbourne
June 1980

Little Boy of Manly.
J. Gillespie & Co., Sydney.
Food; 1899. See 127(o).

BENEATH THE LINO
by Phillip Adams.

How does one define Mimmo Cozzolino, the extraordinary young man responsible for this book? He's not really the author, yet he's far more than an editor. I think I'll settle for a Trade Marxist.

Consider the eerie parallels . . . while Mimmo was born at Herculaneum in 1949, within the shadow of Vesuvius, I was born here, in 1939, within the shadow of the Dandenongs. Well, within a 60-minute drive.

Mimmo spent his childhood at the Herculaneum diggings, peeking under the black curtains at the graffiti of a mythic figure with an enormous phallus. Meanwhile, he studied Latin.

I spent my childhood at the Kew tip, searching through the layers of refuse for interesting artifacts. Such as Mickey Mouse mantels, old car batteries and Marchant's lemonade bottles which were worth threepence at the milk bar. Meanwhile, I studied Latin.

These days, I frequently dart off to Italy where I snuffle into the Tuscan topsoil in the hope of finding the broken shards of an Etruscan chamber pot. In fascinating juxtaposition, Mimmo has established himself as the leading archaeologist of Australian advertising, and is frequently seen peeling the lino from old kitchen floors, in the hope of discovering some yellowed newspaper that, in turn, will yield an undiscovered Abo brandname.

It is well known that every intelligent, educated person with a refined sensibility despises and detests advertising, regarding all who toil for Mammon as the moral equivalents of used-car salesmen and the social equals of lepers. Yet *old* advertising is different. Already 1960s TV commercials have lost their commercial sting, metamorphosising into the iconography of nostalgia. Like popular songs, faded photographs and old Boomerang Songsters, they give us a sense of our past, reminding us of what went on beneath the newspaper headlines and the epic concerns of academic historians. Like Carter at the tomb of Tut, Mimmo takes us into forgotten times. And as he blows the dust from his invaluable collection of engravings and scraper-boards, the counterpart to Tut's priceless jetsam, our earliest tycoons and financial pharaohs live again.

Australians are very *embarrassed* about patriotism. Amongst most of my Labor-voting colleagues, it's been renounced since the Kerr coup. Yet I defy any Oztralian to turn Mimmo's pages without feeling the goose bumps (if not the goose steps) of nationalism. True, many of the symbols are racist or involve appalling puns. Yet somehow they seem infinitely preferable to those of the 1980s where the overwhelming majority of brands on our TV screens or supermarket shelves are alien. Or to be more specific, American. To hell with Colonel Sanders – give me Ballarat Bertie any time. And I'd love to see Mimmo's gun-toting kangaroo give Mickey Mouse, Esso's tiger and Uniroyal's steel cat their marching orders.

But enough of this tub thumping. Let me tell you about Mimmo. Twenty years ago, his parents decided to migrate to Argentina, only to discover that immigration to that country had been cancelled. They subsequently chose Australia because it was 'the second furtherest place to migrate to'. On arrival at Port Melbourne, they were immediately plonked in a cattle train to Bonegilla migrant camp where they suffered from both AC and DC culture shock. It seems the camp was run by a German who'd learnt to strut his stuff with the SS.

Mimmo spent the next five years trying to learn English which he describes as 'a funny language'. His father, a printer by trade, is still trying.

To the general dismay of parents, relatives and teachers, Mimmo enrolled at Prahran College, studying art and design. In his final year he picked up a $1000 prize for winning the Australian section of an international Sugar Mark competition. Thus began his commitment to Trade Marxism.

I first met Mimmo when he was in partnership with a young Greek named Con Aslanis. Their company was called 'All Australian Graffiti' and was motived by 'a mad desire by two crazy wogs to prove themselves in a WASP industry.' In the past immigrants like William Dampier and James Cook had discovered Australia. In the early 1970s, Mimmo and Con discovered it all over again.

In *Symbols of Australia* Mimmo

Kerr's Shares.
Tattersall tickets vendor,
Hobart; 1934.

confronts Australians with a host of ancient hieroglyphs which, I think, add weight to my hypothesis that this nation was founded by ancient Egyptians who dropped off on their way to South America. (In South America they were known as the Aztecs: here, the Anzacs.) Their arrival, in small craft, is celebrated each year in the Henley Regatta on the Yarra, which earned its name from the ceremonial cry of the Anzacs . . . 'Yea! Ra!'. This ritual would have been observed by the high priest standing on the steps of their pyramid, the Shrine of Remembrance, so reminiscent of Cheops, soaring above the Nile.

Rather than directing you to specific hieroglyphs, I will let you enjoy a voyage of discovery. And if you're feeling hot and sweaty by page 141, fear not – you'll be rejuvenated by that aromatic shandy (the quintessence of prickly pear) Eau de Queensland.

Phillip Adams
June 1980

Unsurpassed Australian Made.
J. H. Sharwood, Melbourne.
Footwear; 1917.

NOTES ON THE TEXT

We believe that this is a picture book. But it is a picture book with a story to tell. In symbols, characters, words and slogans. All contained within the individual trademarks. When arranged chronologically, they reflect the history, the values, the development and the nationalism that has gone into building an Australian heritage.

Their authors are the forgotten individuals who commissioned them, and the unsung artists who created them. Although many of these marks may now seem flippant or trivial, there was a time when each one was thought about, discussed and paid for. Our notations merely enlarge their story by giving the reader a better perspective on the role and source of individual marks.

Unfortunately, the real history of most trademarks is lost in the discarded guard books of printers and advertising agencies, or it is seldom recorded in corporate archives.

Method of selection:
In making our choice of visual material, we used a definition of a trademark that is, perhaps, wider than traditionally accepted. To us a trademark is any image, word, symbol, colour, emblem, coat of arms, shield, seal, signature, slogan, label, package, object, jingle, or personality which is presented and used consistently over a period of time so as to be recognised and associated with a product, service, manufacturer, organisation, or person.

The material selection was based on our personal preference. We have not offered a complete representation of all major Australian companies. A few, in fact, are conspicuous by their absence. The material was primarily chosen for its visual or verbal interest, and to a minor extent, for its historical relevance. In essence, if we liked it, or we liked what it reflected, it was included.

The marks in this book can be broadly classified as:
1. Marks that contain obvious Australian symbolism, e.g.: nationalism, maps, flora, language, landmarks.
2. Marks for products that, although not containing any specific Australian symbolism, have become part of our consumer heritage, e.g.: Aspro, Arnott's, Vegemite, Minties, Aeroplane Jelly and Foster's Lager.
3. Marks for unknown products or marks lacking in Australian symbolism but representing absurd, humorous or obscure thinking that was an integral part of the 'try anything once' attitude of a developing nation.

Sources:
Our research covered four specific areas:
1. Directly from packaging, posters and advertising or correspondence with companies and individuals.
2. The State Library of Victoria for periodicals and newspapers.
3. The Commonwealth Government Patents, Trademarks and Designs Office for applications of trademarks from 1906 to the present.
4. The Australian Archives, Canberra, for colonial registers of trademarks prior to 1906.

Span:
The earliest surviving records of registered trademarks are the individual colonial registers. Laws relating to the registration of trademarks were enacted in South Australia in 1863, Queensland and Tasmania in 1864, New South Wales in 1865, Victoria in 1876 and Western Australia in 1885. We therefore set the opening date of research at 1860. We found, however, very little value or interest in any of the colonial registers before the 1880s. Even newspapers and journals from the same period had little to offer. The closing date of 1960 marked the introduction, to Australia, of a new wave graphic approach to trademarks. This date has been adhered to; the only exception being the inclusion of current marks which show a design progression.

Dating:
The date of a trademark shown in the text is, unless otherwise stated, the date of *application* for registration. But, because registration is not required by law, many trademarks were in use long before they were registered. For example, page 81 would have read:

> (c) Evenden's Spring Head.
> Sidney Cooke Pty Ltd,
> Melbourne.
> Nails; 1906.

Our correspondence with Sidney Cooke Ltd

revealed that this product was patented in 1892 and the trademark was used as early as 1895. The delay in applying for registration was probably due to Sidney Cooke's perceiving no need to register the mark as they felt the product was adequately protected by the patent.

When the new Commonwealth Trademarks Register was introduced in 1906, the resultant publicity would have made them revise their thinking and apply for registration.

Wherever possible we have verified dates supplied by individuals or companies, but inconsistencies may still arise. In such cases we would appreciate readers' comments.

Structure:

The book is divided into two sections. The first, 'Reflections', contains marks with a unique Australian flavour. The second, 'Observations', contains marks arranged in product classifications. Each sub-section is arranged chronologically, the only exception being specific corporate histories or pages requiring special design consideration. With individual entries the usual text format is:

Product or brand name	(f) Gum Tree.
Individual, company or organisation owning the mark, or the applicant for its registration (We have used the earliest title even though this may not be the current title.)	J. Wardle & Co., Adelaide.
Product description or use, and the year of application	Metals; 1915.
Notation	This trademark features the 'Old Gum-tree', Glenelg, where the establishment of South Australia was proclaimed in 1836.

The visuals at the foot of the text column are either contemporary, of special interest, or of a supportive nature.

Conclusions:

Australian commercial symbology is sadly overlooked by most Australians. The Trademarks Office now accepts mere photostats as possibly the only surviving record of a trademark. Corporations shed their identities with increasing regularity, discarding them without record. And commercial artists continue to work without personal credit.

As we have already stated, this book was written by the forgotten businessmen who commissioned the trademarks and the unknown artists who created them. It is our hope that after reading *their* book, individuals will be inspired to keep detailed corporate archives ensuring a comprehensive record of this revealing area of Australia's heritage.

G.F.R. & M.C.

GUMLYPTA
COO-EE
NATIONAL
O.K.
PERTH
BRISBANE
ADELAIDE
SYDNEY
MELBOURNE
Aussie
Independent
Fairisle
AUSTRALITE
TUNGSTEN
A.N.P

Book I: REFLECTIONS

(a)

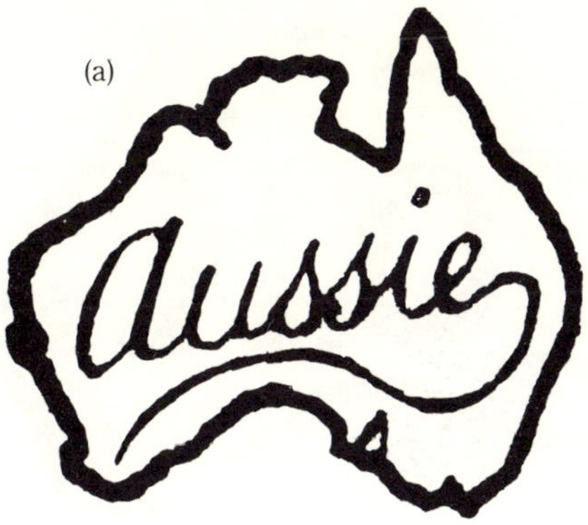

(b)

(c)

1. ALL UNDER ONE ROOF.

With an area of 7,682,300 square kilometres, Australia is the largest island in the world. It is slightly smaller than the United States of America. About 25 times the size of the British Isles. And is the only continent to contain one country.

This awareness of a nation under one roof has dominated many of Australia's trademarks.

(a) Aussie.
National Trustees Executors and Agency Co. of Australasia Ltd, Melbourne.
Pianos and organs; 1924.

(b) Independent.
Lukes Ltd.
Machine and motor accessories; 1926.

(c) Fairisle.
Frieze Bros. Pty Ltd, Melbourne.
Articles of clothing; 1940.

(d) Patent Asphaltum Co. of New South Wales, Sydney.
Bitumen roofing felt; 1901.

(e) Berts Soft Drinks.
Bertshell Pty Ltd, Arncliffe, NSW.
Cordial and carbonated waters; 1969.

(d)

(e)

All under one roof

The map.

The simplest and most common method of representing an Australian company is to place a map of Australia in its trademark. From a design point of view, the map is self-contained, easy to draw and instantly identifiable. Aspects that have all been exploited in a multitude of ways.

(a) Pacific.
The Standard Shoe & Leather Co., Adelaide.
Boots and shoes; 1906.

(b) Sunbeams.
Gustave Rypens, Sydney.
Raw and partly prepared wool; 1906.

(c) O.K.
Orme, Keigwin & Co., Sydney.
Fermented liquors and spirits; 1907.

(d) Bryta.
The Healtheries Mfg. Co., Sydney.
Metal polish; 1908.

(e) Kaldo.
The Kaldo Mfg. Co., Geelong, Vic.
Refrigerating paints; 1909.

(f) Ward Bros., Melbourne.
Sewing machines; 1909.

(g) Thomas Mackenzie Kirkwood, Melbourne.
Collars, hats, hosiery; 1910.

(h) Cozmon.
Cohen & Sons, NSW.
Costumes; 1911.

(i) Early Riser.
Lichtner Ltd, Sydney.
Self raising flour; 1911.

(j) Webb & Webb, Melbourne.
Photographers; c. 1900.
Because of its extremity, Tasmania is left off most trademarks incorporating a map of Australia. Webb & Webb discovered that, if Tasmania was placed under Western Australia, the complete Australian map fitted neatly into a box design.

(a)

(b)

(c)

(d)

(e)

(f)

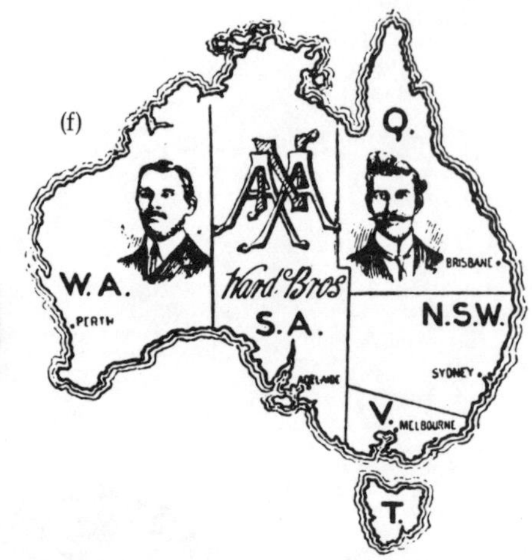

(g)

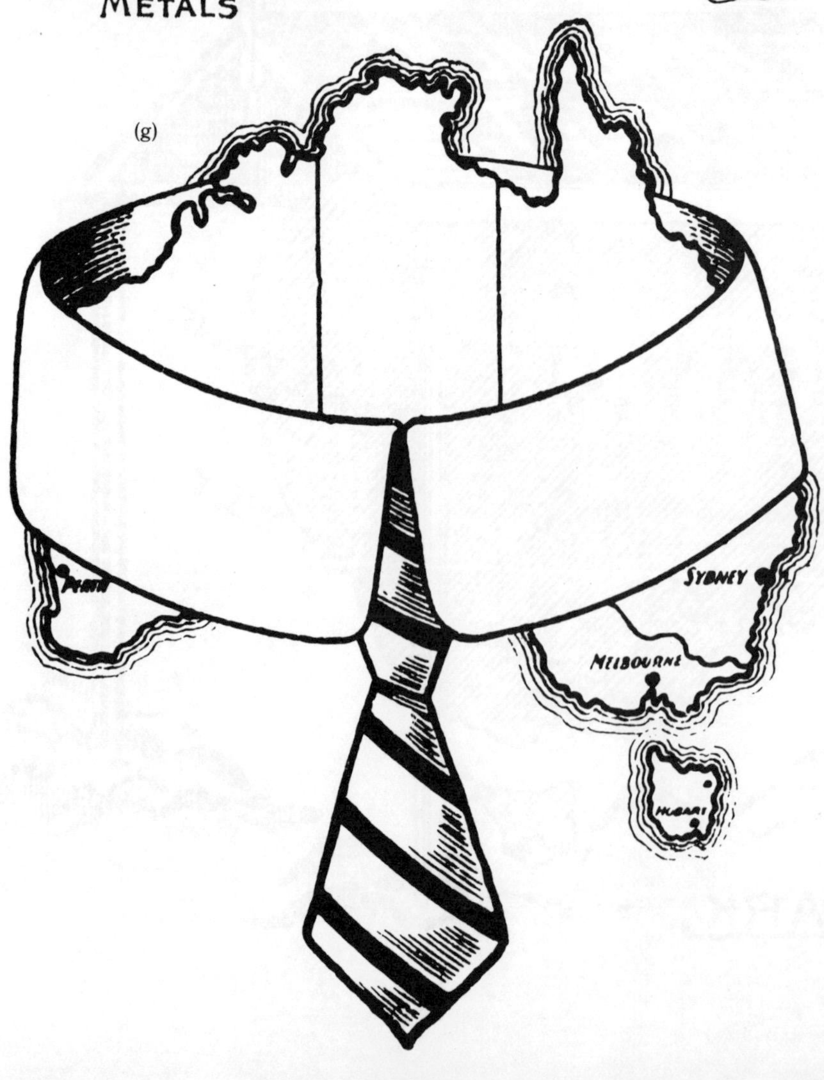

(h)

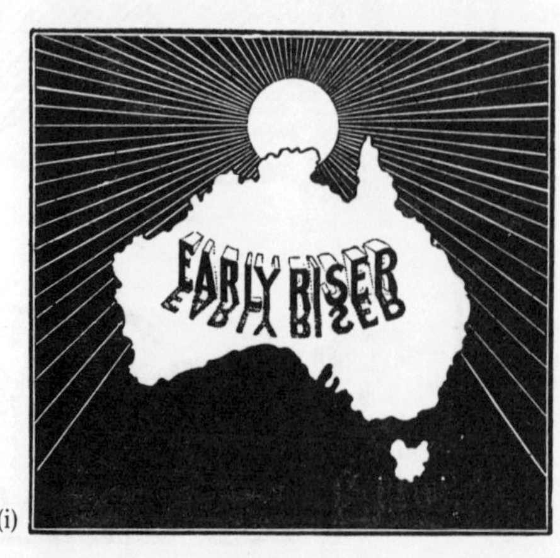

(i)

(j)

(a)

(b)

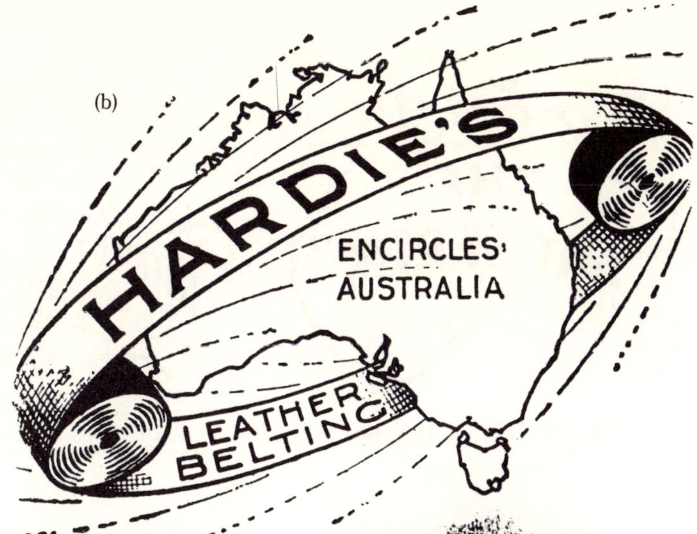

(c)

(d)

(e)

(f)

(g)

(h)

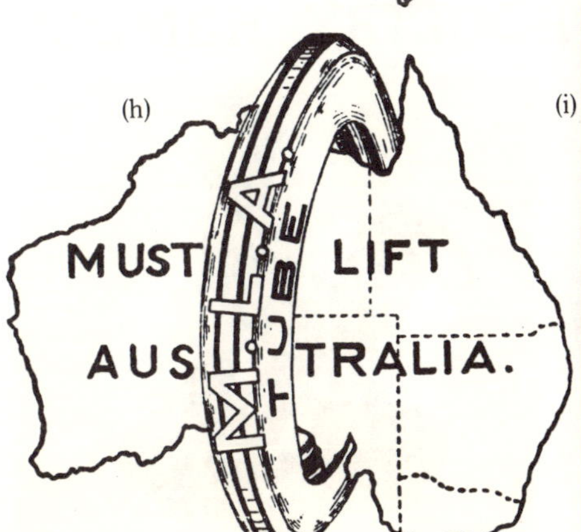

(i)

(j)

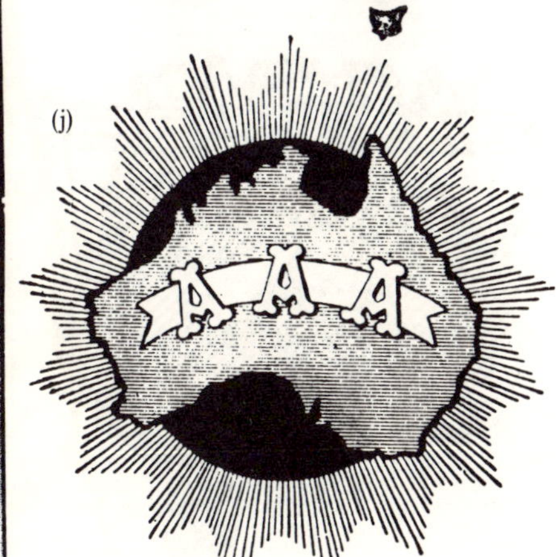

(k)

All under one roof

The map.

(a) Lion Brand.
Downs & Sons Pty Ltd, Melbourne.
Rope; 1916.
(b) James Hardie & Co. Pty Ltd, Melbourne
Leather belting; 1919.
(c) Gluca.
Mills Industries Ltd, NSW.
Glue; 1922.
(d) Olofone
Olof Henry Olson, Sydney.
Talking machines; 1922.
(e) The Australian Vitamite Co., Sydney.
Agricultural chemicals; 1923.
(f) The Katoomba Thousand.
Edgar Booth, Katoomba, NSW.
Lottery; 1923.
(g) Swann Mfg., Sydney.
Disinfectants; 1924.
(h) M.L.A. Tube – Must Lift Australia.
C. H. Murphy, NSW.
Rubber tyres; 1924.
(i) B.H.P. Benzol.
The Broken Hill Pty Co. Ltd, Melbourne.
Petroleum products; 1924.
(j) AAA.
Alcock Bros., Sydney.
Cotton goods; 1924.
(k) A.L.P. (Australian Labor Party).
Unity of Labor is the Hope of the World.

All under one roof

The map.

(a) The Antiseptic.
Paterson, Laing & Bruce Ltd.
Cloths and stuffs of wool; 1925.
(b) The Koala Quilt.
D. H. Clarke Ltd, Sydney.
Quilts, cushions, cosies; 1926.
(c) Surize.
C. G. Brown, Blacktown, NSW.
Baking powder; 1926.
(d) Dome.
H. McMahon & Co., Sydney.
Wearing apparel; 1927.
(e) Sweethearts Joy.
G. Yet Ting Quoy, Sydney.
Nuts; 1928.
(f) Austlpully.
Australasian Steel Split Pulleys Ltd, Sydney; 1930.
(g) Spark-o.
H. T. Sparks, Melbourne
Metal polish; 1931.
(h) Amat-ice.
General Refrigerating Co., Sydney; 1931.
(i) Konkrete.
Webb Bros. Pty Ltd
Melbourne.
Paint; 1932.
(j) Australian Telephone Development Association, Sydney; 1934.
(k) Elephant Brand.
Edward Bentley & Sons Pty Ltd, Sydney.
Linen and hemp yarn and thread; 1939.
(l) Poultry Humoss.
Humoss Products, NSW.
Poultry manure; 1943.
(m) Symbol of The Wool Textile Manufacturers of Australia; 1980.
It signifies Australian manufacture of a cloth or garment using Australian wool.
A literal extension of the old saying 'Australia rides on the sheep's back'.

(a)

(b)

(c)

(d)

(e)

(f)

(g)

(h)

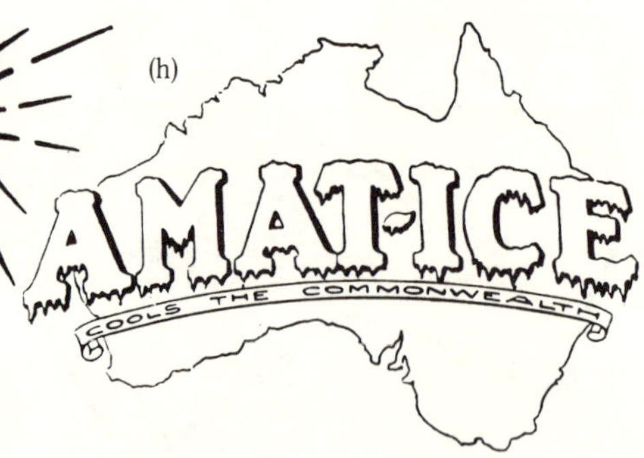

(i)

(j)

(k)

(l)

(m)

All under one roof

The map.

(a) Sunnyvale Orchard.
J. H. Klar, SA.
Fruit; 1949.
(b) Clipper Caravan, Sydney; 1950.
(c) Exclusive Service.
R. F. Graham, Sydney; 1954.
(d) Leo Buring Pty Ltd, Sydney.
Fermented liquors and spirits; 1956.
(e) Nail-Pak.
John Brunton Pty Ltd, Sydney.
Nails; 1956.
(f) Miss Australia Club.
Dowd Associates Pty Ltd; 1957.
(g) The Virite Co. Ltd, Sydney.
Explosives; 1900.
(h) Oceanic.
The Dunlop Rubber Co. of Australasia Ltd, Melbourne.
Hose and packing; 1906.
(i) R. S. Don.
Games and sporting articles; 1907.
(j) Don.
J. & T. Muir, ironfounders, Melbourne; 1910.
(k) Nuvarno Mfg. Co., Melbourne.
Polish; 1912.
(l) The Union Stores Ltd, WA.
Food; 1913.
(m) Jabez Gadsden, Melbourne.
Bags and sacks of jute and cotton; 1917.
(n) Ecco Lightning.
F. R. Johnson.
Metal goods; 1919.
(o) The Sinclair Weaving Co. Ltd, Melbourne.
Tweed; 1921.
(p) B.C.
A. L. Chavasse, Sydney.
Foods; 1924.
(q) Ay Kay M.
Australian Knitting Mills, Vic.; 1925.
(r) The Australia Hotel Co. Ltd, Sydney; 1925.
(s) Attracto.
Richard Allen & Sons (1919) Pty Ltd, Melbourne.
Shirts, pyjamas; 1926.
(t) Montrose Wood Working Co. Pty Ltd, Hobart.
Clothes pegs; 1927.
(u) Davies-Kitchen (Australia) Ltd, Sydney.
Chemicals; 1928.

Continued on page 179

All under one roof

The States.

Although on a local basis the States perform the same function as the map of Australia and provide a quick regional identification of the mark, they have rarely been used to the same extent. This would indicate stronger corporate feelings to nationalism than to State allegiance.

(a) P. W. Heyman, Melbourne.
Milk, cream, butter, bacon, honey; 1907.
(b) Centralian.
D. & J. Fowler Ltd, Adelaide.
Food ingredients; 1908.
(c) Elco.
P. O. Fysh & Co. (1920) Ltd, Launceston, Tas.
Woollen blankets; 1918.
(d) Westral Brand.
Great Southern Roller Flour Mills Pty Ltd, WA; 1924.
(e) Everlite.
O. H. Gray, Proserpine, Qld.
Louvres; 1933.
(f) Department of Main Roads, New South Wales, Sydney; current.

(a)

(b)

(c)

(d)
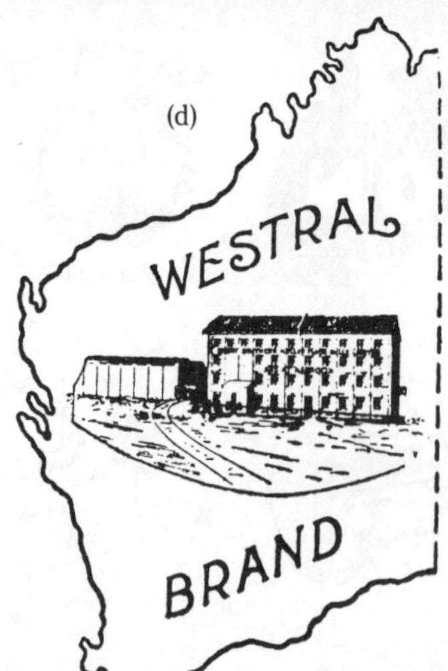

(e)

(f)

(a)

(b)

(c)

(d)

(e)

(f)

(g)

(h)

(i)

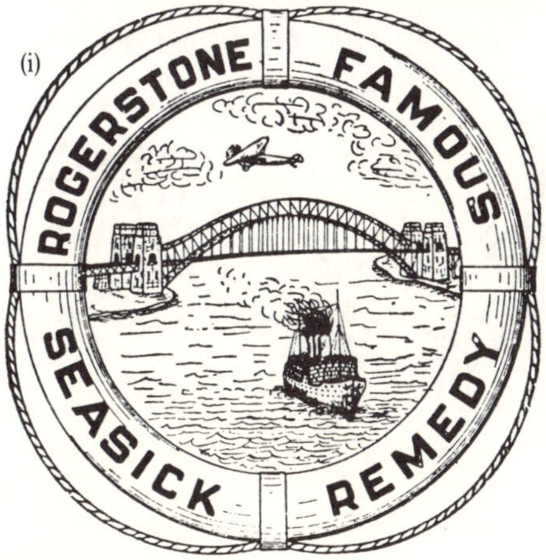

(j)

(k)

All under one roof

The landmarks.

Famous Australian locations and landmarks have been used as trademarks in an attempt to achieve instant fame.
(a) The (Sydney) Town Hall Brand.
Robert Reid & Co., Sydney.
Cotton tapes; 1893.
(b) Burke & Wills.
Robert Harper & Co. Pty Ltd, Melbourne.
Food; 1906.
The statue of Burke and Wills, Melbourne.
(c) The Exhibit Boot.
Whybrow & Co., Melbourne.
Boots and shoes; 1907.
The Exhibition Buildings, Melbourne.
The lake appearing in this mark has since been shrunk to a pond.
(d) Kosciusko.
W. H. Gardiner, Melbourne.
Food; 1917.
(e) Canberra, a Capital Cigar.
Myon A Cigar Co.; 1921.
Canberra is an Aboriginal word. The meaning is uncertain, but is claimed to refer to a woman's breast.
(f) Mallee Eye Drops.
V. & J. T. Howard; 1924.
The Mallee District, Western Victoria.
(g) Wambidgee Lime.
J. H. Grant, Wambidgee, NSW; 1924.
Inspired by the ballad *Nine miles from Gundagai* this earlier live characterisation was created by J. H. Grant to advise customers of their location – 19 miles from Gundagai. It was registered eight years before the unveiling of the 'Dog on the Tucker Box' statue – see (j).
(h) Coys Capitol Pickles.
Thomas Coy, Sydney; 1927.
This trademark was registered the same year Parliament House, Canberra, was completed.
(i) Rogerstone Famous Seasick Remedy.
Rogerstone Supply Co., Sydney; 1932.
(j) The Tucker Box Dog & Cat Food Co., Vic.
Pet food; 1938.
The Dog on the Tuckerbox statue, Gundagai, NSW – see (g).
(k) Barriereef Fashions.
The Myer Emporium Ltd, Melbourne.
Silk piece goods; 1940.

To our knowledge, no one has ever registered *Ayers Rock* as a trademark.

All under one roof

The name.

Derived from the Latin word *australis*, meaning southern, not even the word *Australia* was free from commercial exploitation.

(a) Austral Cycle Agency Ltd, Melbourne; 1897.
(b) Austral.
W. H. Blackham, Melbourne.
Milking machines; 1907.
(c) Austral Brand.
A. J. Jenkins.
Chemical substances; 1909.
(d) The Austral.
Gowing Bros., Sydney.
Umbrellas, walking sticks; 1911.
(e) Austrawool.
D. & W. Murray Ltd, Melbourne.
Shirts; 1912.
(f) Australino.
A. Pringle Stewart, Sydney.
Hats; 1912.
(g) Australite.
W. McLean & Co., Melbourne.
Lamps; 1913.
(h) Custalia – The Custard of the Commonwealth.
A. S. Price & Co., England; 1914.
(i) Aussie's.
S. Frazer, Brisbane.
Cigars; 1920.
(j) The Austrola.
R. S. Taylor.
Talking machines; 1921.
(k) The Austrella.
J. A. Booth & Co., Sydney and Newcastle.
Talking machines; 1925.
(l) Austral Gut Co., Sydney.
Gut for racquets; 1932.
(m) Ausette.
H. Arendsen & Sons Pty Ltd, Melbourne.
Safety razors; 1942.

(a)

(b)

(c)

(d)

(e)

(f)

(g)

(h)

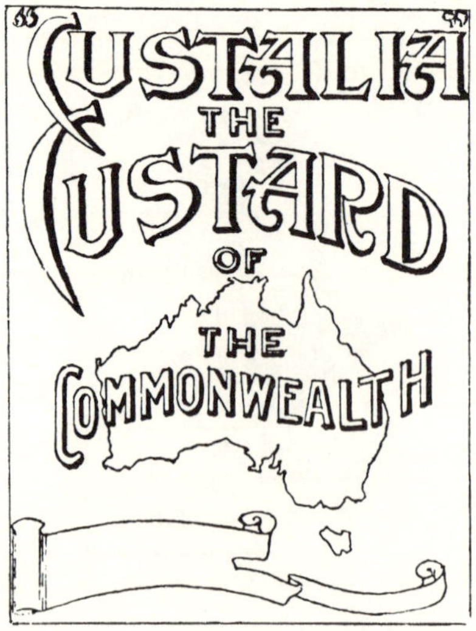

(i)

(l)

"THE GUT THAT KEEPS THEM HOPPING"

"THE CHOICE OF THE CHAMPIONS'

(j)

(k)

(m)

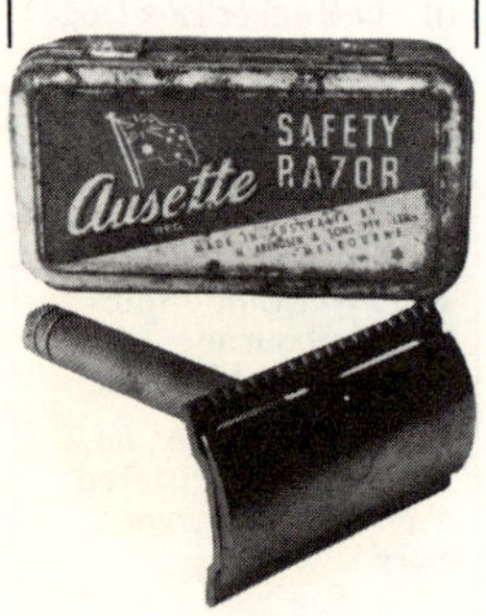

(a)

(b)

(c)

(d)

2. AUSTRALIANS FIRST.

As early as 1857, W. C. Wentworth, the famous explorer and politician, was suggesting a Federation for Australia. In 1870 a Royal Commission was appointed to consider the concept but it proceeded no further than submitting a preliminary report. Then, in 1889, Sir Henry Parkes launched an all-out campaign. In the 1890s depression the concept grew rapidly and was finally accepted. In 1900, Queen Victoria gave her assent to an Act that united the six colonies into the Commonwealth of Australia on January 1, 1901.

(a) Made in Australia from Australian cloth by Australian workmen for Australian people.
W. Dodgshun & Sons, Melbourne.
Clothing; 1906.

(b) Australians First.
Hugo Wertheim, Melbourne.
Machinery; 1906.

(c) Australians First.
W. E. Lewer, Sydney.
Fruit agent; 1932.

(d) Australian Made.
Launched in 1961 to promote awareness and interest in Australian made products, this symbol is still in use today. Copyright is held by the Confederation of Australian Industry, Canberra. If 75% of the cost of production of an item is made up of Australian labour or materials, then the symbol can be applied to that item.

Australians first

Coats of arms.

The marriage of the kangaroo and the emu appears to have had its beginnings in the Bowman flag of 1806. They continued to be used as supporters in numerous business coats of arms which laid the foundation for the Commonwealth coat of arms.

(a) The Bowman flag. Designed by John Bowman, this flag was flown on his property at Richmond, NSW, to celebrate Nelson's victory at Trafalgar. *Courtesy Mitchell Library*.

(b) Creswell & Co. Seed Merchants, Melbourne. 'Exporters of eucalyptus of sorts, catalogue of native trees and shrubs forwarded on application' said their advertisement in 1882.

(c) United Australian Blend. Barnes, Crosby & Co. Melbourne. Tea; 1889.

(d) Brewer's Plastic 'Silex', Melbourne. Boiler covering; 1894.

(e) Wallworth & Co. Melbourne. Hats, umbrellas; from an advertisement appearing 1897.

(f) E. S. Williams. Perfumery, toilet articles; 1900.

(g) Fountain Brand. F. W. Edwards, Sydney. Foods; 1901.

(h) Union. John Hooper & Co., SA. Foods; 1901.

(i) Advance Australia. A. E. & S. Tolley, Adelaide. Wines and spirits; 1902.

(j) Advance Tasmania. P. O. Fysh & Co. Launceston, Tas. Clothing; 1906.

(k) Bang! Remember them? The symbol used in a 1969 'Save the Kangaroo' campaign created by Monahan Dayman Adams. Illustration by Jim Rae.

(k)

Remember them?

(a)

(b)

(c)

(d)

(e)

(f)

FOUNTAIN BRAND.

(g)

(h)

(i)

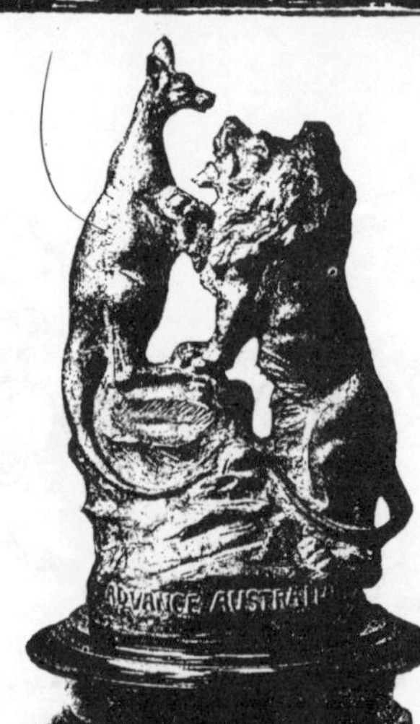

(j)

28

Australians first

Coats of arms.

(a) W. Jno. Baker, Sydney. Ale glasses, cutlery; 1906.
(b) The Advance Brand. Beath, Schiess & Co. Melbourne.
Hosiery; 1906.
(c) Empire.
Harrington & Co. Ltd, Sydney.
Photographic papers; 1907.
(d) W. Dodgshun & Sons, Melbourne.
Woollen goods; 1910.
(e) A.J.C. Advance Australia.
A. J. Cottee.
Clothing for animals; 1901.
(f) Campbell's No. 1.
Campbell Bros. Ltd, Brisbane.
Soaps; 1916.
(g) Henderson's Federal Spring Works Pty Ltd, Melbourne; 1924.
(h) Duraloid.
Pabco Co. (Australia) Ltd, Sydney.
Roofing dampcourse and building papers; 1932.
(i) (j) (k) The Commonwealth of Australia coat of arms.
Symbol of the Commonwealth Government, it is used to indicate Government ownership of property, to authenticate official documents and for other official purposes.
In 1908 the first coat of arms was granted to the Commonwealth of Australia by King Edward VII (i). In view of recurrent criticism, this coat of arms was revised and a new design granted in 1912 (j). There has been no change to the coat of arms since 1912, although a stylized version (k) is currently used where simplicity is required.
(l) Let's Advance Australia.
A campaign launched in 1979 by the Australian Manufacturing Council with support from the C.A.I. and the A.C.T.U. The times have changed but the slogans haven't. *Advance Australia* was being used as early as 1850. Today, 130 years later, it is still seen as the best way to promote national pride.

(a)

(b)

(c)

(d)

(e)

(f)

(g)

(h)

(i)

(j)

(k)

(l)

Australians first

The Southern Cross.

Use of the constellation of the Southern Cross had its beginnings in the Anti-Transportation League flag of 1851 and the Eureka Stockade flag of 1854. A symbol of independence and Australian nationalism, it later dominated the Australian flag as well as a number of trademarks.
(a) Southern Cross.
Thorn Brothers, Melbourne.
Roof cooling composition; 1899.
(b) 'Be true to the Southern Cross'.
J. P. Jones, tailors, Melbourne; 1905.
(c) Australian Labour Conditions.
The Commonwealth Trade Mark; 1906.
(d) The Southern Cross Brand.
F. J. Baily, Tas.
Woollen goods; 1922.
(e) The Southern Cross.
Sir Charles Kingsford-Smith's Fokker aircraft in which he made the first trans-Pacific flight from the USA to Australia in 1928. This plane became *Smithy's* personal trademark.
(f) Southern Cross Information and Press Agency, Sydney; 1957.
(g) Federal Flag.
Robert Harper & Co. Pty Ltd, Melbourne.
Foods; 1906.
(h) C. D. Haywood, Hobart.
Biscuits, confectionery, condiments; 1906.
(i) Flag.
Wallace, Hirst & Co., Brisbane.
Articles of clothing; 1907.
(j) Keep Australia Beautiful Council.
This symbol was first used in 1968, Australia-wide.

(a)

(b)

(c)

(d)

(e)

(f)

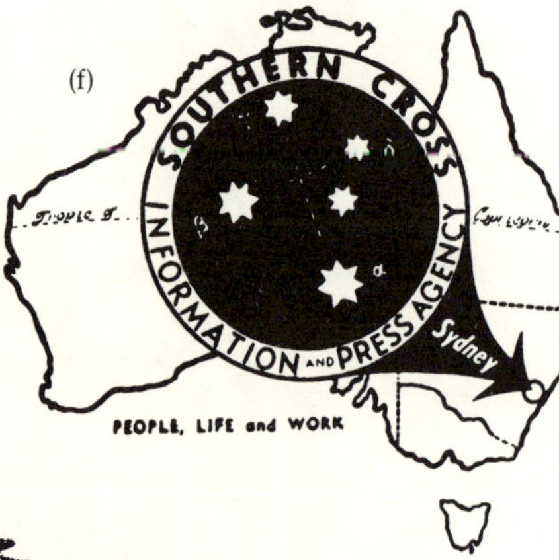

(g)

(h)

(i)

(j)

Australians first

The Anzacs.

With the arrival of the First World War came a whole new form of nationalism and a wealth of material for the trade-mark artist to exploit. No sooner had the word *ANZAC* (Australian and New Zealand Army Corps) come into use in Egypt and Gallipoli, than an architect in Melbourne attempted to register it as a trade-mark. The Defence Regulation Act of 1921 restricted its use commercially, but war related substitutes were soon found. Returning soldiers from the French Front brought back new words like *treybon* which was applied to tea. And as the Second World War started, so did the knitting and the registration of slang terms like *Dinkum Digger* for wool.

(a)

(b)

(c)

(d)

(e)

(f)

(a) ANZAC.
T. W. Pearce, architect, Melbourne.
Joinery; 1915.
Application for registration was cancelled.
(b) Treybon Brand Tea.
The Diggers Commerce Agency, Melbourne; 1921.
(c) Digger.
The Young District Producers' Co-op. Association, NSW.
Prunes, dried fruits and nuts; 1931.
(d) Dinkum Digger.
The Myer Emporium Ltd, Melbourne.
Knitting wool; 1939.
(e) Digger Junior.
Telephone Rentals Ltd, Adelaide.
Toys; 1946.
(f) Help us to make Australia strong.
From a block in the *Ebes Collection*.

Australians first

The Anzacs.

Public attitudes to the Armed Forces were quickly transferred to products.
(a) Dependon.
Theo. Felsted & Good, Melbourne.
Cotton goods; 1915.
(b) Our Wounded Hero Brand.
J. Alexander.
Foods; 1915.
Application for registration of this trademark was refused.
(c) United Service.
J. A. Mitchelson-Watson, Melbourne.
Foods; 1919.
(d) The Digger.
J. Hunter & Son Ltd, Sydney.
Footwear; 1919.

As a compensation for hardships, the Government allocated money for the resettlement of returning soldiers. Some used this money to establish businesses and, via their trademarks, used their wartime hardships as unique selling propositions.
(e) Aussie.
The Pikedale Soldiers Settlement Co-op. Canning, Jam & Preserving Co. Ltd, Amiens, Qld.; 1921.
(f) The Army & Navy Stores Ltd, SA.
Food; 1922.
(g) BST.
The New South Wales Blinded Soldiers Tea Co.
Tea, coffee; 1923.
(h) Limbless Soldiers' Association of Victoria; 1927.
(i) (j) In 1916 the Returned Services
Continued on page 179

(i)

(j)

(a)

(b)

(c)

(d)

(e)

(f)

(g)

(h)

(a)

(b)

(c)

3. DINKUM BONZA COO-EE.

Since the first fleet *chucked* its anchor into Botany Bay, the Australian environment, the unique fauna and flora, and the Aboriginal language have resulted in a wealth of indigenous words and phrases. *Local lingo* that has been reflected in trademarks and, in some instances, even derived from them.

(a) Dinkum Tea.
Kinlyside & Winslow; 1919.

(b) Bonza Sheen.
F. E. Smith, Sydney.
Brilliantine, creme, shampoo; 1938.

(c) Coo-ee.
Jessie Ireland, Newcastle, NSW.
Butter, bacon, cheese; 1893.

(d) Fair Dinkum Graphics, Arti Studio.
Malcom Enright, Brisbane.
A creative advertising studio; 1975 to 1978.

(d)

Dinkum bonza coo-ee

Coo-ee.

Coo-ee, an Aboriginal word meaning 'come here', was often used as a penetrating cry in the bush.
(a) Cooee.
Dixon & Sons, Sydney and Brisbane.
Manufactured tobacco; 1893.
(b) Coo-ee Tomato Sauce.
M. Richards & Co.; 1910.
(c) Coo-ee Brand.
J. M. Moore, Melbourne.
Galvanized iron; 1910.
(d) Coo-ee.
Price Griffiths & Co., Melbourne.
Fermented liquors and spirits; 1913.
(e) Coo-ee.
Bell & Spence, Melbourne.
Motor cycles; 1913.
(f) Coo-ee.
Brown & Dureau Ltd. Melbourne.
Flour; 1924.
(g) Coo-ee Cigarettes.
The British Australian Tobacco Co. Pty Ltd, Melbourne; 1934.
(h) Coo-ee Clothing Co.
Newcastle, NSW; 1935.
(i) Coo-ee Kola.
Mauri Bros. & Thompson Ltd, Sydney.
A non-alcoholic refreshing beverage; 1912.
(j) Coo-ee.
The Castlemaine Brewery and Wood Bros. Co. Ltd, Newcastle, NSW; 1880s.

(a)

(b)

(c)

(d)

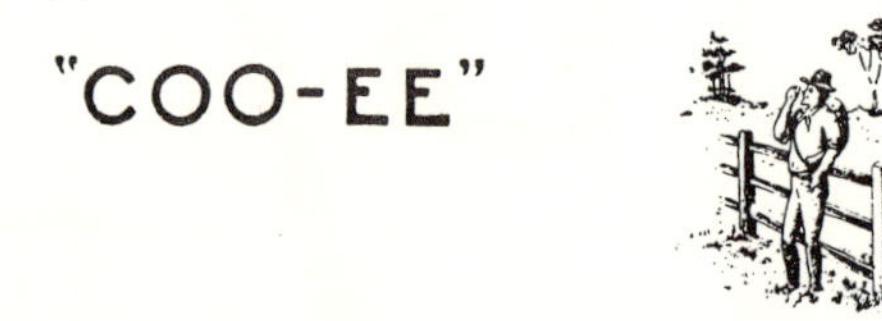

(e)

(f)

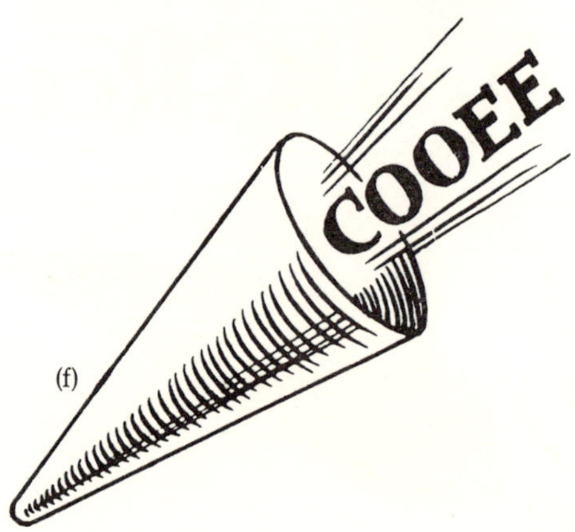

(g)

(h)

(i)

(j)

(a)

(b)

(c)

(d)

(e)

(f)

(g)

(h)

(i)

(j)

(k)

(l)

(m)

Dinkum bonza coo-ee

Local language.

(a) Bod-e-line.
John Sackville Pty Ltd. Melbourne.
Trousers and knickers; 1933.
Bodyline was a term created to describe the aggressive style of bowling used by the English in the Australian Cricket Tour of 1932-33. This trademark was registered during that same season.

(b) True Blue.
T. W. Cotton Pty Ltd, Melbourne.
Candles, soap; 1919.
True Blue was first used to describe the colour of the flag of the Australasian Anti-Transportation League in 1851.

(c) Bluee.
The Sterling Soap & Candle Co. Pty Ltd.
Common soap; 1922.
Application for registration was refused. Possibly it was deceptively close to (b) above.

(d) Bonser.
Edward Butler & Son Ltd, Sydney.
Saddlery; 1925.
Bonza, a general exclamation of approval, is an Australian adaptation of the American *bonanza*, used to describe a rich gold mine.

(e) Easo.
Edward Crafti, Brisbane; 1927.

(f) Smokettes.
Vere Le Roi Stokoe, Geelong, Vic.
Tobacco; 1927.

(g) Kon-Ka-Roo.
George White, Sydney.
Medicine for conquering rheumatisms; 1931.

(h) Billy Bluegum.
J. Jackson & Son, Brisbane.
Native toy bear; 1931.
Billy Bluegum was the name given to Norman Lindsay's famous koala bear character.

(i) Grippo.
M. & A. Thomson, Sydney.
Clothes pegs; 1932.

(j) Ripa.
Ripeners Pty Ltd, Brisbane; 1934.

(k) T-Shoo.
Simpson Hain (1940) Pty Ltd, Sydney.
Tissue paper; 1948.

(l) Drinko.
E. M. Pratt, Melbourne.
Preparation for the treatment of alcoholism; 1948.

(m) Bang-er-oo.
W. Blockli, Melbourne.
Toy projecting devices and targets used in shooting games; 1949.

Dinkum bonza coo-ee

Registered ideas.

As well as visual marks, tradenames have been used to record entrepreneurial ideas. Some eventuating into products. Some not. Smart operators never missed an opportunity to make a quid. As *ute* became a generic word for utility motor vehicles, it was quickly registered for wheelbarrows. But would you know that *Strip-Teasies* was a brand of sausage casings?
(a) Lu-Pol.
E. C. Robertson & Co.
Cattle and poultry food; 1914.
(b) Pasho.
N. & F. Ashelford, Bathurst, NSW.
Passion fruit flavour aerated beverage; 1925.
(c) Choc-A-Bloc.
Myers Bros. & Ellis, Brisbane.
Food products; 1926.
(d) Num-Ba-Won.
B. Blumenthal, Brisbane.
Perfumery and toilet articles; 1929.
(e) O-Ke-Doke.
Kraft Walker Cheese Co. Pty Ltd, Melbourne.
Milk products, cereals including pop corn and cereal preparations of all kinds; 1936.
(f) Plonk.
John Bookallil and James Donovan, Sydney.
Liquid insecticide; 1938.
(g) Piedagree.
John Martin & Co. Ltd, Adelaide.
Health shoes; 1939.
(h) Ant-I-Dope.
R. B. Findlay, Valley, Qld.
Ant powder; 1939.
(i) Quick Lay.
W. Thomas & Co. (W.A.) Ltd, Cottesloe.
Poultry food; 1946.
(j) Rat-Menu.
A. B. Gibson & Sons Pty Ltd, Melbourne.
Vermin destroying preparations; 1946.
(k) Choke-A-Mouse.
Barnes and Howard, Hay, NSW.
Mousetraps; 1947.
(l) Plasti-Roo.
The Simons Leather Goods Co., Sydney.
Leather wrist watch bands; 1947.
Continued on page 179

(y)

(a) **Lu-Pol**

(b) **Pasho**

(c) **Choc-A-Bloc**

(d) **Num-Ba-Won**

(e) **O-Ke-Doke**

(f) **Plonk**

(g) **Piedagree**

(h) **Ant-I-Dope**

(i) **Quick Lay**

(j) **Rat-Menu**

(k) **Choke-A-Mouse**

(l) **Plasti-Roo**

(m) **Mae Vest**

(n) **Abbo-Liter**

(o) **Strip-Teasies**

(p) **Chickemite**

(q) **Ute**

(r) **Diminuentoe**

(s) **Go-Poof**

(t) **Olitalia**

(u) **Calfeteria**

(v) **Car-B-Que**

(w) **Downunda**

(x) **Moo-Vellous**

(a)

(b)

(c)

(d)

(e)

(f)

(g)

(h)

(i)

Dinkum bonza coo-ee

The blokes.

'The ringer looks around and he's beaten by a blow' goes the line of a popular Australian ballad. The *ringer* is the fastest shearer in a shed. In the ballad he looks around to check the progress of a fellow shearer—a pause that loses his title.

Australia, with its unique industries, has created many unique vocations that are remembered in story, song and even trademarks.

(a) Ringer.
Rundel & McMillan, Vic.
Agricultural and horticultural machinery; 1896.

(b) Bushman.
Jewell Davis & Co., Sydney.
Metal goods; 1902.

(c) The Digger.
The Bendigo & District Farmers & Fruitgrowers Co-op. Society Ltd, Vic.
Jams, pickles, sauces; 1906.
Digger – a man who worked the gold diggings.

(d) Stockrider Brand.
Clarke & Co., Melbourne.
Eucalyptus oil; 1908.

(e) Swagman.
William McKenzie & Co., Townsville, Qld.
Tents, tarps, rope, twine; 1909.
Swagman – the Australian nomad who carries his clothing and possessions in his bedroll or *swag*.

(f) Stockman Brand.
T. H. Wiggins, Karoonda, SA.
Veterinary ointments; 1916.

(g) Drover.
Clarton Hodgson & Co. Ltd, Sydney.
Foods; 1919.

(h) Sundowner Brand.
W. A. Blake Pty Ltd, Melbourne.
Jams; 1928.
As for swagman.

(i) Buckjumper Brand.
Craig, Mostyn & Co., Sydney.
Hams and bacon; 1939.

Dinkum bonza coo-ee

Part of the lingo.

Trademarks have been based on the Australian language and, in some cases, have added to it.
(a) Norco.
The North Coast Co-op. Co. Ltd, Byron Bay, NSW.
Butter; 1915.
From the Norco trademark *norks* was derived as a slang term for women's breasts.
(b) W. Menz & Co. Ltd, Adelaide.
The company began manufacturing biscuits in the 1850s. The design shown here is c. 1935. The company name led to South Australians referring to a visit to the male toilets as *going to the biscuit factory*.
(c) Zam-Buk.
C. E. Fulford trading as 'The Bile Bean Manufacturing Co.'
Cure-all cream; 1906.
Zam-Buk was carried at sporting events by first aid attendants, who consequently became known as *Zam-Bucks*. The term is now obsolete. During the same period, the Zam-Buk tradename was also applied to soap.
(d) Bobby Dazzler.
L. L. Leyshon, Melbourne.
Clothing; 1923.
An expression for anyone or anything possessing superlative qualities.
(e) Fuzzy Wuzzy.
W. Bennett & J. McNeil, Penshurst, NSW.
Foods; 1946.
A term for New Guinea natives.
(f) Wacker (or whacker) is a slang term used to describe a simpleton. It is also the surname of the founder of a German pneumatic equipment company that has been operating in Australia for the past fourteen years.

(a)

(b)

(c)

(d)

(e)

(f)

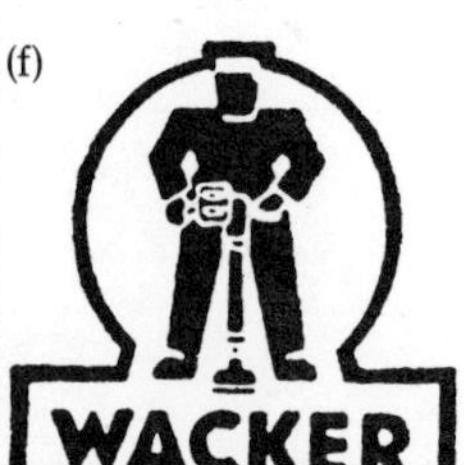

(a)

Dinkum bonza coo-ee

Puns.

A pun is the use of a word having several meanings, or of two words having the same sound but different meanings, so as to create a startling or humorous effect. Across the broad spectrum of Australian trademarks, puns have been used with extremely startling and, indirectly, humorous effects.

(a) Hones-Tea.
G. H. O'Brien, Sydney; 1896.
Hones-Tea incorporates every style of pun – word pun, sound pun and visual pun. *Poll on 'is 'T'* is the basic visual device of a cockatoo or poll (a shortened version of polly) on his 'T' shaped perch. This is linked to *The best poll-I-see is Hones-Tea* and the corporate line *Honesty is the best policy and my Hones-Tea is the best of T's* with some almost punishing results.

(b) More Pork.
William Stokvis.
Pork smallgoods; 1922.
Everything has an explanation. The illustration is a Mopoke bird.

(b)

Dinkum bonza coo-ee

Puns.

(a) W. S. Husbands.
Sun and dust shades;
1892.
The slogan for these early sunglasses was *Husbands' sun & dust shades to suit son & daughter too*.
(b) Palm Brand Ham.
A. J. Davis, Brisbane;
1896.
(c) Globe Capital Tea.
Atcherley & Dawson,
Sydney; 1904.
(d) Geisha.
Scott Henderson & Co.,
Sydney.
Dressed rice; 1908.
Rice was used as a slang term for Orientals. A *Geisha* is a gaily dressed Oriental.
(e) Intestone.
H. Aitcheson, chemist,
Charters Towers, Qld;
1907.
As well as the obvious *Intestone/intestine* word play for this bowel mixture, H. Aitcheson went one step further by branding them *Dr Potter's*.
(f) The Eye and Bee.
Isherwood & Bartlett,
Melbourne.
Clothing; 1909.
*I*sherwood and *B*artlett – *Eye* and *Bee*.
(g) Melrose Hop Ale.
The Adelaide Brewery
Co. Ltd, Mitcham, SA;
1937.

(a)

(b)

(c)

(d)

(e)

(f)

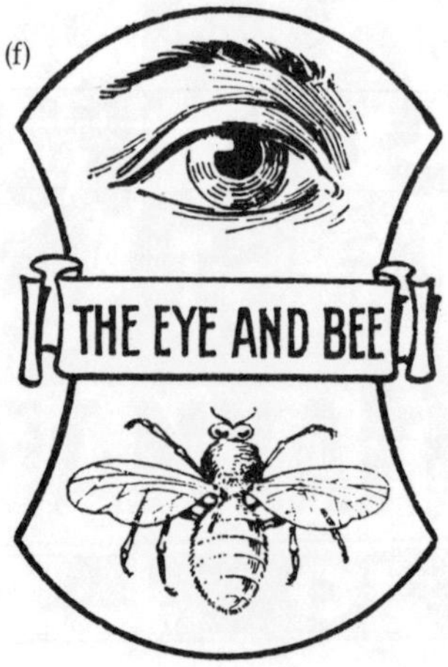

(g)

(a)

(b)

(c)

(d)

(e)

(f)

(g)

(h)

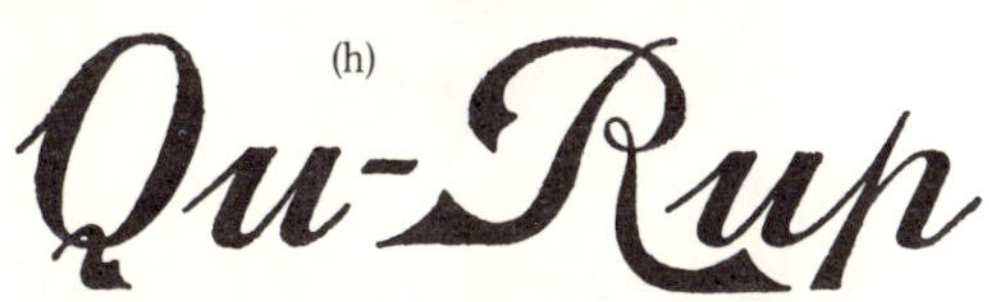

(i)

(j)

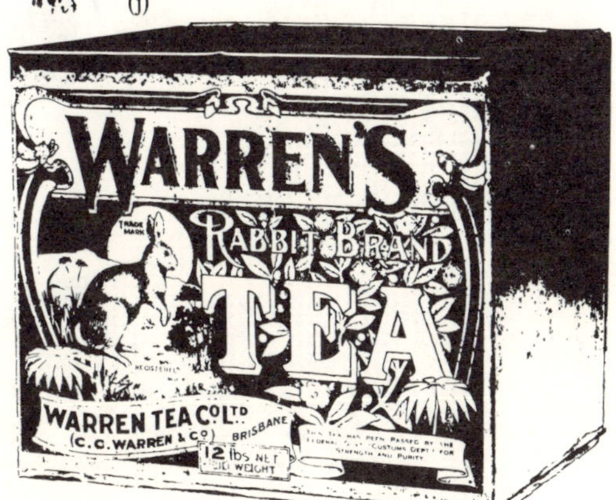

(k)

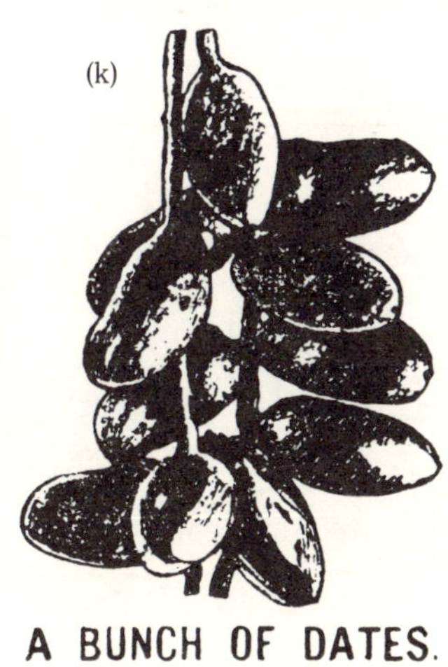

(l)

Dinkum bonza coo-ee

Puns.

(a) Sayso.
A. Triggs, Melbourne.
Ice cream biscuits; 1909.
'It's up to you to have a Sayso.' *Say-so* was a slang term for boss or leader.
(b) The Match.
Made in Sweden.
Matches; c. 1910.
(c) Curit.
C. A. Bevan, storekeeper, Broken Hill, NSW.
Medicinal powder; 1910.
(d) Kure-ettes.
T. J. Holmes, Melbourne.
Medicine; 1938.
Puns based on curate, the assistant to a parish priest. Can we conclude that two *Kure-ettes* equal one *Curit*?
(e) Drummer Boy.
Gregory & Davidson Ltd, Brisbane.
Foods; 1911.
A broken drum can't be beat.
(f) Fay-mos.
B.B. Company, Sydney.
Articles of clothing; 1911.
(g) Nolyte.
H. Peach, dentist, Sydney.
Shields for eyes; 1912.
(h) Qu-Rup.
Urettra Edwards, Melbourne.
Salve for human use; 1912.
(i) Buchanan's Cat Brand.
J. D. Buchanan, Brisbane.
Paints; 1915.
A tale of paint.
(j) Rabbit Brand Tea.
The Warren Tea Co. Ltd, Brisbane; c. 1915.
(k) A bunch of dates.
Graham Bros., Brisbane.
Calendars and stationery; 1916.
(l) QP – Queensland Preserves Ltd, Brisbane.
From the 1926 *Commonwealth Trades Alphabet*.
A Q P doll.

Dinkum bonza coo-ee

Puns.

(a) Teddy Beer.
J. H. Foureur Ltd, West Mitcham, SA; 1921.
(b) Thorp's Walnut Whipped Creams.
Thorp Bros., Melbourne.
Confectionery; 1921.
(c) Shoe-R Cure Liniment.
W. Wilson; 1921.
A sure cure for horses' hooves.
(d) APL.
Aluminium Pty Ltd; 1921.
*A*luminium *P*ty *L*td = Apple. Simple when you work *fru-it*.
(e) Appy-Tiza.
C. G. Ward, Melbourne.
Foods; 1921.
(f) Catamaran Coal.
Catamaran Colliery Pty Ltd, Hobart; 1922.
(g) Nightingale, The Mop of Australia.
The Nightingale Supply Co., Sydney; 1922.
(h) Possum Brand.
E. N. Ansell & Sons, Melbourne.
Teats for babies' bottles; 1923.
(i) Dux.
Walter Stubbs, NSW.
Electric water heater; 1924.
(j) Pyramints.
Griffith Sweets Pty Ltd, Melbourne; 1957.

(a)

(b)

(c)
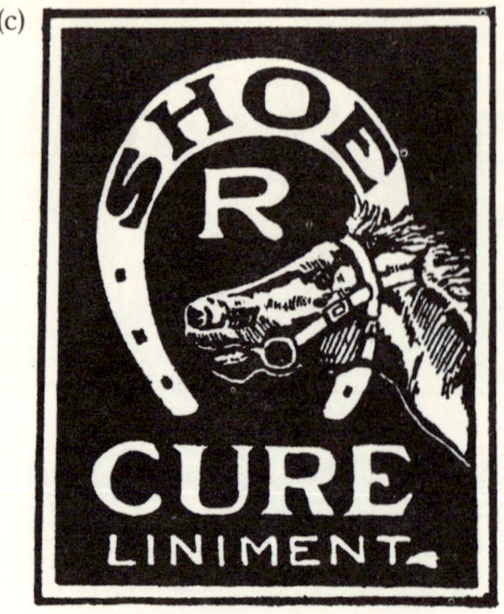

(d)

(e)

(f)
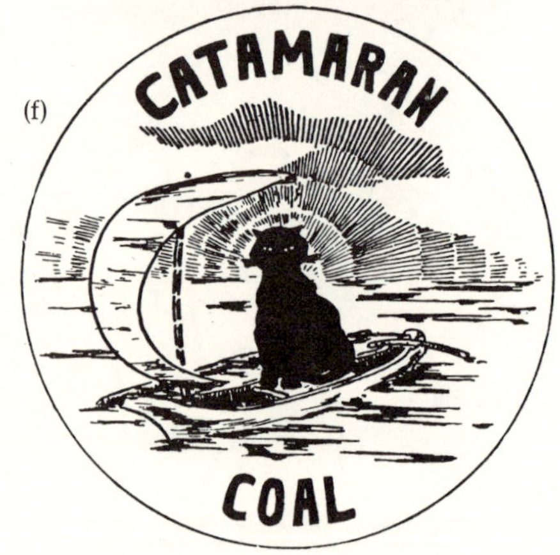

(g)

(h)

(i)
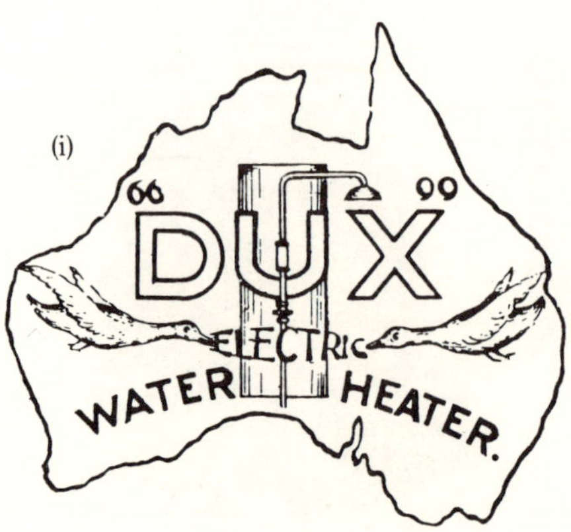

(j)

(a)

(b)

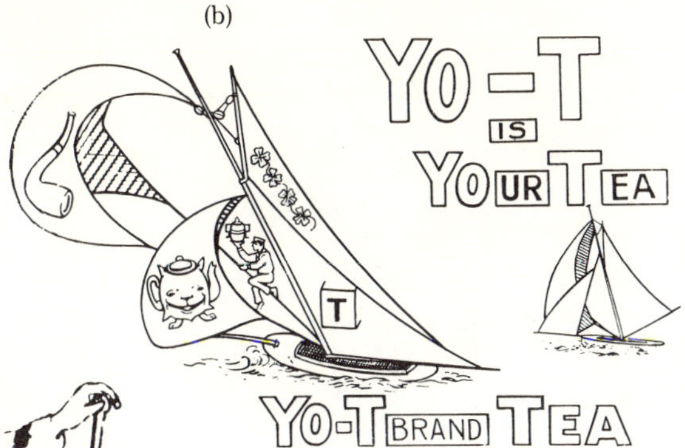

(c)

(d)

(e)

(f)

(g)

(h)

(i)

(j)

(k)

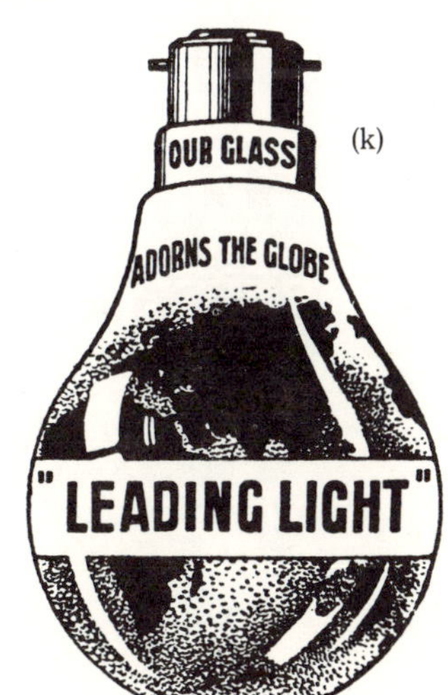

Dinkum bonza coo-ee

Puns.

(a) The Prince of WA ALES.
The Swan Brewery Co. Ltd., Perth; 1924.
(b) YO-T Brand Tea.
Frederick Thomson, Melbourne; 1925.
(c) Can't Be Beat.
Australian Chemical Products Co., Melbourne; 1927.
(d) Royal Flush.
Sureflush Cistern Co. Ltd, Perth; 1928.
(e) WoolRuss.
G. J. Russell & Son Pty Ltd, Melbourne; 1928.
*Wool*len clothes made by J. *Russ*ell. Their name: *WoolRuss*. Their symbol: a walrus.
(f) Berg Pure Silk Ties.
Greenberg & Co. Ltd, Sydney; 1936.
Greenberg & Co. made *Berg* brand ties. Their symbol: an iceberg.
(g) Brisbon.
Brisbane Chemical & General Supply Co., Brisbane.
Liquid soap; 1943.
(h) Storpedo.
Air Supply Packs Pty Ltd, Melbourne.
Containers; 1943.
(i) Link-on-Fish.
Port Lincoln Fisheries Pty Ltd, SA; 1948.
(j) Mat-A-door.
B. M. Larnach, Sydney.
Rope mats; 1956.
(k) Leading Light.
Bent Glass Pty Ltd, Melbourne.
Glass; 1957.
(l) Mag-Pies Supreme.
Collingwood, Vic.; current.
A pie shop named after the *Magpies* (Collingwood Football Club).

(l)

Dinkum bonza coo-ee

Parwill – the pun that didn't work.

In 1910, the popular English spread *Marmite* was registered in Australia. Made from beef extract, the product is still in existence today.
In early 1923, Fred Walker, an enterprising general merchant, produced a vegetable extract.
To position it in direct competition with Marmite, he called it *Parwill*: Marmite – mother might, but Parwill – father will.
The brand didn't take on and Walker assumed it may have had something to do with the name. Late 1923 he conducted a public competition to rename it.
The result was *Vegemite*, which Walker duly registered.
At the same time, Walker employed an up-and-coming microbiologist, Dr Callister, who had been working on a yeast extract. With Walker's support he succeeded in developing the product we know today.
(a) Marmite.
The Marmite Food Extract Co. Ltd, London.
Extract of yeast; 1910.
(b) (c) (d) Vegemite.
Fred Walker & Co. Pty Ltd, Melbourne.
Vegetable and yeast extract; 1923. (b) Early jar, (c) c. 1955,
(d) Vegemite is currently owned and manufactured by Kraft Foods Ltd.

The maids.

(e) Australian Maid.
Brown & Dureau Ltd, Melbourne.
Foods; 1917.
(f) Colonial Maid.
J. E. Bartleet Perry, Melbourne.
Metal goods; 1919.
(g) Quick Maid.
Leo Bloom, Qld.
Foods; 1922.
(h) Mrs B. Thrifty.
Fowlers Pty Ltd, Melbourne.
Sterilizing cooking apparatus; 1931.

(a)

(b)

(c)

(d)

(h)

(e)

(f)

(g)

(a)

(b)

4. FAMOUS SINCE CAPTAIN COOK.

The Australian Aborigines have been at the wrong end of the stick since the *white man* set foot in their timeless land.

Advertising and commercial communications are by no means innocent of the degradation of this proud race.

In the form of trademarks, public attitudes have been reflected and perhaps even developed by the business sector.

(a) Abo Brand. Australian Paint Mfg. Co. Ltd, Sydney; 1921.

(b) (c) Whacco Pty Ltd, Melbourne.

Self raising flour, custard, jelly powder, spices, essences; (b) 1935, (c) 1945.

(c)

Famous since Captain Cook

'Abo Brand'.

Not only the Aborigines but all facets of their life have been exploited in trademarks.
(a) Mia-mia
Charles W. Nance, Sydney; 1892.
Mia-mia – bark shelter.
(b) Lubra Brand.
Woods & Co., Kangaroo Island, SA.
Chemical substances used in medicine and pharmacy; 1892.
Lubra – young Aboriginal woman.
(c) John Eckersley, St Arnaud, Vic.
Medicine; 1893.
'Bubonic plague can be prevented by using Eckersley's Mentholine,' said one of their advertisements.
(d) Silver's Woorayl.
J. Silvers, Vic.
Medicine for human use; 1896.
Woorayl – lyre bird.
(e) The Graziers' Meat Export Co. of New South Wales Ltd, Sydney; 1896.
Warrigal – dingo or native dog.
(f) Yarraman Tea.
United Australian Tea Co., Sydney; 1897.
Yarraman – horse.
(g) Womerah.
J. A. O'Shea, Sydney; 1904.
Womerah – throwing stick.
(h) Hansen Butter Factory.
Hansen Dairy Co., Vic.; 1906.
(i) The Woomera.
A. M. Hertzberg & Co., Brisbane.
Musical instruments; 1907.
(j) Competition.
A. J. Cotton, orchardist, Kettering, Tas.
Fruit cases; 1913.
(k) Municipal shield of the City of Brighton, Vic.; current.

(a)

(b)

(c)

(d)

(e)

(f)

(g)

(h)

(i)

(j)

(k)

(a)

(b)

(c)

(d)

(e)

(f)

(g)

(h)

(i)

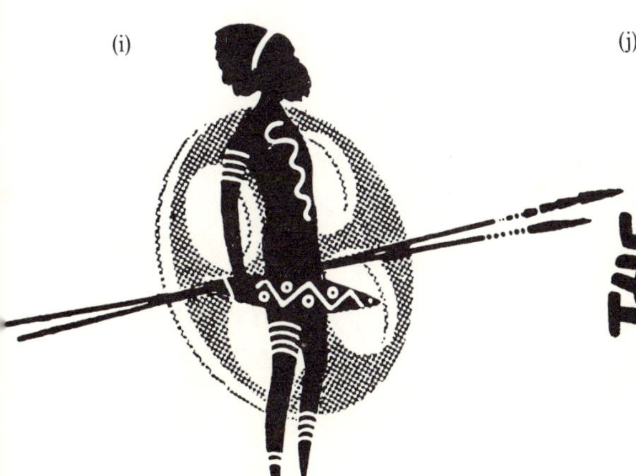

(j)

(k)

(l)

Famous since Captain Cook

'Abo Brand'.

(a) Australian Black. Plymel 1914 Ltd, Sydney. Carbon paint; 1915.
(b) Budgeree. W. N. Hutchison, inventor, Sydney. Preparation for the destruction of blowflies; 1918. *Budgeree* – excellent or good.
(c) Nulla-nulla. M. O'Riordan & Sons, Sydney. Soap; 1920. *Nulla-nulla* – club or hitting stick.
(d) White Way. Nutt & Jones, Sydney. Cleaning preparation; 1926.
(e) Blackboy Brand. F. R. Mellor, Melbourne. Fresh fruit; 1929.
(f) 'Abo' Brand. A. J. Wiley, Adelaide. Souvenirs from the native mulga tree; 1932.
(g) Budgerree Doll. The Australian Souvenir Co., Sydney. Ornamented souvenirs; 1938.
(h) Good-oh. Realest Pty Ltd, merchants, Sydney; 1942.
(i) Avondale Studios Pty Ltd, Sydney; 1951.
(j) The Gunyah. A. V. Hopkins, Sydney. Tents; 1954. *Gunyah* – hut or shelter.
(k) Victor. Corowa Milling Co. Ltd, NSW. Flour; 1954.
(l) Municipal shield of the City of Preston, Vic.; current.

Famous since Captain Cook

The boomerang.

Of all the Aborigines' artifacts, the boomerang became their most succinct symbol. This weapon encompassed many of the early European misconceptions of the Aborigines as a *violent race of savages*. In terms of commercial symbology, the boomerang was quickly removed from its Aboriginal context to symbolize 'returning' and more broadly, Australia.

(a) Boomerang.
F. A. Turner.
Metal goods; 1921.
(b) Bain's White Ant Exterminator.
William Bain, Casino, NSW; 1898.
(c) The Boomerang Brand.
Webendorfer Bros., Sydney.
Explosives; 1898.
(d) Joshua's Boomerang.
Joshua Bros., Melbourne.
Brandy; 1899.
(e) Boomerang.
Stokes & Sons, Melbourne.
Goods of precious metals; 1908.
(f) Boomerang Brand.
E. A. Adams.
Foods; 1920.
(g) The Boomerang.
F. A. Turner.
Glass; 1921.
(h) Boomerang.
H. J. Evans.
Stock licks and remedies; 1929.
(i) Allcourt.
Barnet Glass Rubber Co. Ltd, Melbourne.
Rubber footwear; 1933.
(j) The Bond Street.
Sargood Gardiner Ltd., Sydney.
Hats and caps; 1935.
(k) Boomerang Cigarette Papers Pty Ltd; current.
(l) The Boomerang Harmonica – Alberts' system.
From an advertisement appearing 1923.

(a)

(b)

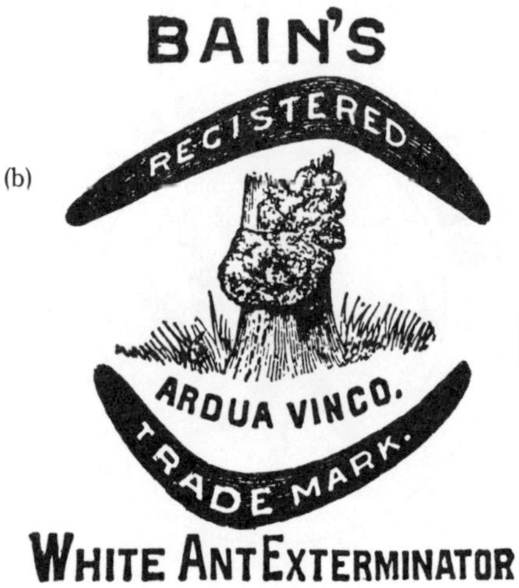

(c)

(d)

(e)

(f)

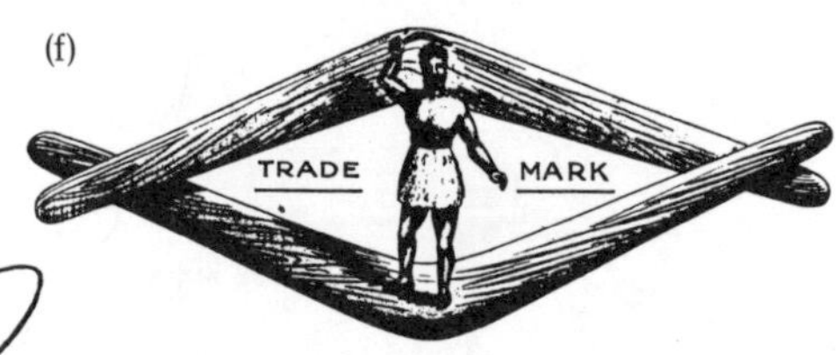

(g)

(h)

(i)

(j)

(k)

(l)

Famous since Captain Cook

A White Australia.

These trademarks reflect the infamous *White Australia Policy* – a term used to describe the multitude of government policies devised during the first part of this century to restrict immigration.
(a) Parsons' Starch. Parson Bros. & Co. Pty Ltd, Sydney; 1903.
(b) Champion Gold-Top. L. W. Craw, Australian Gold-Top Co., Melbourne. Non-alcoholic beverages; 1906.
(c) White Australian Pineapple. M. Finucan Bros., Brisbane; 1910.
(d) King's Compo. King & Co., Perth. Refrigerating paint; 1911.
(e) Golden Fleece Soap. John Cahill & Co., Sydney. Common soap; 1924.
(f) White Australia. Randolph Bedford, publisher, Brisbane; 1925.
(g) Bon-wash. Bon Mfg. Co. Pty Ltd, Sydney. Antiseptic soap; 1944.

(a)

(b)

(c)

(d)

(e)

(f)

(g)

Famous since Captain Cook

Jolly niggerboys.

Racial exploitation was not restricted to Australia's coloured people. American and African Negroes, as well as products, were branded *sambo, coon* and *nigger*.
(a) (b) Miller's Feather Shop, 213 Chapel St., Prahran, Vic.
Ostrich feathers; (a) 1906.
(b) from a post card dated 1908. A direct mail piece developed from the registered trademark.
(c) Nubian Paint.
William Adams & Co. Ltd, Melbourne; 1906.
(d) Darkey Brand.
G. W. Beal, Melbourne.
Ground sand soap; 1906.
(e) Coon Stick.
Long & Smith, Melbourne.
Lollie sticks; 1911.
(f) Sambo Brand.
Robertson & Young Ltd.
Foods; 1913.
(g) Zulu.
Pacific Mfg. Co. Ltd, Sydney.
Boot polish; 1916.
(h) You're Next.
Harry Greave, Sydney.
Reptile and other skins; 1931.
(i) Jolly Niggerboys.
Bryant & May Pty Ltd, Melbourne.
Matches; 1938.
(j) Nigger Boy.
National Licorice Co., Melbourne; 1945.

(a)

(b)

(c)

(d)

(e)

(f)

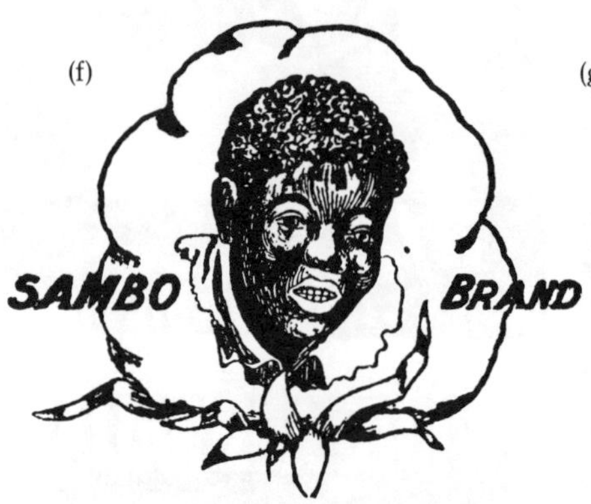

(g)

(h)

(i)

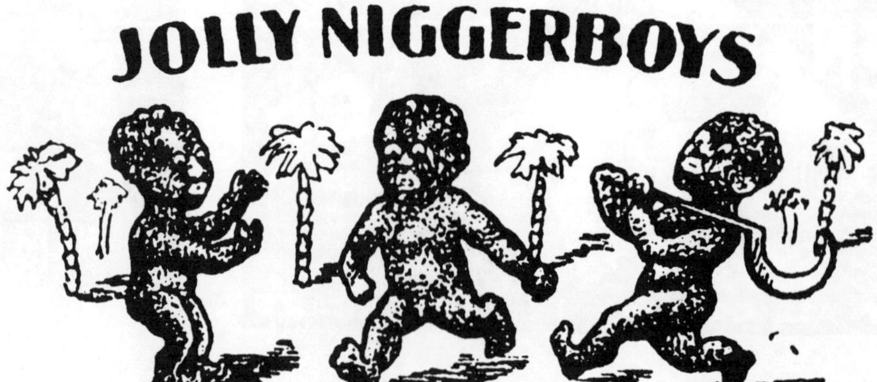

(j)

5. NATIVE COMPANIONS–FAUNA.

Because of their uniqueness, native animals have always been fascinating to Australians and foreigners alike. The kangaroo is by far the most popular symbol of Australia. But lately, possibly due to threats of its extinction, the koala is rising in popularity. All the native companions, even mythical, have offered countless opportunities to the Australian trademark artist.

(a) Native Companions. Mungo Scott Ltd, Sydney. Flour; 1934.

(b) Lithgow Valley Colliery Company, Lithgow, NSW, began production of industrial and domestic pottery in 1876, but by the turn of the century had virtually closed down. Only some of the Lithgow pottery bore the kangaroo mark.

(c) Richard Lohn, Melbourne. Ornamental confectionery; 1907.

(d) Gazeka Paints. Alice Farley, Melbourne; 1909. See Gazeka story, page 143.

(e) Taronga Zoo, Mosman, Sydney. Designed in 1968 by C. Wetton in conjunction with R. Straun, Zoo director at the time.

(a)

(b)

(c)

(d)

(e)

Native companions – fauna

Koalas.

The word *koala* comes from the Aboriginal name for this appealing, but difficult to illustrate native marsupial.
(a) Dr Blue Gum. Neale, Constable & Co. Ltd, Perth. Eucalyptus oil; 1916. The Billy Bluegum koala bear was created by Norman Lindsay in the pages of the *Bulletin* and *Lone Hand* of 1907. Lindsay's bears continued to appear in the *Bulletin* up until 1956. Some of the bears on these pages were obviously influenced by his illustrative style or could even be his work.
(b) (c) Bear Brand. A. & R. Ingwersen, Melbourne. Chemical substances for agricultural and veterinary uses; (b) 1909, (c) 1928.
(d) Australite Paint, Melbourne. 'Australian pigments, oils and labour'; from an advertisement appearing 1910.
(e) While I live I'll climb. A. Harcourt, Tamworth, NSW. Boots, shoes and all gent's wearing apparel; 1910.
(f) Koala Brand. Morrows Ltd, Brisbane. Foods; 1915.
(g) Perdriau Rubber Co. Ltd, Sydney. Medicine for human use; 1916.
(h) Koala. Koala Mfg. Co., Melbourne. Wood stains; 1920.
(i) Koala Brand. P. W. Heyman, Melbourne; 1933.
(j) Koala Jelly Crystals. From an undated advertisement.

(a)

(b)

(c)

(d)

(e)

(f)

(g)

(h)

(i)

(j)

Native companions – fauna

Koalas.

(a) Gumlypta.
Gillard Gordon Ltd, Sydney.
Chemical substances for agricultural and veterinary uses; 1919.
(b) Koala.
Karmel Bros. Pty Ltd, Melbourne.
Jewellery; 1938.
(c) Aussie Bear.
Thurlstane (Australia) Pty Ltd, Sydney.
Leather, skins and articles of leather; 1944.
(d) Koala – the Kooler Kola.
J. B. Baker, Melbourne.
Mineral and aerated waters; 1945.
(e) Bear Brand.
A. Simpson & Son, SA.
Hollow ware; 1947.
(f) Winkin & Blinkin.
Malcolm Hepburn & Co., Melbourne.
Children's dressing gowns; 1948.
(g) Associated Day Tours, Melbourne; 1950.
(h) H.C.P. Cola.
Healesville, Vic.
Mineral and aerated waters; 1953.
(i) 3 Koalas.
Lewis Ornstien, Melbourne.
Sound records; 1958.
(j) Joe the Koala.
Salisbury Travel Goods Co., Sydney.
Compressed fibre travel goods; 1935.

(a)

(b)

(c)

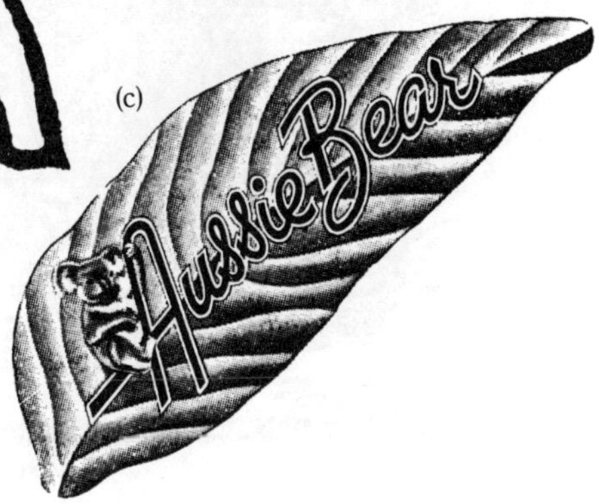

(d)

(e)

(f)

(g)

(h)

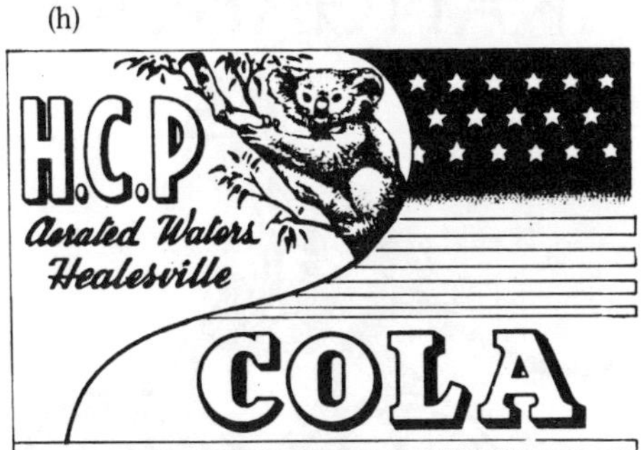

(i)

(j)

Native companions – fauna

Kangaroos.

In Australian trademarks the kangaroo has been depicted performing all manner of activities for all manner of products. Its visual treatment ranges from perfect realism through to the contemporary design of the current 1982 Commonwealth Games symbol where the kangaroo has been reduced to a mere three bands.

(a) Arnold V. Henn & Co., Sydney.
Calico and other fabrics; 1892.

(b) Goldsmiths Alliance.
Aaron Spitzel, Brisbane.
Jewellery and imitations; 1886.

(c) Walla Walla Brand.
Yung, Shollenberger & Co., 2 Change Alley, Pitt Street, Sydney.
Leather and skins; from an advertisement appearing 1890.
Walla Walla is Aboriginal for rain. Yung, Shollenberger & Co. boasted in their advertisements to be the largest buyers of kangaroo skins in Australia.

(d) Kangaroo Desiccated Potatoes.
H. Saltau & Sons, Warrnambool, Vic; 1894.

(e) Kangaroo.
Robert Lascelles & Co., Melbourne.
Velocipedes; 1896.

(f) The XII Commonwealth Games Australia (1982) Foundation Limited, Brisbane.
The symbol of the XII Commonwealth Games was designed by Hugh Edwards in a nation-wide competition held in 1978. It is derived from the form of a kangaroo in full flight and represents a stylized 'A' for Australia.

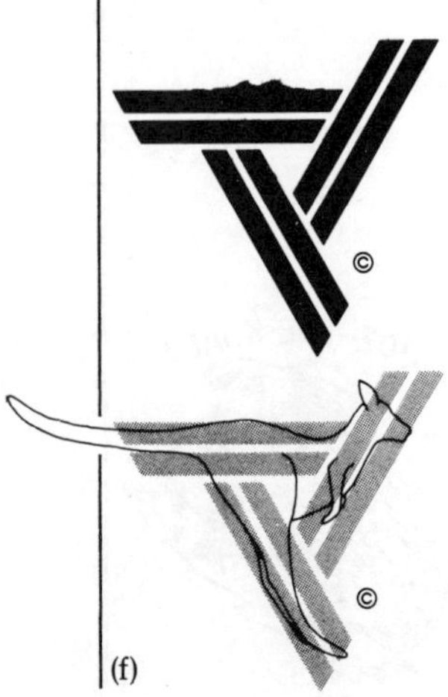

(f)

(a)

(b)

(c)

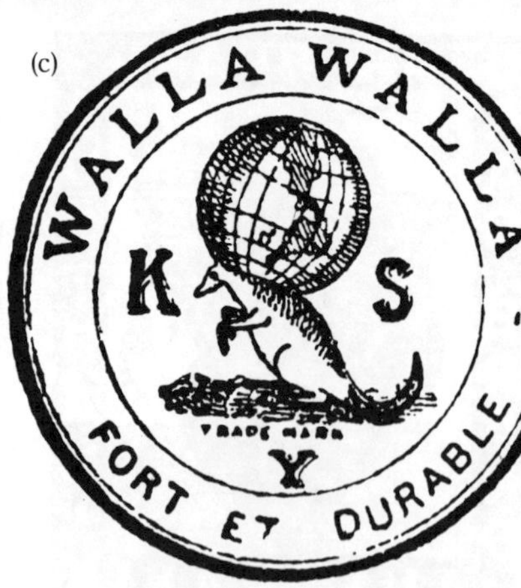

(d)

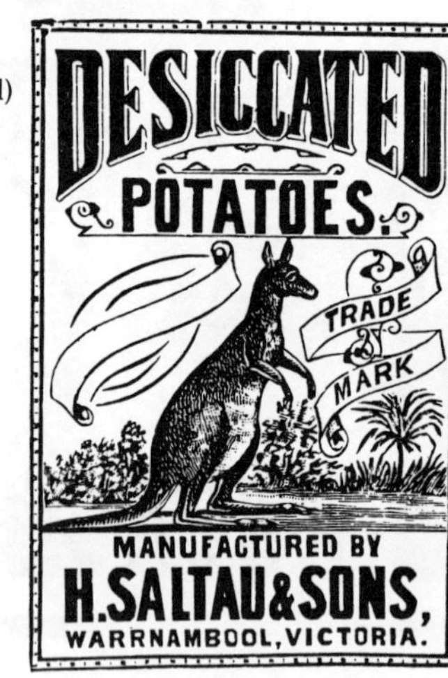

(e)

Native companions – fauna

Kangaroos.

(a) 'Karroo Roo' Soap. The Soap Works; 1901.
(b) The Kangaroo. Made in Japan. Safety matches; early 1900s.
(c) Rooide. John McEvoy & Sons, Sydney. Boots and shoes; 1909. Around the turn of the century, the wholesale slaughter of kangaroos led to a huge hide industry and the start of kangaroo preservation groups.
(d) Kangaroo. Commonwealth Oil Corporation Ltd, Sydney. Paraffin wax, grease; 1909.
(e) Eli Bannister. Paper, stationery and book binding; 1916.
(f) Surefit. Maurice & Connell, Sydney. Shirts and costumes; 1917.
(g) Kango: the sole survivor. Kango Mfg. Pty Ltd, NSW; 1922.
(h) Kicking Roo Brand. Tropical Traders, WA. Fresh and dried fruits; 1923.
(i) The Voice of Australia. V.O.A. Sound Productions Film House, Sydney; 1938.
(j) Ken the Kanga. Salisbury Travel Goods Co., Sydney. Compressed fibre travel goods; 1935. Joe the Koala's partner.

(a)

(b)

(c)

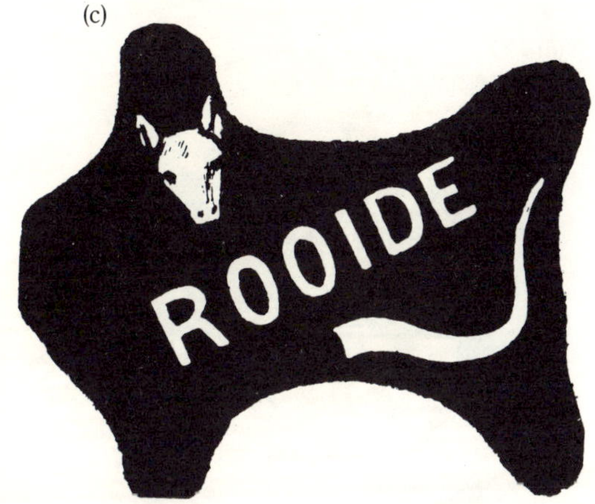

(d)

(e)

(f)

(g)

(h)

(i)

(j)

Native companions – fauna

Kangaroos.

(a) Dominion.
Light Aircraft Pty Ltd, Sydney.
Parachutes, balloons, life savers and floaters; 1939.
(b) Champion.
Paterson Laing & Bruce Ltd, Sydney.
Clothing; 1941.
(c) Aussie Roo.
Thurlstane (Australia) Pty Ltd, Sydney.
Leather, skins and articles of leather; 1944.
(d) Kanga.
Wright Varnish Co., New Hindmarsh, SA.
Paint; 1944.
(e) Auski Mfg. Co., Melbourne.
Skis; 1949.
(f) Roo Beauty Brand.
Paterson & Co. Ltd, Fremantle, WA.
Apples; 1958.
(g) S. E. Shooboudge, orchardist, Hobart; 1889.
(h) Kangaroo Brand.
James Spicer & Sons, Melbourne.
Paper; 1908.
(i) Kangaroo.
A. J. Sage & Co., Melbourne.
Dry cells; 1908.
(j) Good Luck.
George Summers, Qld.
Mineral and aerated waters; 1908.
(k) (l) Kangaroo Brand.
Lohmann & Co., Sydney.
Gums and resins; 1909.
(m) W. A. Brushware Co., Fremantle, WA.
(n) The Kangaroo Coupon Tea Co., Qld.; 1915.
Continued on page 179

(ad)

(a)

(b)

(c)

(d)

(e)

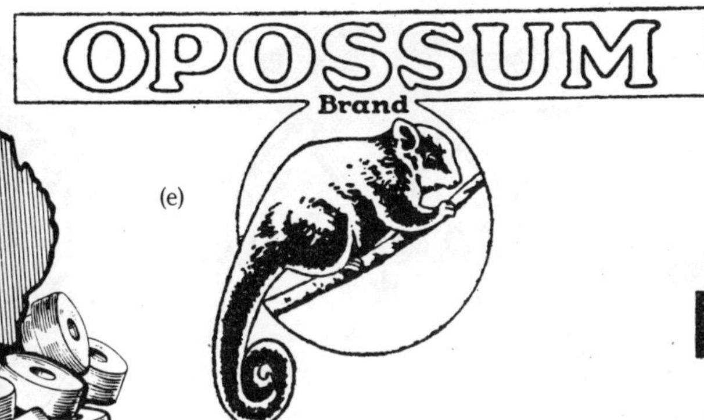

(f)

(g)

(h)

(i)

(j)

(k)

(l)

(m)

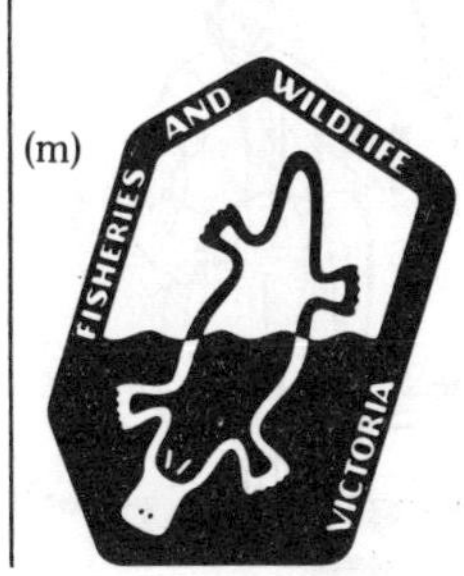

Native companions – fauna

Possums.

(a) Possum Brand. Tuomy & Co., Melbourne. Wines and spirits; 1899.
(b) Possum Brand. Allans & Stark, drapiers and clothiers, Brisbane; 1910.
(c) Apos Drug Co., Melbourne. Chemicals; 1913.
(d) Possum Brand. A. J. Thomas & Co., Sydney. Paper and stationery; 1925.
(e) Opossum Brand. F. Cave & Co. Pty Ltd, Melbourne. Fresh fruit; 1928.
(f) Possum. Taffelshone Pty Ltd, Sydney. Paint; 1952.

Platypuses.

(g) The Platypus. W. Dodgshun & Sons. Melbourne. Oil baize floor cloth; 1906.
(h) Platypus Brand. The Tasmanian Eucalyptus Oil Co. Ltd, Melbourne; 1906.
(i) Platypus Brand. The Orchardists' Chemical Works, Melbourne. Vermin destroyer; 1908.
(j) Platypus. F. A. McCarthy & Co. Pty Ltd, Melbourne. Lubricating oils and greases; 1913.
(k) R. C. Henderson Ltd, Sydney. Hats; 1918.
(l) Platypus. C. E. Mann, Adelaide. Foods; 1921.
(m) Fisheries and Wildlife Division, Ministry for Conservation, Victoria. This symbol was introduced in 1960 to coincide with the renaming of the Department from 'Fisheries and Game' to 'Fisheries and Wildlife'.

Native companions – fauna

Dingoes.

(a) Dingo Brand.
James Bond, Wingello, NSW.
Eucalyptus oil; 1892.
(b) Lister's Dingo Trail.
John Lister, Sydney; 1899.
(c) Dingo Brand.
D. J. Tuomy & Co., Melbourne.
Wines and spirits; 1916.
(d) Warrigal.
Peapes & Co. Ltd, Sydney.
Clothing; 1917.
(e) Dingo.
John Kees & Sons Ltd, hardware merchants, Sydney; 1920.

Wombats.

(f) Wombat.
American Trading Co. of Australia, Sydney.
Flour; 1919.
(g) Wombat.
The Tamar Valley Co-op. Ltd, Blackwall, Tas.
Fresh and preserved fruit; 1919.
(h) The Wombat Boot Mfg. Co. Ltd; 1921.

New breeds.

(i) Kangarooster Brand.
York Flour Milling Co. Ltd, Perth; 1930.
Kangarooster – the suggested name for offspring of Australian-US marriages.
(j) Chock-aroo.
Nestle & Anglo-Swiss Condensed Milk Co. (Australasia) Ltd, Sydney.
Chocolate; 1931.
(k) Zanic.
Imperial Industries of Australia and New Zealand; 1937.
(l) Kevin Pappas, Greek/kangaroo symbol of All Australian Graffiti Pty Ltd, illustration and design studio, Melbourne; 1975 to 1978.
The symbol was designed by Con Aslanis.

(a)

(b)

(c)

(d)

(e)

(f)

(g)

(h)

(i)

(j)

(k)

(l)

(a)

(b)

(c)

(d)

(e)

6. NATIVE COMPANIONS-AVIFAUNA.

Like the unique fauna, the Australian avifauna has captured the flights of fancy of many a trade-mark designer.
(a) Diggaburra.
The Digger Tea Supply Co., Qld.; 1922.
(b) Cockatoo Brand.
J. Gillespie, East Northam, WA.
Flour; 1902.
(c) Lyre Bird Brand.
G. Sutherland Smith & Sons, Sydney and Melbourne.
Wines and spirits; 1906.
(d) Magpie.
Richards Bros., Melbourne.
Self raising flour; 1909.
(e) Emu Pilsner Beer.
The Emu Brewery Co., Perth; 1956.

Native companions – avifauna

Kookaburras.

A member of the Kingfisher family, the kookaburra (Aboriginal) has been tagged with a multitude of names: bush alarm, bushman's clock, jack, jackie, jackass.

(a) Kingfisher Brand – 'Our Jack'.
A. M. Bickford & Sons, Adelaide; 1899.
A. M. Bickford & Sons used this trademark for a range of products.

(b) Kookaburra.
Birt & Co. Ltd, Sydney.
Frozen meat; 1907.

(c) Kookaburra.
Australian Knitting Mills Ltd, Melbourne.
Hosiery; 1913.

(d) Kookaburra Brand.
A. G. Thompson, Melbourne.
Leather sporting goods; 1913.

(e) Jackass.
G. Gunnersen & Co., Melbourne.
Manufactures from mineral and other substances for building or decoration; 1915.

(f) Kookaburra 'Our Jacks'.
D. & W. Murray Ltd, Adelaide.
Hats; 1920.

(g) Kookooburra Brand.
A. Forsyth & Co., Ltd, Sydney.
Ropes; 1925.

(h) Municipal shield of the Shire of Korumburra, Vic.; current.

(a)

(b)

(c)

(d)

(e)

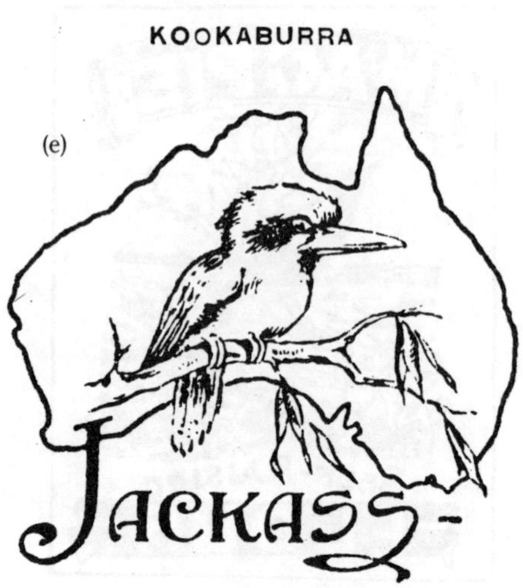

(f)

(g)

(h)

Native companions – avifauna

Kookaburras.

(a) The Commonwealth of Australia Hall Mark Co.; 1921.
(b) National Motor Car Mfg. Co. Ltd, Sydney; 1926.
(c) Cookaburra. Briggs Bros. Pty Ltd, Melbourne. Patty pans; 1927.
(d) Jackie Brand. E. F. Martin, Vic. Leather goods; 1927.
(e) Kookaburra. Stinton & Son, Geelong, Vic. Bulbs and seeds; 1930.
(f) Kookaburra. Duval Trading Co., Sydney. Blind hollands; 1936.
(g) Kingfisher. R. Fisher Pty Ltd, Melbourne. Shelving, racks, storage; 1956.
(h) Kookaburra Cotton Shoe Laces; current pack.

(a)

(b)

(c)

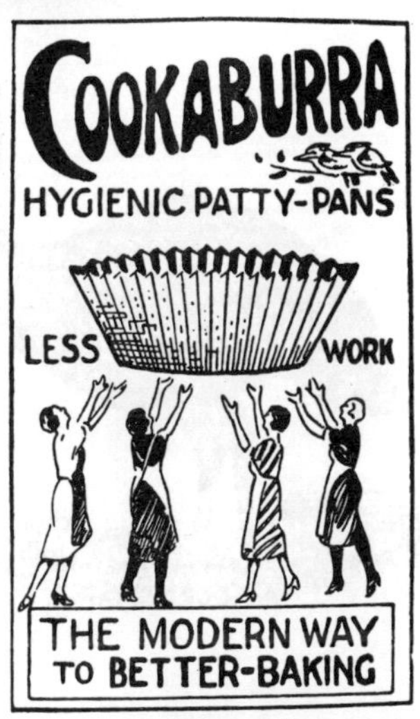

(d)

(h)

(e)

(f)

(g)

Native companions – avifauna

Emus.

The word emu was derived from the Portuguese *ema* (crane or ostrich).
(a) Emu. Webendderfer Bros., Sydney. Frame moulding; 1891.
(b) Mac Robertson. Macpherson David Robertson, Melbourne. Chocolate and cocoa; 1893.
(c) Emu Brand. Dyason & Son, Melbourne. Cordial sauce; 1894.
(d) Emu Brand. James Allard, Melbourne. Pottery wares; 1906.
(e) F. H. Faulding & Co. Adelaide. Eucalyptus oil and extracts; 1906.
(f) Emu Brand. The Emu Bay Butter Factory Co., Burnie, Tas. Butter and cheese; 1908.
(g) Emu Brand. Kent Town Preserving Co., SA. Canned foods; 1914.
(h) Clark & Fauset Ltd. Machinery; 1921.
(i) Emu Brand. Rosenfeld & Co. Pty Ltd, Sydney. Australian hardwoods; 1926.
(j) Emu Brand. G. Kinnear & Sons Pty Ltd, Melbourne. Rope; 1928. The emu is still being used on some of Kinnear's packaging.

(a)

(b)

(c)

(d)

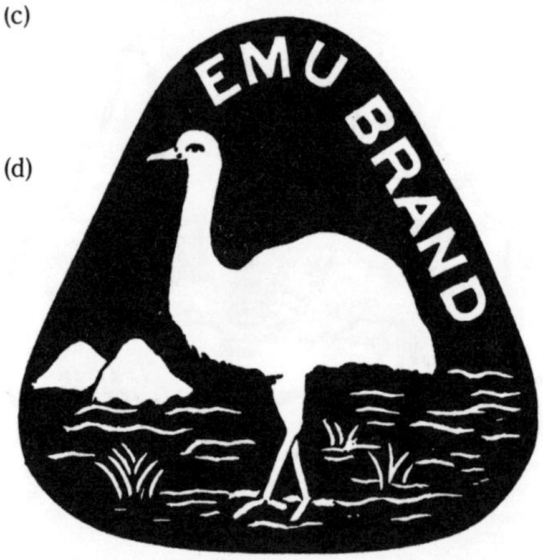

(e)

(f)

(j)

(g)

(h)

(i)

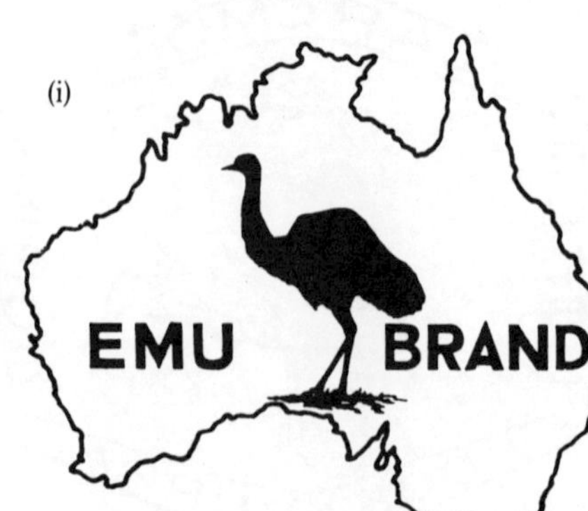

(a)

(b)

(c)

(d)

(e)

(f)

(g)

(h)

(i)

(j)

(k)

Native companions – avifauna.

Lyrebirds.

(a) Coote's Harp Tail Pheasant Brand.
J. Might Coote & Co., Melbourne.
Foods; 1893.
(b) A. A. Simpson.
Baking powder; 1892.
(c) Lyre Bird.
Downer & Co., Adelaide and Melbourne.
Fermented liquors; 1907.
(d) Lyre Bird Brand.
Davis Bros., Melbourne.
Smallgoods; 1909.
(e) Lyre Bird.
Sniders & Abrahams Ltd, Melbourne.
Tobacco; 1920.

Magpies.

(f) Turner & Henderson Ltd, printers and stationers, Sydney; 1915.
(g) Magpie Brand.
J. Kitchen & Sons Pty Ltd, Melbourne.
Soap; 1927.
(h) Magpie.
The Bunyip Soap Co. Ltd, Adelaide.
Soap; 1927.

Cockatoos.

(i) Cockatoo.
W. H. Blackham.
Luncheon cheese; 1916.
(j) Cockatoo Brand.
Cockatoo Preserves Ltd, Melbourne.
Jams and preserves; 1919.
(k) W. J. Ledger, Melbourne.
Wines; 1941.

7. NATIVE COMPANIONS-FLORA.

Although the gumtree is the most popular, like the native animals and birds, most major species of flora have been represented in trade-marks.

Black boys.

(a) Black Boy Eczemacura.
W. Paterson, Whitby Falls, WA.
Cure for eczema; 1895.
(b) A.N.P.
Australian Natural Products (Stains) Ltd, Melbourne.
Wood stains; 1915.
(c) S.A. Black Boy Products Ltd, Adelaide; 1928.

Wattles.

(d) Silver Wattle.
Pure creamery butter, Vic., 1906.
(e) Blossoms.
A. L. Benjamin, Brisbane.
Tobacco; 1914.
(f) Golden Wattle Elastic.
Elastic Webbing (Australia) Pty Ltd, Melbourne; 1939.

Waratahs.

(g) Waratah Brand.
The Rosella Preserving & Mfg. Co. Ltd, Melbourne; 1911.
(h) Waratah.
R. Lee & Co. Ltd, Sydney.
Paints, stains; 1918.
(i) Waratah.
Ryland Bros. (Australia) Ltd, Port Waratah, NSW.
Wire netting, barbed wire, nails; 1933.
(j) Department of Railways, New South Wales.
From an advertisement appearing 1959.

(a)

(b)

(c)

(d)

(e)

(f)

(g)

(h)

(i)

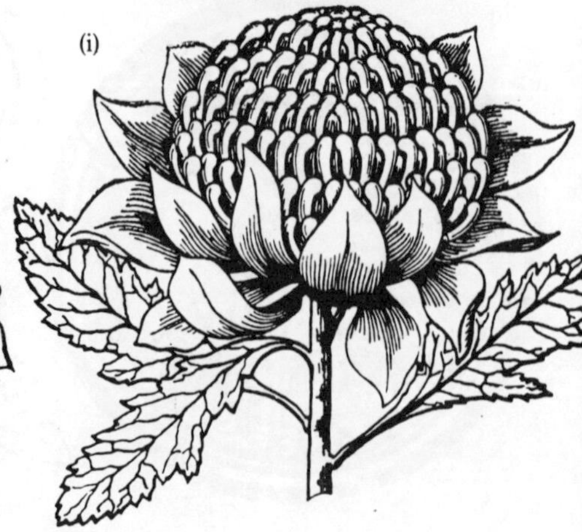

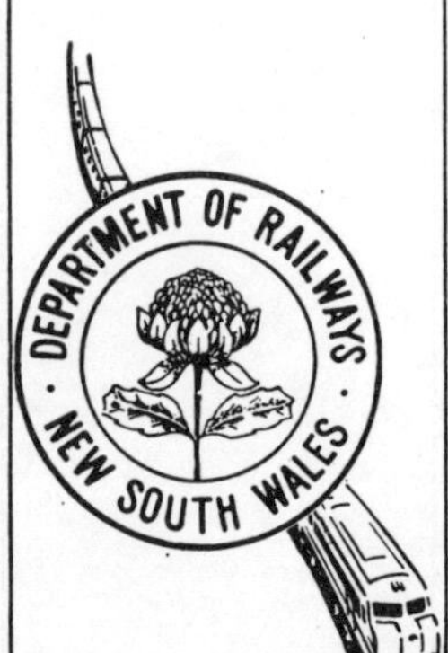

(j)

(a)

(c)

(b)

(d)

(e)

(f)

(g)

(h)

(i)

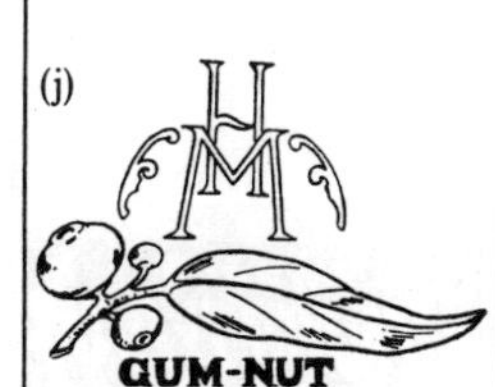

(j)

Native companions – flora.

Gums.

(a) Blue Gum Oil. B. A. Atwell, Hobart; 1887.
(b) The Mallee Brand. The Mildura Fruit Preserving Co., Vic. Fruit; 1893.
(c) Ironbark. The Sydney Paper Mills Ltd; 1905.
(d) Gum Tree Brand. A. T. Hammond & Co., Melbourne; 1906.
(e) Gum Leaf Brand. J. Perry, Melbourne. Wooden shafts and poles; 1912.
(f) Gum Tree. J. Wardle & Co., Adelaide. Metals; 1915. This trademark features the 'Old Gum-tree', Glenelg, where the establishment of South Australia was proclaimed in 1836.
(g) Golden Gum. Australian Mfg. & Importing Co. Ltd, Sydney. Food; 1920.
(h) Gum Leaf. Pacific Mfg. Co. Ltd, Sydney. Disinfectants; 1925.
(i) Prima Hosiery Pty Ltd, Melbourne; 1928.
(j) Gum-nut Chocolates. G. Malin; 1920.

Native companions – flora.

Gums.

(a) Gum Tree.
Crosby Mann & Co. Ltd, Adelaide.
Flour; 1928.
(b) Red Gum Pack.
Paterson & Co. Ltd, Perth. Apples; 1934.
(c) Arbon.
Die Casters Pty Ltd, Melbourne; 1936.
(d) Toyala.
N. Burnet, Sydney.
Toys; 1939.

Etc..

(e) Kurrajong.
H. W. Salkeld & Co. Sydney; 1906.
(f) Ti-Tree Brand.
W. H. Archer, Melbourne.
Butter, cheese; 1908.
(g) Banksia.
R. Holmes & Co. Ltd, Perth.
Fermented liquors; 1917.
(h) Fern Brand.
Lilydale Aerated Water Co. Pty Ltd, Vic.
Mineral and aerated waters; 1923.
(i) Mentho-Lyptus Pastilles.
Payne's Ltd, Sydney; 1935.

(a)

(b)

(c)

(d)

(e)

(f)

(g)

(h)

(i)

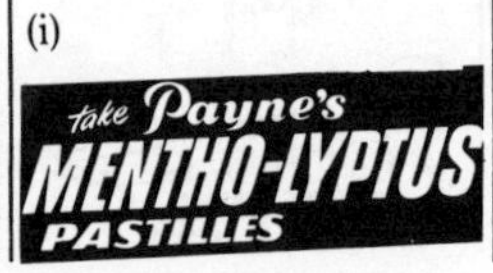

Bushells TEA
ROSELLA
MINTIES
The Universal Sweet
PER 1/- TIN
NOVELTIE
MADE IN AUSTRALIA
MORLAY POULTRY FOODS
TO BANK
MORLAY – MORE PAY
NOW BOND'SET
TO CUT SHRINKAGE
GUARD YOUR
HEALTH SMOKE
LIFEGUARD
ONE PINT
HEENZO
COUGH MIXTURE
F

Book II: OBSERVATIONS

8. DON'T WORRY.

After the gold rush and Federation, the 'Emerging Australians' rode on the sheep's back into rural settlement. But, they weren't alone in the conquest of the outback. Other 'New Australians' followed: the rabbit and the prickly pear cactus. Before them all lay poor soil, scrubby timber and a climate that raged from flood to drought. Behind them, the opportunists, quick with innovations and ideas designed to take the worry out of being a farmer.

(a) Grazcos Co-op. Ltd, Sydney; 1955.
Grazcos were in operation by the 1930s as *The Graziers' Co-operative Shearing Co. Ltd* – merchants of most farm needs.

(b) The Oil Sheep Dip Co., Bathurst, NSW; 1909.

(a)

(b)

Don't worry

About the sheep.

Australia's breeding of sheep was only surpassed by its breeding of blowflies.
(a) Antibuzzbuzz.
F. Lassetter & Co. Ltd, Sydney.
Fly preventive; 1907.
(b) Eclipse Drench.
Banks Property Co., Rockdale, NSW.
Agricultural chemicals; 1911.
(c) Ben Trovato Wormecide.
James Wilson, Melbourne.
Drench for sheep and domestic animals; 1913.
(d) Hoggite.
H. Daly, Sydney.
Preparation for preventing blowflies in sheep; 1915.
(e) S.O.S. (Save Our Sheep).
S.O.S. Chemical Co., Sydney.
Veterinary chemicals; 1917.
(f) Blo-Fli-Di.
H. H. Hinds Ltd, Sydney.
Veterinary chemicals; 1918.
(g) Defiance.
Bagley Sanoleo Chemical Co., Broken Hill, NSW.
Blowfly oil; 1920.
(h) Arsenical.
J. H. Swan, NSW.
Marking oil for sheep; 1923.
(i) Pinko.
Pinko Remedy Co., Sydney.
Eye powder for sheep; 1928.
(j) Notix.
Oliver Smith, Emmaville, NSW.
Sheep dipping powder; 1937.
(k) Billabong Windmills.
John Danks & Son Pty Ltd, Melbourne; from an advertisement appearing 1944.

(a)

(b)

(c)

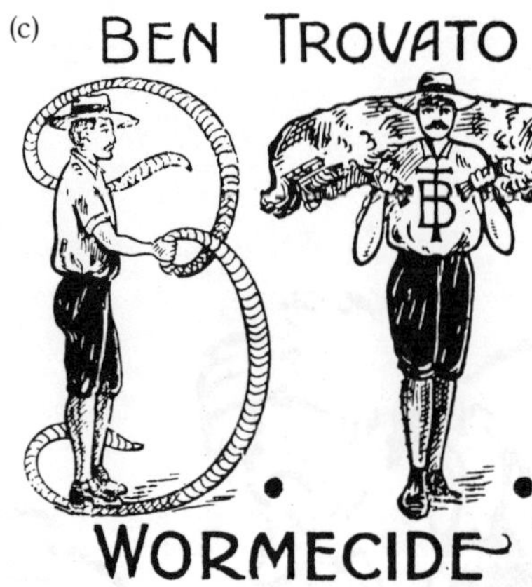

(d)

(e)

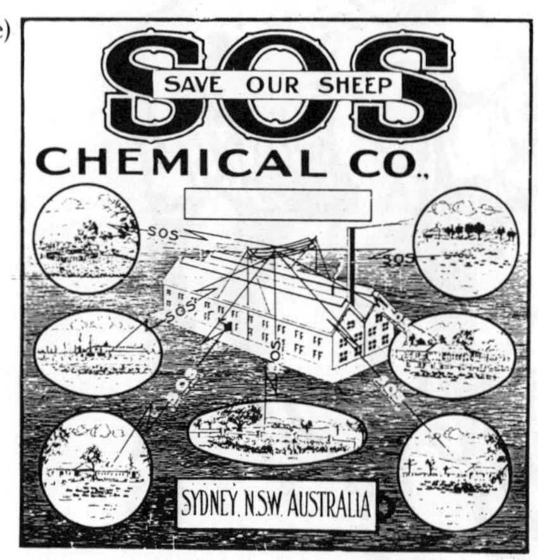

(f)

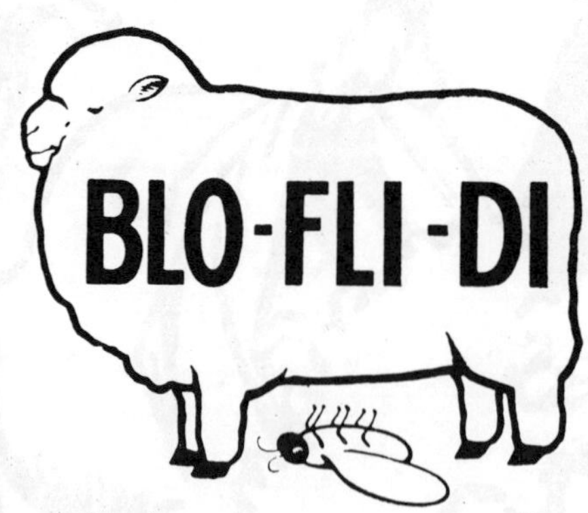

(g)

(k)

(h)

(i)

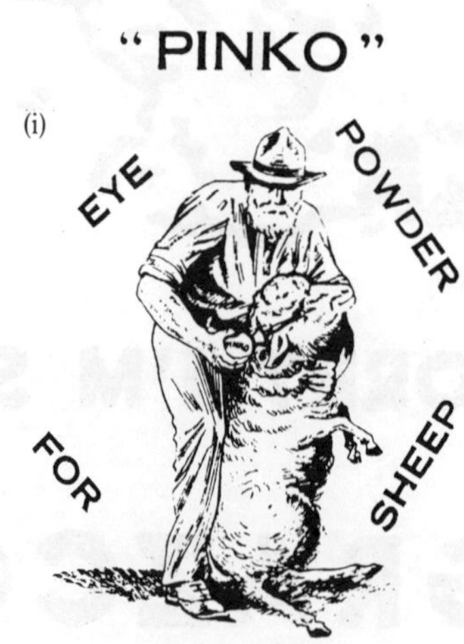

(j)

Don't worry

About thc pests.

If you can't shear it, shoot it. If you can't shoot it, spray it. If you can't spray it, work out a way to shear it.

(a) Dog Dynamite.
E. A. Scammell, Blanchetown, SA.
Chemical for the destruction of dogs; 1909.
(b) Silex Weed Destroyer.
W. H. Brewer, Melbourne; 1907.
(c) White Frog.
Jaques Fisher & Co., Melbourne.
Fungicide; 1911.
(d) Mustdie.
Hudsons Eumenthol Chemical Co., Sydney.
Insecticides; 1913.
(e) Deathdust.
Sayers, Allport Pty Ltd, Sydney.
Chemical substances for agriculture and horticulture; 1925.
(f) Cloudform Dusts.
Gibbs, Bright & Co., Adelaide.
Insecticides and fungicides; 1925.
(g) Noxo.
Noxo Products Pty Ltd, Melbourne.
Weed killers; 1926.

(a)

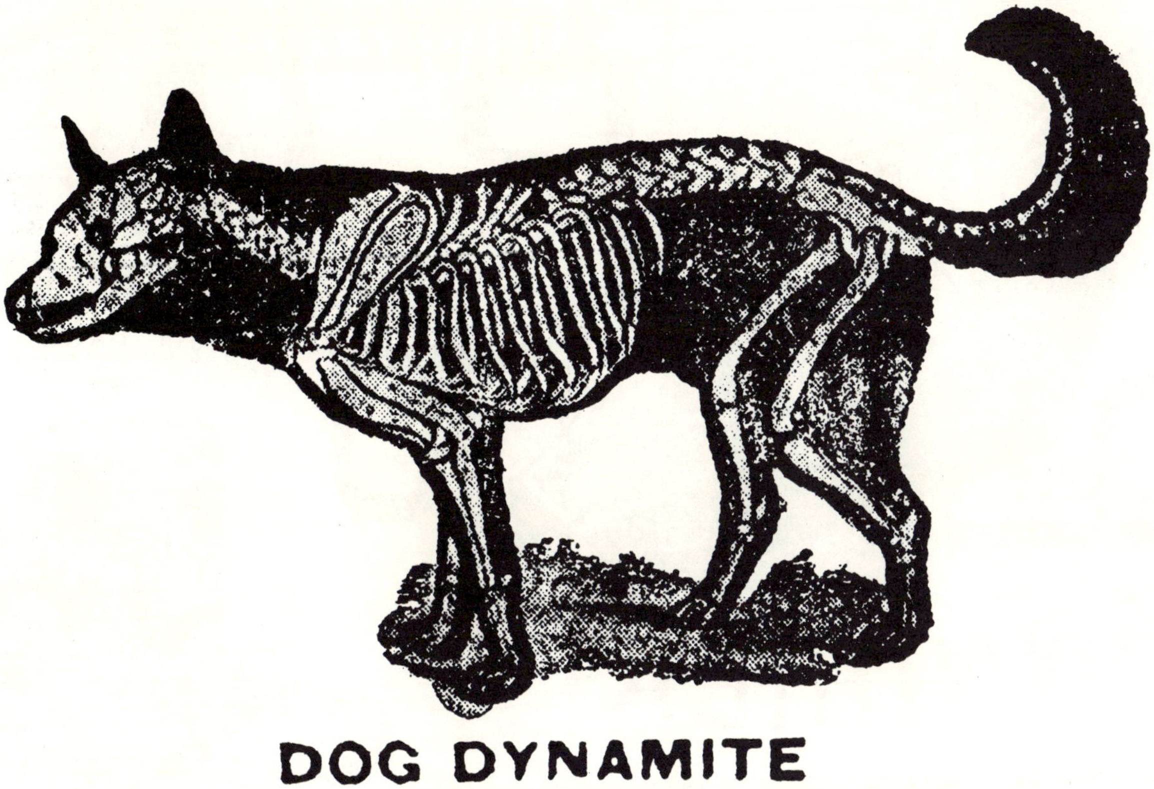

(b)

(c)

(d)

(e)

(f)

(g)

Don't worry

About the rabbit plague.

In 1859, twelve imported wild rabbits were released on Thomas Austin's property at Barwon Park, Victoria. By 1880 they had covered half the continent and reached plague proportions. There were reports of farmers wading knee-deep in rabbits, bashing them to death with sticks. For the less energetic, the agricultural chemist provided poisonous liquids, pellets and gases to help with the whole-sale *bunnycide*.

(a) PPP Annihilator.
Rucker & Mackenzie, Melbourne.
Rabbit destroyer; 1896.

(b) Bosker.
Elliott Bros. Ltd, Sydney and Brisbane.
Rabbit poison; 1905.

(c) Presto.
J. H. Grant, Sydney.
Rabbit poison; 1910.

(d) S.A.P.
Sayers, Allport Pty Ltd, Sydney.
Rabbit poison; c.1916.

(e) Decoy-Em-All.
F. D. Cox and C. H. Parker, Warrabah, NSW.
A vermin destroyer; 1917.

(f) Magnetic.
The P. D. Magnetic Rabbit Poison Co.; 1921.

(g) Bunni-Di-Brickette.
Lancelot Le Souef, Melbourne.
Rabbit exterminator; 1934.

(h) Smokogas.
Hart & Co. Pty Ltd, Melbourne.
Rabbit poison; 1941.

(i) Bunnycide.
F. H. Faulding, Adelaide.
Rabbit destroyer; 1904.

(a)

(b)

(c)

(d)

(e)

(f)

(g)

(h)

(i)

BUNNYCIDE

(a)

(b)

(c)

(d)

(e)

(f)

Don't worry

About the rabbit plague.

While to some the rabbit was a menace, to others it was a new source of income. Not only as Fresh Rabbit, Frozen Rabbit and Preserved Rabbit, but as the tenacious spirit of a new product that *could not be exterminated*.

(a) Cannot Be Exterminated.
W. C. Marshall & Co., Brisbane.
Articles of clothing; 1898.
(b) Worregil.
Country Freezing Co. Ltd, Sydney.
Frozen rabbits and hares; 1907.
(c) Rabbito.
W. Harris.
Eating rabbits; 1918.
(d) Fresh Rabbit & Bacon Pie.
S. F. Jarrett, South Melbourne; 1923.
(e) C. R. Cole, Melbourne.
Preserved rabbits; 1933.
(f) Freshcort.
Luke Wright Marine Industries Pty Ltd, Sydney.
Eating rabbits; 1949.
(g) Best Australian Roller Flour.
E. Hayes, Melbourne; 1905.

(g)

Don't worry

About cures and manures.

As well as killing just about anything, the agricultural chemist could cure just about anything. And mark it, clean it, or fertilise it.

(a) W. A. Graham. Mary Emily Moss, Sydney. Veterinary chemicals; 1906.

(b) Pegasus. Elliott Bros. Ltd, Sydney. Veterinary remedies; 1907.

(c) Scougall's 'Uwanta'. Seaton Dun Scougall, Brisbane. Cattle medicine; 1907.

(d) Kwik Heal. Denyer Bros., Melbourne. Chemicals; 1907.

(e) Torpedo. H. D. Evans, Melbourne. Veterinary patent medicine; 1907.

(f) AWU. John Sanderson & Co., Melbourne. Agricultural and veterinary chemicals; 1910.

(g) Carbine Remedies. United Distributing Companies Ltd, Sydney. Veterinary chemicals; 1911.

(h) Phosphatum. The Australian Produce Co., Melbourne. Cattle medicine; 1911.

(i) The Sun. F. S. Falconer, NSW. Condition powder for horses; 1912.

(j) Wallaroo Super. Wallaroo Phosphate Co. Ltd; from an advertisement appearing 1910.

(a)

(b)

(c)

(d)

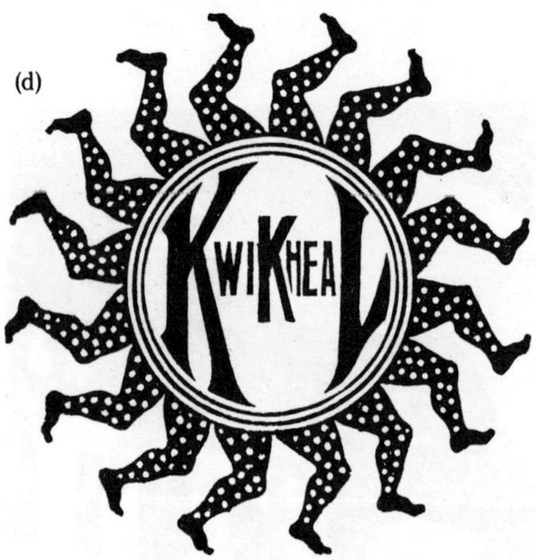

(e)

(f)

(g)

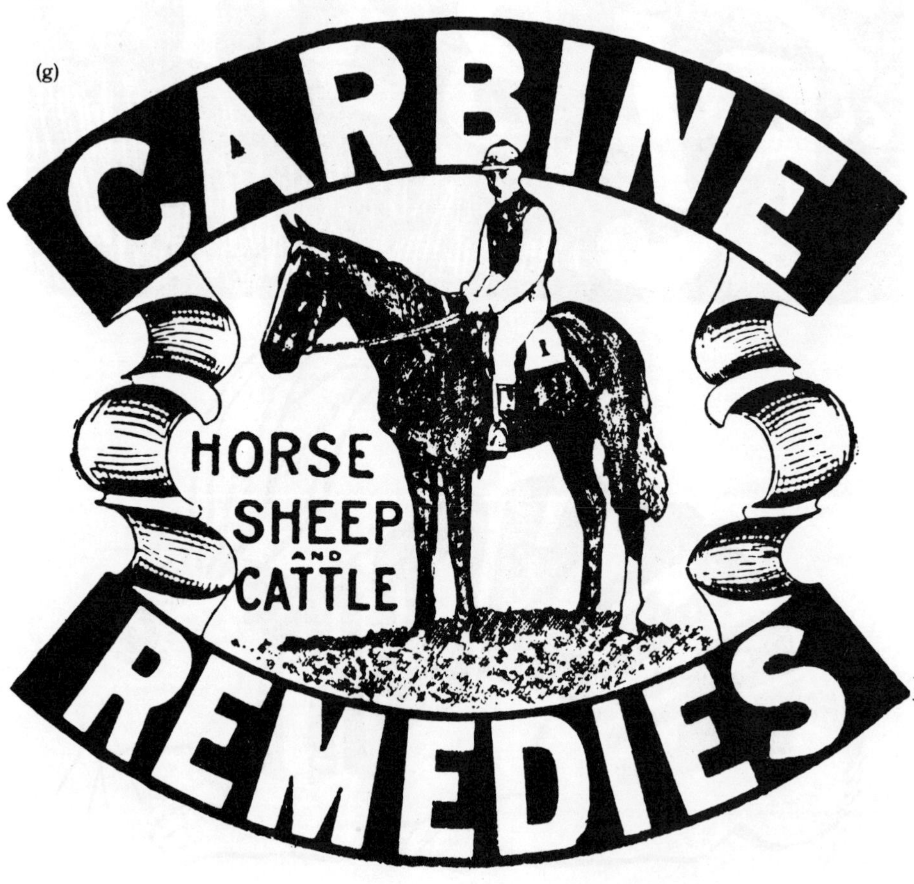

(h)

(i)

(j)

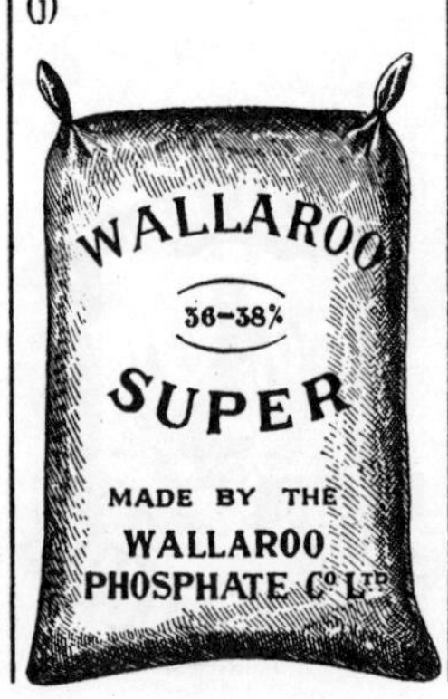

Don't worry

About cures and manures.

(a) Katalo Brand.
The Veterinary Remedy Co., Sydney; 1914.
(b) Aero Brand.
A. M. Bickford & Sons Ltd, Adelaide.
Agricultural chemicals; 1916.
(c) Marko.
The Oil Sheep Dip Co., Sydney.
Sheep branding oils; 1917.
(d) Digger Brand.
The Scientific Garden Utility Co.,
Chemical substances; 1919.
(e) Equivita.
A. E. Maxwell, Melbourne.
Cure for bot-worm and sand in horses and cattle; 1924.
(f) Rhino.
Commonwealth Fertilizers & Chemicals Ltd, Melbourne; 1934.
(g) A.S.D.
J. H. Wagstaff, Melbourne.
Stock medicines and disinfectant; 1936.
(h) Martin R. Freney, Sydney.
Agricultural chemicals; 1951.
(i) Elder Smith & Co. Ltd.
Stock agents.

(a)

(b)

(c)

(d)

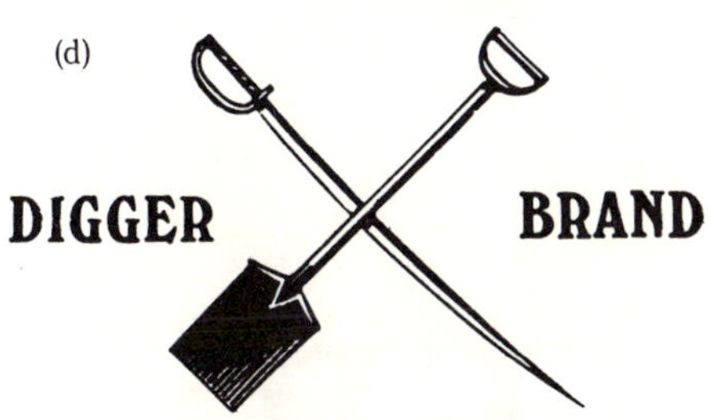

(e)

(f)

(g)

(h)

(i)

Don't worry

About the chooks.

In his advertisement, Bill Manning of Bendigo proved that a good dose of trademark could make any rooster stand erect.

(a) Before and After.
William Manning, Produce and seed merchant, Bendigo, Vic.
Poultry spice; from an advertisement appearing 1893.

(b) Morlay Poultry Foods.
R. B. Young, Perth; 1935.

(c) La-By.
A. E. Watson, Warracknabeal, Vic.
Egg preservative; 1935.

(d) A square deal.
Poultry Breeders Better Chick Association, Sydney; 1936.

(e) The Top Note Mixture.
Arthur Yates & Co., Sydney.
Canary seed; 1898.

(f) Sweeter Song.
The Producers' Co-op. Distributing Society Ltd, Sydney.
Bird food; 1939.

(g) J. Cockbill, Melbourne.
Poultry grit, meat meal and bone meal; from an advertisement appearing 1941.

(a)

(b)

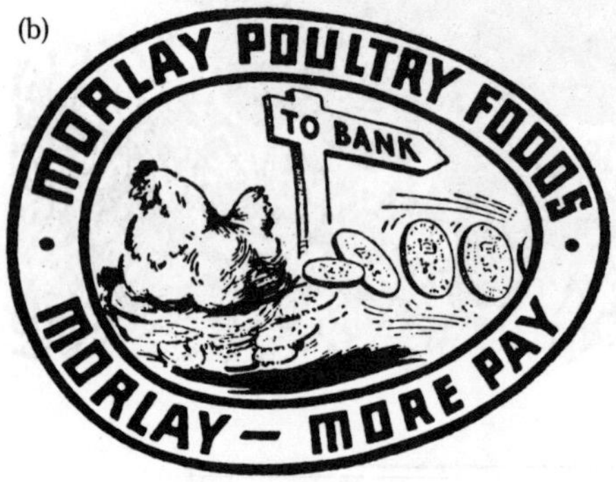

(c)

(d)

(e)

(f)

(g)

(a)

(b)

(c)

(d)

(e)

(f)

(g)

(h)

(i)

(j)

(k)

(l)

Don't worry

All around the farm.

There were products to help the farmer make money. And spend it.
(a) Eureka.
S. Howe Co.
Wheat cleaning machine; from an advertisement appearing 1899.
(b) The National Cattle Food Co., Melbourne; 1904.
(c) Neptune Unrivalled Steel Wire.
Barbed and fencing wire; 1910.
(d) £.s.d.
G. Shirley Ltd, Sydney.
Manure; 1912.
(e) Something to crow about.
Mitchell & Co. Pty Ltd, Melbourne.
Agricultural and horticultural machinery; 1913.
(f) Cicada.
The Tootgarook Estate Pty Ltd, Melbourne.
Manurial soil; 1917.
(g) Leakpruf.
Arthur G. Wilson Ltd, Sydney.
Cotton piece goods; 1929.
(h) Gippsland & Northern Co-op. Ltd, Melbourne.
Pedigree seeds; 1937.
(i) Bacal.
The Australian Cotton Co-op. Association Ltd, Brisbane.
Cattle and sheep food; 1938.
(j) Glenora Seeds.
M. F. Hodge & Sons Ltd, Adelaide.
Seeds; 1953.
(k) The Hunter Gate & Fence Co. Ltd, Islington, NSW; 1954.
(l) F. H. Purcell, Maylands, WA.
Aluminium horseshoes; 1958.
(m) L.S.D.
Pounds, shillings and pence – it was used to sell everything from manures (d) to cures like this preparation for the relief of stomach troubles by F. C. Moore of Southport, Qld.; 1931.

(m)

Don't worry

About the prickly pear.

The *Opuntia stricta*, or prickly pear cactus, was introduced into New South Wales in 1839.
By 1900 it covered an area of 4,000,000 hectares. By 1920, 23,000,000 hectares.
It seemed nothing could stop the steadily spreading succulent.
But, in the late 1920s and early 1930s an imported insect called *Cactoblastis cactorum* lived up to its name and ate the prickly plague away, leaving behind a range of useless exterminators and a soap for farmers to wash their hands of the whole incident.

(a) The Adder Prickly Pear.
L. E. Griffith, Mirumbri, NSW.
Prickly pear exterminator; 1911.

(b) Pear-Stroyer.
Kolter & Co., Gatton, Qld.
Prickly pear destroyer; 1921.

(c) Prickly Pear Soap.
Prickly Pear Products Pty, Dulacca, Qld; 1921.

(a)

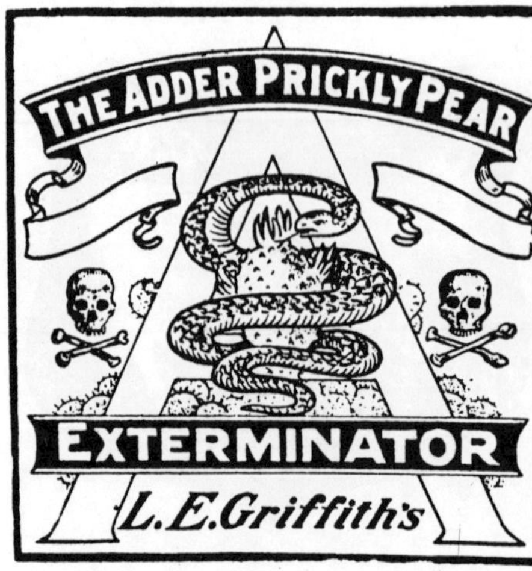

(b)

(c)

(a)

9. THE HALF BACK.

While the man on the land was slowed by rabbits and cacti, the wheels of industry gained speed.
Australia needed machines. From automobiles to the *Auto-pie*.
As the Farmer cried, 'Full forward', the Urbanite demanded, 'Half back'.
(a) We give you the half back.
The Australian Life Agencies Ltd, Melbourne; 1913.
(b) F. E. Lyton; 1913.

(b)

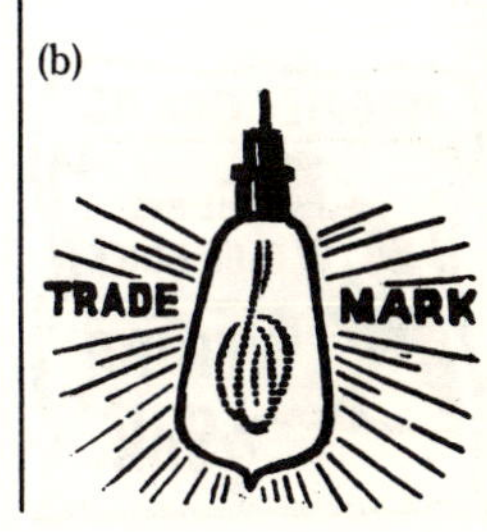

The half back

On glue.

Clag – one of the great substances of the Australian education system. There was not a child who had not sniffed, tasted or been covered in it.
(a) Clag.
J. Angus, Melbourne.
Paste; 1898.
(b) Strength.
De Meric Ltd, Sydney.
Glue; 1914.
(c) Jimmy the Granite.
Z. E. Williams, Brisbane.
Cement; 1921.
(d) Glyco.
J. H. Granville, Perth.
Pastes; 1917.
(e) Rubbagrip.
Rubber Adhesives Pty Ltd, Sydney; 1937.
(f) Tarzan's Grip.
R. G. Whitehead, Sydney.
Cement; 1935.
(g) Keegan Bros, Sydney.
Cement; 1944.
(h) Styx Malayan Mucilage, Sydney; 1948.
(i) Magpie Brand.
F. C. Nicholls.
Writing ink; 1910.

(a)

(b)

(c)

(d)

(e)

(f)

(g)

(h)

(i)

The half back

On industry.

A telephone call to one of Chandler's stores enquiring as to the relevance of the Kangaroo shouldering arms, abruptly concluded with the current Italian proprietor's reply: 'I dunno.'

(a) D. J. & W. H. Chandler, Melbourne. Hardware merchants. Established 1876. The mark was in use by the turn of the century.

(b) M. Ferguson, Melbourne. Wrought iron pipes; from an advertisement appearing 1890.

(c) Evenden's Spring Head. Sidney Cooke Pty Ltd, Melbourne. Nails; c. 1895, registered 1906.

(d) Australian Explosives & Chemical Co. Ltd, Melbourne; from a letterhead dated 1902.

(a)

(b)

(c)

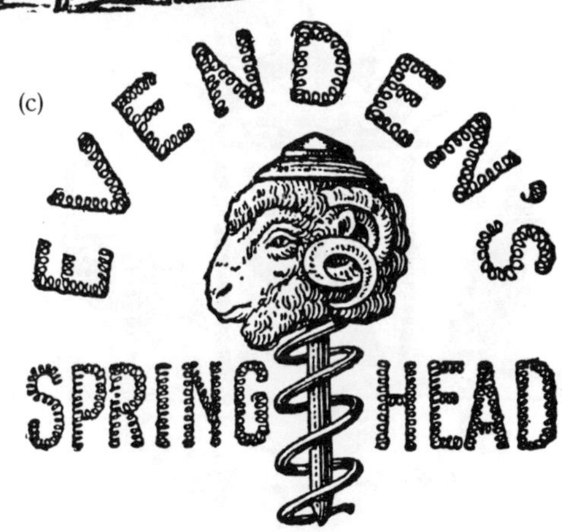

(d)

The half back

On industry.

(a) Kangaroo Brand.
M. Donaghy & Sons, Melbourne.
Rope, cordage and twine; from an advertisement appearing 1892.
(b) Pearl Rich, Broome Hill, WA.
Mallet bark and wood; 1906.
(c) The Gripwell.
The Sydney Soap & Candle Co. Ltd, Sydney.
Driving belts; 1907.
(d) Python.
Edward Butler & Sons, Brisbane.
Hooks and chains; 1911.
(e) T. Duff & Bros., Melbourne.
Shopfitters; 1909.
(f) Cosmopolitan Import Agency, Melbourne.
Machinery; 1909.
(g) Calopedes.
William Lewis, Sydney.
Lasts for shoes; 1911.
(h) Patch.
E. H. James, Melbourne.
Rubber and gutta percha; 1911.
(i) Tui.
The Victorian Hardwood Milling & Seasoning Co. Pty Ltd, Melbourne.
Prepared timber; 1915.

(a)

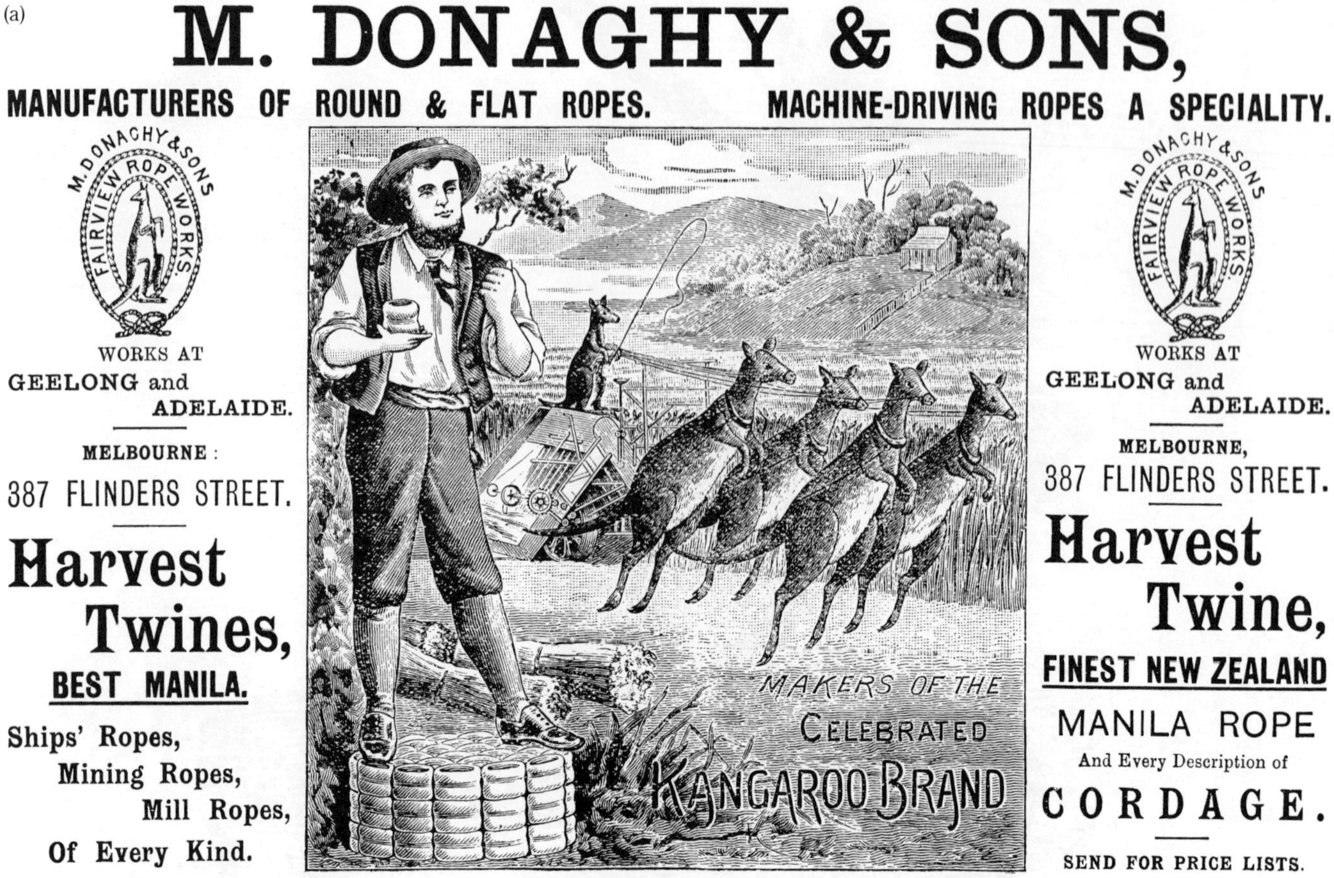

(b)

(c)

(d)

(e)

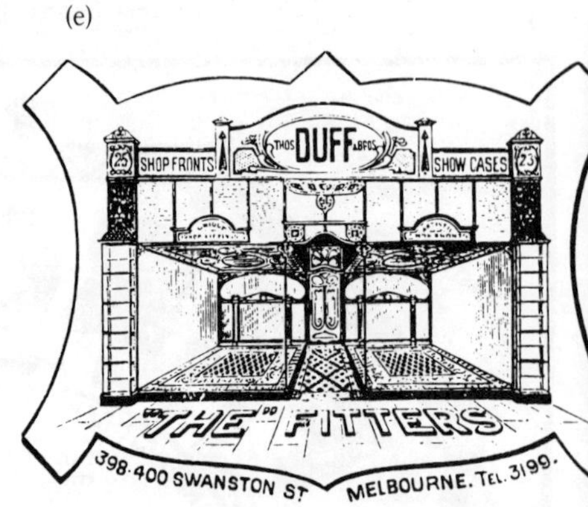

(f)

(g)

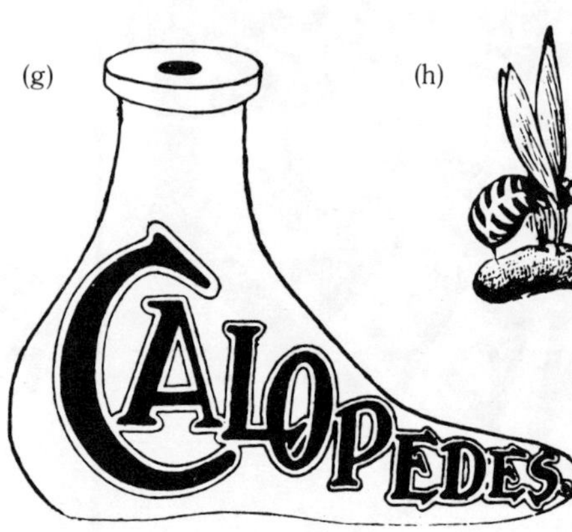

(h)

(i)

The half back

On industry.

(a) Knight's Lal Lal. Fire Brick & Pottery Works Pty Ltd, Lal Lal, Vic. Fire clay bricks; 1913.
(b) Hardite. C. A. Stewart, Sydney. Case hardening compound for iron; 1914.
(c) Fibrolite. James Hardie & Co., Melbourne. Asbestos sheeting; 1917.
(d) United States of Australasia Mfg. Works – W. E. Cash, Melbourne. Engineering contrivances; 1916.
(e) (f) The Broken Hill Pty Co. Ltd, Melbourne. Iron, steel; (e) 1920, (f) current symbol designed by Richard Beck in the early 1960s.
(g) Hitch your wagon to a star. Commonwealth Aircraft Corporation Ltd.; 1920.
(h) Cyclone Pty Ltd, Sydney. Metal gates and fences; from an advertisement appearing 1921.
(i) F. E. Myers & Bros. Co. Pumps, hay tools and door hangers; 1923.

(a)

(b)

(c)

(d)

(e)

(g)

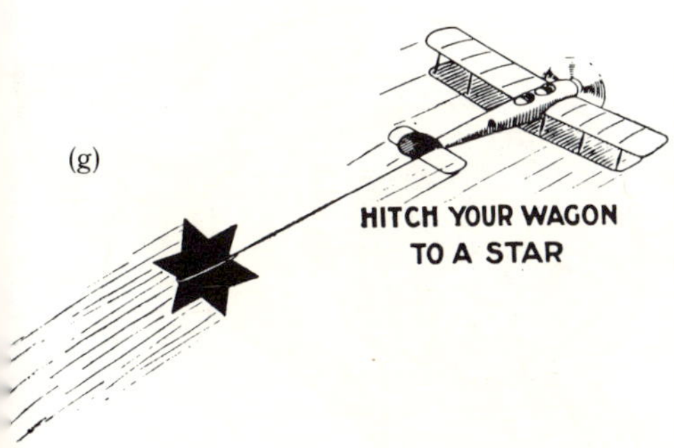

(h)

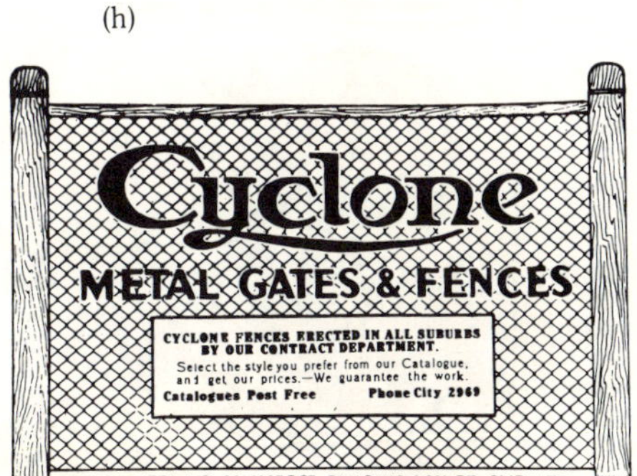

(i)

(f)

The half back

On industry.

(a) Corax.
Marie Dorin, Melbourne.
Fire extinguisher; 1925.
(b) Brownie Steel Products.
E. T. Brown Pty Ltd, Melbourne.
Steel furniture; 1926.
(c) Old Everything.
James Campbell & Sons, Brisbane.
Undressed timber; 1926.
(d) Central Spring Works, Melbourne.
Springs of all kinds, bumper bars; 1926.
(e) Aut-O-Pie.
J. E. Nobbs, Rose Park, SA.
Machinery; 1929.
(f) Python.
H. W. Cox, Sydney.
Wire tying machines; 1931.
(g)(h) 'Screw Man'.
Sidney Cooke Pty Ltd, Melbourne.
Metal fasteners; 1940.
This trademark was originally designed by Paton Advertising Services and, with a minor variation, is still in use today (h).
(i) Cutler.
Austral Otis Andebar Cannery Equipment Pty Ltd, Melbourne; 1935.
(j) M.I.A.
National Wire Products Pty Ltd, NSW; 1938.
(k) Steelbilt.
Wormald Bros. Pty Ltd, Sydney.
Steel furniture; 1938.
(l) Spitfire.
Estee Trading Co.
Pty Ltd, Melbourne.
Blowlamps; 1942.

(a)

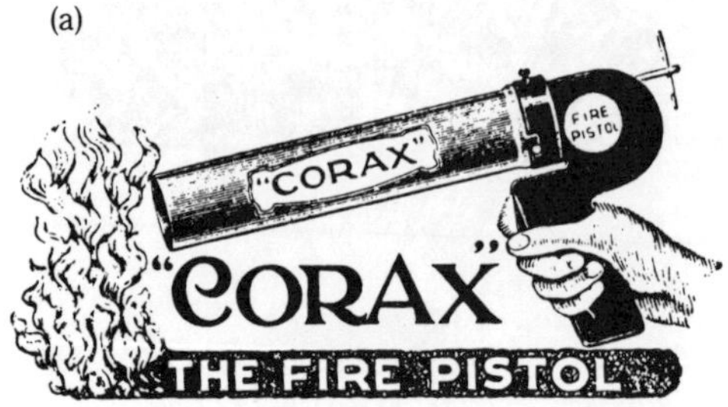

(b)

(c)

(d)

(e)

(f)

(g)

(h)

(i)

(j)

(k)

(l)

(a)

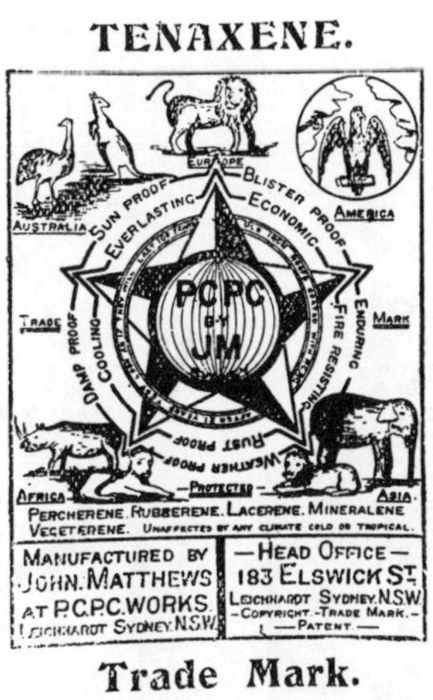

(b)

(c)

(d)

(e)

(f)

(g)

(h)

(i)

(j)

(k)

(l)

The half back

On paint.

Industry had an answer for everything. *Roofcool* made hot weather bearable. *Fly-Fire* prevented your house and clothes from burning, and through it all, *Sunny Bill* and *Bill Brush* agreed with S. N. Castle & Sons – 'Repaint or repent'.

(a) Tenaxene.
John Matthews, Sydney; 1904.

(b) Auto Brand.
Taubmans', Sydney.
Varnishes, paints and colors; 1906.

(c) Sun Brand.
William Docker, Sydney.
Paints, colors and varnishes; 1907.

(d) C. G. Moore, Sydney.
Waterproofing and preserving paints; 1909.

(e) Roofcool.
J. Church, Fremantle, WA.
Paint; 1911.

(f) United.
Australasian United Paint Co. Ltd, Adelaide.
Paints and enamels; 1912.

(g) Zenith.
Australian Paint Co., Herberton, Qld.
Paints; 1912.

(h) Fly-Fire.
The Fly-Fire Syndicate, Melbourne.
Material for rendering articles non-flammable; 1913.

(i) Sunny Bill.
R. H. Clark & Co., Sydney.
Paints; 1922.

(j) Bill Brush.
L. Berger & Sons, Sydney.
Paints; 1924.

(k) S. N. Castle & Sons, North Brighton, SA.
Paint; 1952.

(l) T. Kift & Son, Ballarat, Vic.
Painters and decorators; from an advertisement appearing 1911.

The half back

On transport.

The tyranny of distance: miles and miles, or more recently, kilometres and kilometres from city to city, town to town. The results: Qantas is the world's second oldest airline, and the ute, a high speed cross between a car and a truck, was developed and assembled by Ford Australia 20 years before it was manufactured in America.

Distance stood in the way of the developing industry so an industry was developed to conquer it.

(a) Roy W. Sandford Ltd, Sydney.
Motor cars; 1913.
(b) Radio.
G. N. McMicking & Co., Melbourne.
Radiator cleanser; 1914.
(c) Liberty.
A. W. Mather, Adelaide.
Batteries; 1920.
(d) John Victor Wilmoth.
Motor accessories; 1922.
(e) The Streemlyne Body.
Williamson-Page, Melbourne.
Side-car body; 1924.
(f) Beam.
Widdis Diamond Dry Cell Pty Ltd, Melbourne.
Batteries; 1928.
(g) Olympic Tyre & Rubber Co. Pty Ltd, Melbourne.
Sir Frank Beaurepaire commenced manufacturing Olympic tyres in 1934. In his youth he had been a successful Olympic swimmer and this influenced his choice of the brand name and the adoption of the discobolus as his symbol.
(h) X-Press Tyre Services Pty Ltd, Sydney; 1945.
(i) Summit Battery.
A. Carter, Melbourne; 1930.
(j) (k) General Motors Holden, Melbourne.
Motor cars; (j) 1948,
(k) General Motors Dealer Friendly Service sticker.
(l) (m) Repco Ltd, Melbourne.
Machinery; (l) 1951,
(m) 1961.

(a)

(b)

(c)

(d)

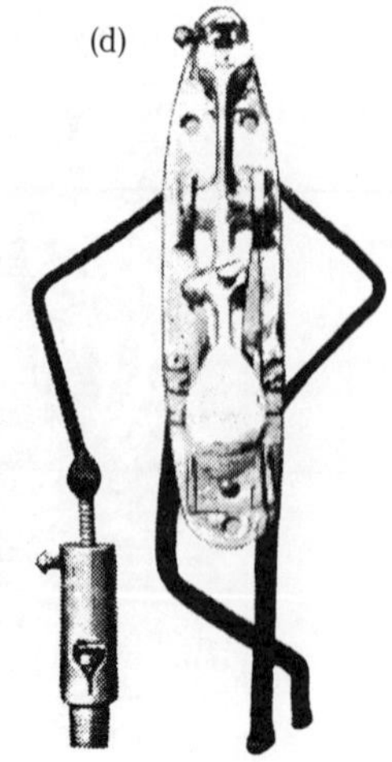

(e)

(f)

(g)

(h)

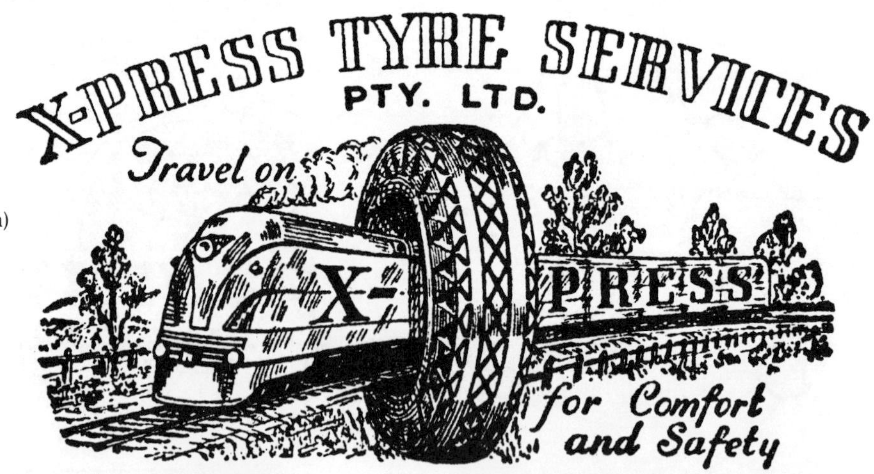

(i)

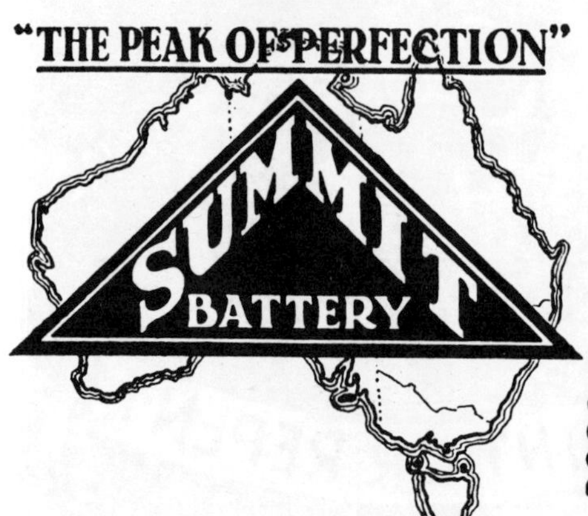

(j)

(l)

(m)

(k)

(a)

(b)

(c)

(d)

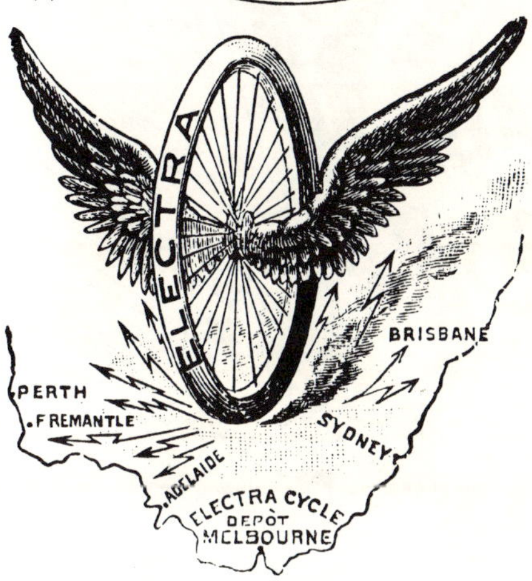

(e)

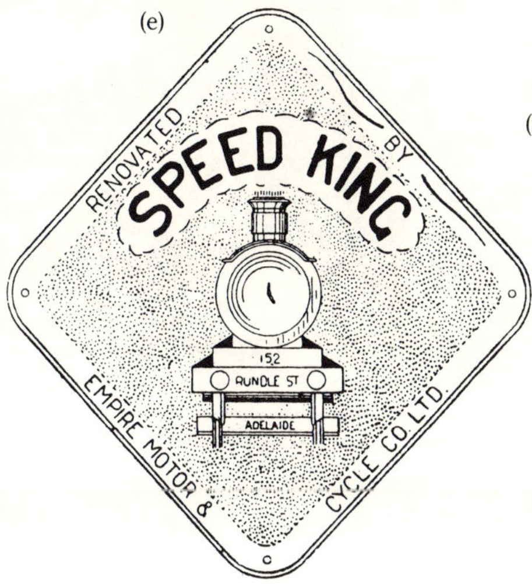

(f)

(g)

(h)

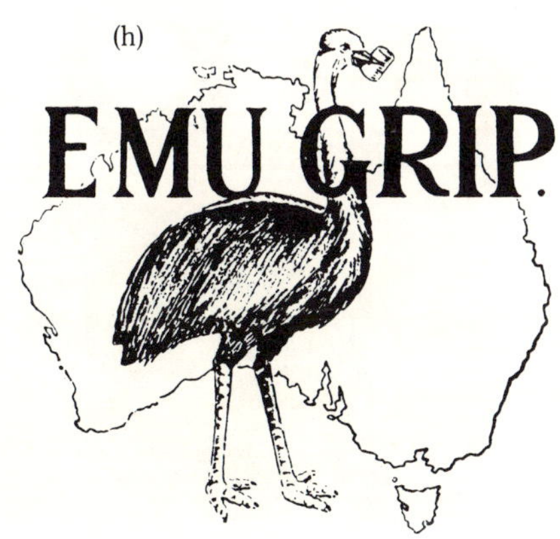

(i)

(j)

(k)

The half back

On transport.

(a) (b) (c) The Hercules, The Explorer, The Greyhound.
H. S. Chipman, Sydney.
Bicycles; 1896.
(d) Electra.
Hugo Wertheim, Melbourne.
Bicycles; 1890s.
(e) Speed King.
Empire Motor & Cycle Co., Adelaide.
Cycles; 1910.
(f) The Wheeler.
W. Wheeler, Melbourne.
Repairing compound; 1913.
(g) Gumleaf Brand.
John Perry Pty Ltd, Melbourne.
Spokes and naves; from an advertisement appearing 1925.
(h) Emu Grip.
C. M. Glynn Ltd, Sydney.
Tyre repairs; 1930.
(i) Malvern Star.
Bruce Small Pty Ltd, Melbourne.
Bicycles; 1934.
(j) Re-Nu.
M. Herbert, Melbourne.
Rubber repair; 1933.
(k) Cyclo.
General Accessories Pty Ltd, Melbourne.
Metal goods; 1938.

The half back

On lubricants and fuels.

In complete contrast to the huge corporations that exist today, the oil business in Australia had extremely haphazard beginnings.

(a) (b) (c) Neptune Oil Company.
J. Kitchen and Sons entered the oil business via their Sydney Soap and Candle Company – lubricants being traditionally handled by these businesses. They marketed their oils and greases under the brand-name of *Neptune* for at least 15 years before registering the Neptune Oil Company in 1909 (a). Around 1917 Neptune introduced Waratah Brand motor spirit.
(b) The Waratah symbol from an advertisement appearing 1947.
(c) Redesign of the Neptune trademark by Richard Beck; 1956.
(d) (e) (f) C.O.R.
B.P., originally the Anglo-Persian Oil Company, was established in England by William Knox D'Arcy with the money he made from the Mount Morgan goldmine in Queensland. In 1920 the Commonwealth Oil Refineries Ltd (C.O.R.) was set up by the Hughes Labor Government with the Anglo-Persian Oil Company and the Commonwealth Government as equal partners.
In 1952 the Government sold its share to the now Anglo-Iranian Oil Co. The C.O.R. tradename was eventually phased out and replaced by B.P. in the 1960s. (d) 1923, (e) 1929, (f) a pump; c.1929.
(g) Ronatip Oils. Ronaldson Bros. & Tippett, Ballarat, Vic.; 1914.
(h) Pathfinder. J. Wardle & Co., Adelaide. Lubricants; 1915.
(i) Lubra Brand. Proud Bros. Pty Ltd, Melbourne. Lubricants; 1935.
(j) XL Petroleum; current.

(a)

(b)

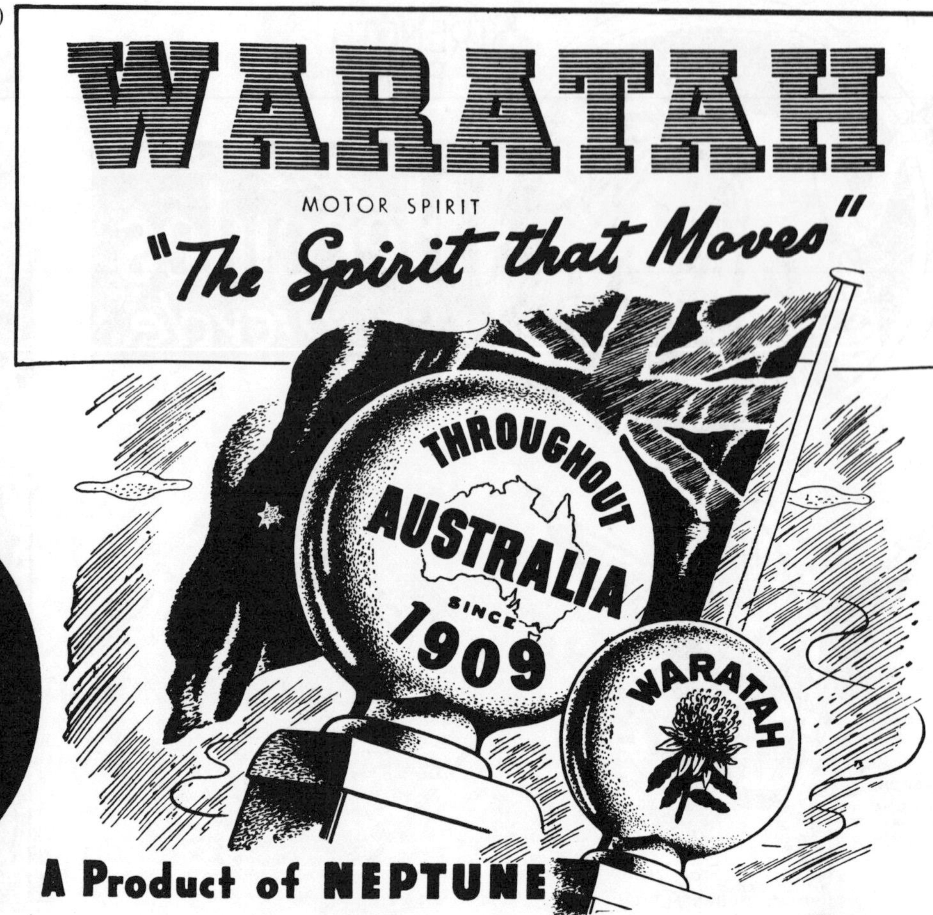

(c)

(d)

(e)

(f)

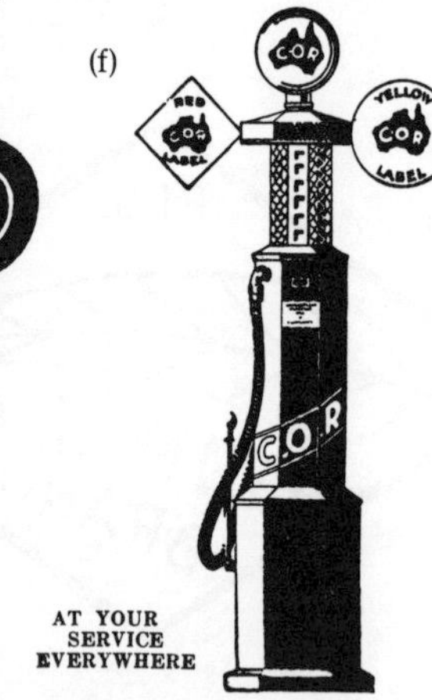

(g)

(h)

(i)

(j)

The half back

On lubricants and fuels.

(a) (b) Golden Fleece. When a consignment of Californian motor spirit arrived in 1913, H. C. Sleigh, a general importer, was asked if he would handle the shipment. He chose the brand name *Golden Fleece*, and from this rather minor incident the organisation grew. (a) In 1951, with the introduction of single branded service stations, Golden Fleece redesigned its trademark and applied it to their complete driveway image. The golden ram was based on 'David', a prize merino owned by the Boonoke Stud.
(b) trademark; current.
(c) Ampol Petroleum Ltd; from an advertisement appearing 1958.
Ampol commenced operations as the *Australian Motorists Petrol Company Ltd*. Founded by W. G. Walkley, a New Zealander, the company was registered in Sydney in 1936. It changed its name to *Ampol Petroleum Ltd* in 1948.
(d) (e) The Kangaroo Petroleum Co. Pty Ltd, Melbourne, commenced in 1959 with a nominal capital of one million pounds. Three years later it was taken over by H. C. Sleigh Ltd. (e) Kangaroo pumps; from an advertisement appearing 1960.
(f) Southern Cross Petroleum.
In 1975 a group of independent Victorian garage proprietors banded together to resist pressures from the multinationals to phase them out. The name was chosen because of its connotations with the spirit of independence. Southern Cross is still in existence.

(a)

(b)

GOLDEN FLEECE

(c)

(d)

WHOLLY AUSTRALIAN OWNED
KANGAROO
Kangaroo

(e)

(f)

SOUTHERN CROSS

The half back

On Qantas.

The kangaroo first took to the air as the emblem for The Royal New South Aero Club (a). Qantas originally used the kangaroo for its 1944 Indian Ocean hop – the Perth office adapting the one used on the Australian penny and painting it on their new Liberator aircraft. This Indian Ocean hop was quickly dubbed the *Kangaroo Service* (b). In late 1946 Qantas developed the winged kangaroo (c) to replace the Qantas Empire Airways symbol (e) featured here in a pre-Government takeover advertisement appearing in *Aircraft*, January 1946. After the Government takeover of Qantas in 1947, the flying Kangaroo was maintained and developed into the current international Qantas symbol (d). This story was adapted from *The Tale of Four Kangaroos*, an article which appeared in *Airways*, January 1947.
Along the way Qantas dropped an early slogan which explained: 'Just as the crow flies only faster.'

(a)

(b)

(c)

(d)

(e)

FLY QANTAS

The half back
On TAA.

From its inception in 1946, the Government-owned Trans-Australia Airlines have used the kangaroo logo design as their corporate symbol on all signage and stationery. The current signature (b) was derived from the basic elements contained in the original symbol (a). The transition from the old to the new took place with the general modernisation of the TAA fleet (c). Advertising material for TAA has not followed a long-term theme but has adopted symbology on a campaign basis:
(d) TAA hostess introduced in 1952.
(e) Animated plane called 'Smiley' introduced in 1972.
(f) T-Jet signature introduced in 1973.
(g) Current signature featuring the recently ordered Airbus.
(h) Advertisement appearing on the first anniversary of TAA.

(a)

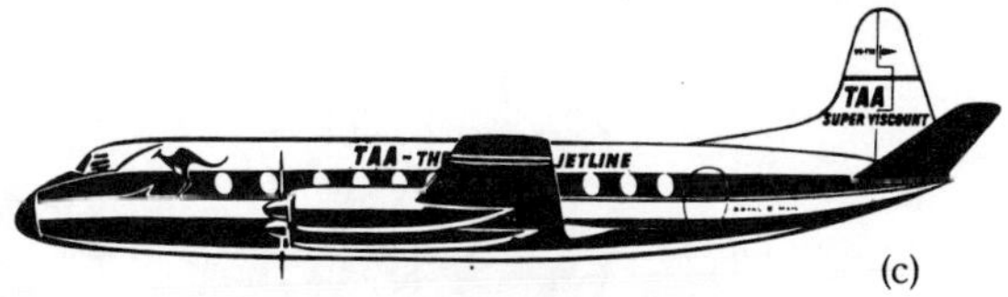

(c)

TAA
TRANS-AUSTRALIA AIRLINES

(b)

(e)

(d)

(f)

(g)

(h)

TAA's first year

On October 7th, 1946, the first Airliner left the tarmac on TAA's inaugural public service. In carrying over 220,000 passengers, 2700 tons of freight and 560 tons of mail, a record has been set for the first 12 months of operation of any Airline. Today, TAA looks forward to greater developments and a continuance of the efficient friendly service that has won the approval and support of Australian travellers and freight consignors during the past year.

"Fly TAA the friendly way"

Trans-Australia Airlines

YOUR AIRLINE. AUSTRALIA'S FINEST

The half back

On banking.

Behind every business was a bank. Banks spread with early settlement, but as the distances were shortened they amalgamated. The Bank of Ballarat, the Royal Bank of Queensland and the Colonial Bank of Australasia are now lost in the history of the National Bank.
The Australian and European Bank, the Town and Country Bank and a host of others – now part of the Commercial Bank of Australia.
In recent times, all major banks have made dramatic stylistic developments to their corporate symbols, from the complex coats of arms of the pioneers to the clinical shapes of computerised business. More than anything else, this has transported their image from the staid solidarity of the founding fathers, to one of aggressive survival in the fast world of modern business.
(a) (b) (c) Bank of New South Wales.
(a) Coat of arms; c.1850.
(b) Coat of arms; 1931.
(c) Current symbol designed by Huveneers Pty Ltd; 1974.
(d) to (g) Commonwealth Bank of Australia.
(d) Coat of arms from 1955 differing in minor degree only to the one originally adopted in 1912. *Courtesy Reserve Bank of Australia, formerly Commonwealth Bank of Australia.*
(e) Commonwealth Banking Corporation; 1961.
(f) Tin money box introduced in the 1920s and still available today.
(g) The elephant has become the Bank's unofficial symbol since the early 1970s.
Continued on page 179

The half back

On stencils.

Stencil trademarks use design simplicity for easy recognition.
Van Cooth's horse's head on a hessian bag says horse feed. Compressed visual information for instant digestion.
(a) Dingo Brand.
The Great Southern Flour Mills Ltd, Narrogin, WA.
Flour; 1917.
(b) G. Graham & Co., Sydney.
Butcher's pepper; 1889.
(c) Van Cooth & Co., Melbourne.
Compressed fodder; 1906.
(d) Boars Head Brand.
Stuart, Walker & Co. Ltd, Sydney.
Sausage casings; 1923.
(e) George Wills & Co.
Frozen meat; 1906.

(a)

(b)

(c)

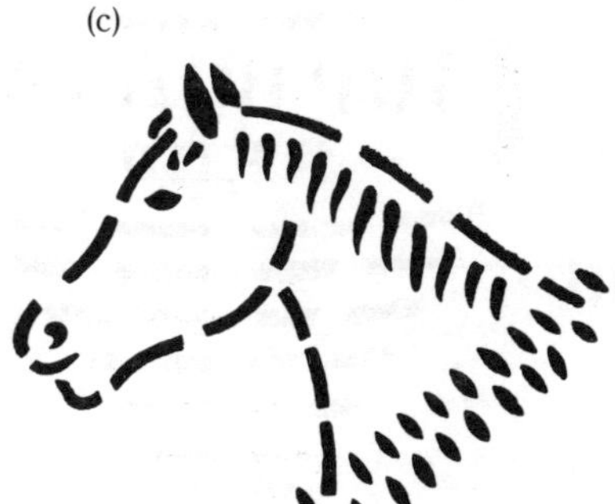

(d)

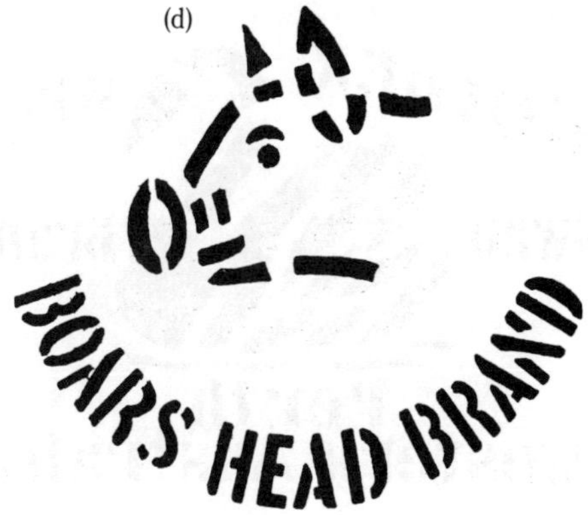

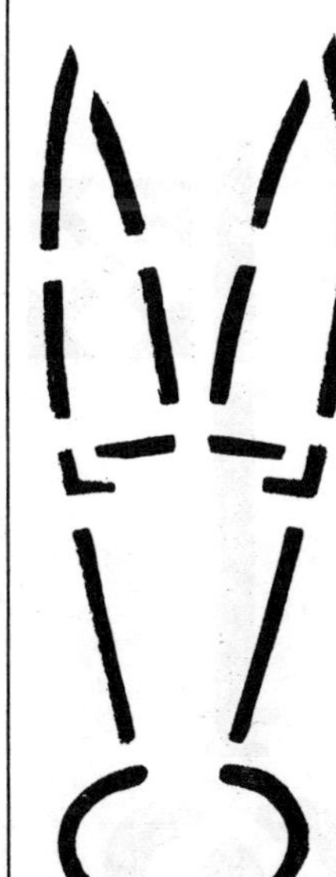

(e)

The half back

On stencils.

(a) Magpie Brand.
A. W. Bayley Sims, SA.
Yacca gum; 1922.
(b) F. Lassetter & Co.
Ltd, Sydney.
Galvanized and tinned shears; 1885.
(c) Vulcan.
R. W. Cameron & Co., Sydney.
Iron and steel; 1906.
(d) Pelican Tobacco.
Justus Scharff, Sydney.
Tobacco; 1906.
(e) Molasses Fodder.
The Colonial Sugar Refining Co. Ltd; 1907.
(f) Swan Brand White Lead.
Australian Mining & White Lead Pty Ltd, Perth; 1921.
(g) Golden West Swan Brand.
The Westralian Farmers Ltd, Perth.
Flour; 1925.
(h) Top Brand.
Adelaide Tent & Verandah Blind Co., SA.
Tents, tarpaulins, blinds; 1928.
(i) Wombat Brand.
George Wills & Co. Ltd, merchants; 1936.
(j) George Wills & Co.
Frozen meat; 1906.

(a)

(b)

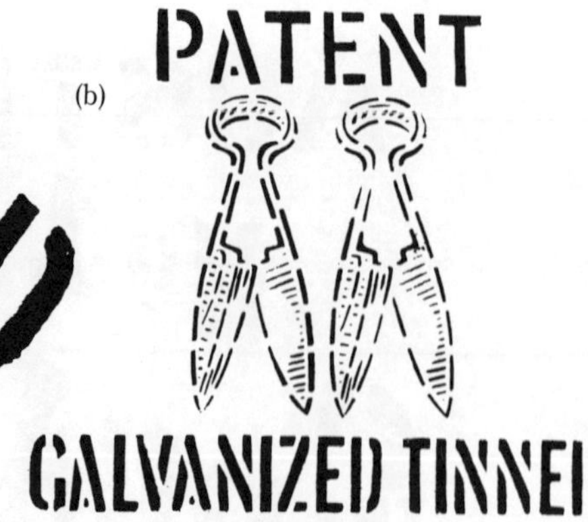

(c)

(d)

(e)

(f)

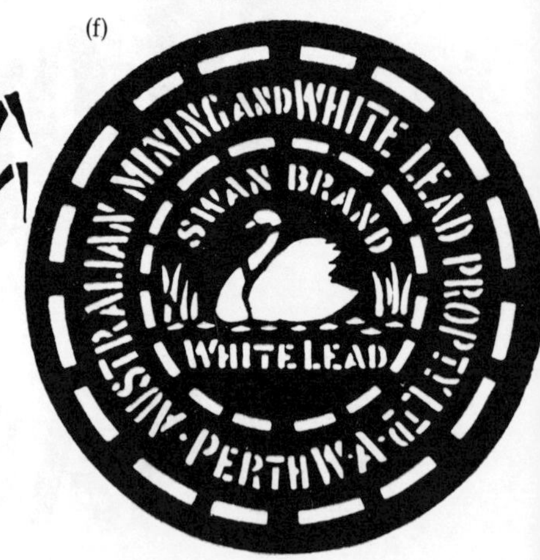

(j)

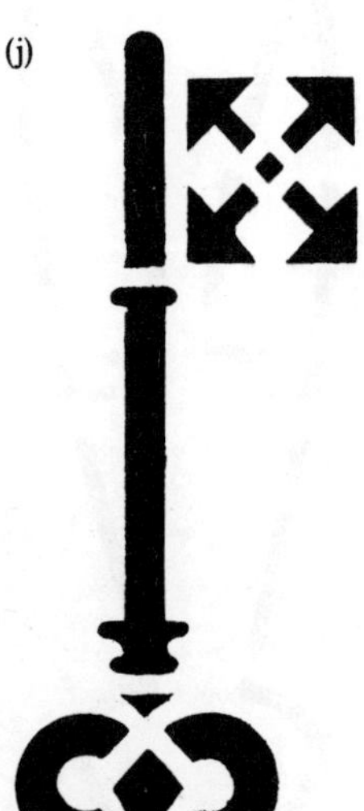

(g)

(h)

(i)

10. EXPORT QUALITY. Roller flour.

With the introduction of metal rollers to the production of flour, there came a need to differentiate between the new *roller* flour and the old *stone ground* flour. Brand names were developed to suit particular export markets.
(a) W. S. Kimpton & Sons, Melbourne; 1917.
(b) Port Flour Mill. C. E. Slee, Fremantle, WA; 1897.
(c) Balloon Brand. Hugh Duff Fleming, Adelaide; 1906.
(d) (e) W. S. Kimpton & Sons, Melbourne; 1908.
(f) Robert Little & Co., Sydney; 1908.
(g) Silver Eye. Robert Little & Co., Sydney; 1909.
(h) Robert Little & Co., Sydney; 1909.
(i) Tjap Semar. Robert Little & Co., Sydney; 1913.
(j) Kooyana. Steele & Baker, Adelaide; 1908.

(a)

(b)

(c)

(d)

(e)

(f)

(g)

(h)

(i)

(j)

Export quality

Roller flour.

(a) Horse on wheels.
W. S. Kimpton & Sons, Melbourne; 1917.
(b) Gillespie Bros. & Co., Sydney; 1917.
(c) Lyre Bird.
Mitsui, Bussan, Kaisha Ltd, Sydney; 1917.
(d) Bungalow Brand.
Handel Maatschappij, Ban Lian, Medan, Sumatra; 1917.
(e) Windmill Brand.
F. A. Waller & Co.; 1919.
(f) Motor Boat Brand.
Jackett Bros. Adelaide; 1919.
(g) Railroad Brand.
The River Murray Milling Co. Ltd, Adelaide; 1922.
(h) (i) Whoop-Whoop Brand, Heknows Brand.
William Charlick Ltd, Adelaide; 1922.
(j) Snowcap.
G. H. Swanton & Co. Pty Ltd; 1926.
(k) Twin Elephants Brand.
Bunge (Australia) Pty Ltd, Melbourne; 1940.
(l) Telephone Brand.
N.V. Handel My; 1952.
(m) Cycle.
E. Davey & Sons, Sydney; 1911.

(a)

(b)

(c)

(d)

(e)

(f)

(g)

(h)

(i)

(j)

(k)

(l)

(m)

Export quality
Butter marks.

Reminders of a time when butter came in 56 pound boxes, for export, or to be sold by the pat at the local grocery store.
(a) Kangaroo Valley Farmers & Settlers Co-op. Society Ltd, Kangaroo Valley, NSW; 1907.
(b) Boomerang. Yinnar Cream & Butter Factory, Yinnar, Vic; 1894.
(c) Heather Bell Brand. Skillen & Walker, Dungog, NSW; 1897.
(d) Australian Egret Brand. Broken River Butter Factory, Benalla, Vic.; 1901.
(e) Boomerang Brand. The Ulladulla Refrigerating Butter Co. Ltd, Milton, NSW; 1905.
(f) Canary Brand. Sims Bros., Echuca, Vic.; 1906.
(g) The Cherry Brand. The Westend Creamery Co-op. Co. Ltd, Bemboka, NSW; 1897.
(h) Echuca Co-op. Butter Factory, Vic.; 1906.
(i) Wonga. The Lismore Co-op. Dairy Co. Ltd, NSW; 1906.
(j) Myee. The North Coast Co-op. Co. Ltd, NSW; 1906.
(k) Emu Factory. Humphris Sons Ltd, SA; 1906.
(l) Acme. J. Newell, NSW; 1906.
(m) Shell. The Coastal Farmers Co-op. Society Ltd, NSW; 1906.
(n) Mincha. John McKay, Vic; 1907.
(o) Northern Central Factory. Foley Bros., Sydney; 1907.
(p) Bushman Brand. Singleton Central Co-op. Dairy Co. Ltd, Hunter River, NSW; 1907.
(q) Snow Drop. Farmers & Settlers Co-op. Society Ltd, Blayney, NSW; 1907.
(r) George John Vagg, Vic.; 1906.

(r)

Export quality

Butter marks.

The beautiful and simple execution of these marks was a vital discipline at a time when butter was sampled before being bought. Quick recognition of the trademark meant consistent brand loyalty from satisfied customers.
(a) Beech Forest Butter Factory Co. Ltd, Vic; 1906.
(b) Yalooka.
The Shepparton and District Co-op. Butter, Cheese and Ice Factory Co. Ltd; Vic.; 1906.
(c) Heron Brand.
Wonthaggi Butter Factory, Vic.; 1906.
(d) Pyramid Hill Butter & Cheese Factory, Vic.; 1906.
(e) Pansy.
Tenterfield Co-op. Butter Factory Co. Ltd, NSW; 1906.
(f) Boort Butter & Ice Co. Ltd, Vic.; 1906.
(g) Abba.
McKeever & Co., Melbourne; 1906.
(h) Mutual.
W. H. Blackham, Melbourne; 1906.
(i) Mulga.
Millthorpe Butter & Bacon Co-op. Co. Ltd, NSW; 1906.
(j) Oakey Co-op. Dairy Co. Ltd, Qld; 1907.
(k) Revolver Brand.
Euroa Butter & Ice Factory Co. Ltd, Vic.; 1907.
(l) Boronia.
Bellinger Central Co-op. Butter Co. Ltd, NSW; 1907.

(a)

(b)

(c)

(d)

(e)

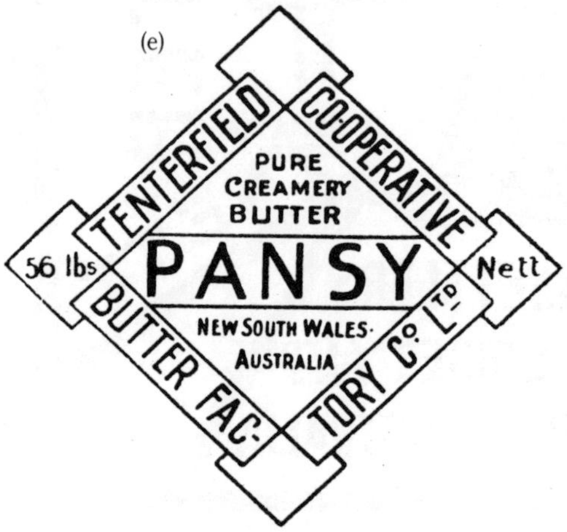

(f)

(g)

(h)

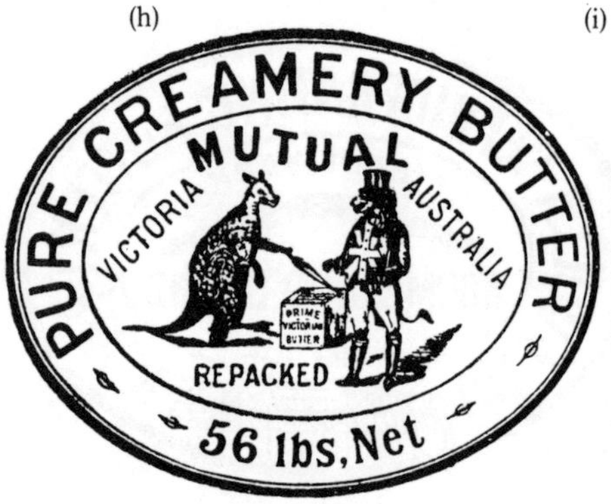

(i)

(j)

(k)

(l)

(a)

11. EATMORE.

There are more trademarks registered in Australia for food and drink than for any other product category. But, with all these products, there has been little development of a national cuisine. At best, Australians have supported a host of locally branded products. Vegemite, Aeroplane Jelly, and Foster's Lager have become the things to *eatmore*.

(a) Eatmore.
H. R. Hallo, Melbourne.
Fruit; 1923.
(b) Brooke's Oros Ltd, Melbourne.
Cordials; 1937.
(c) Liquid Sunshine.
Resch's Waverley Brewery.
Beer; 1906.
(d) Mac's Famous Big Boy Hamburgers.
L. & S. McLaws, Melbourne; 1955.
(e) Vegemite.
Kraft Foods Ltd, Melbourne.
Single serve container; current — see page 44.

(b)

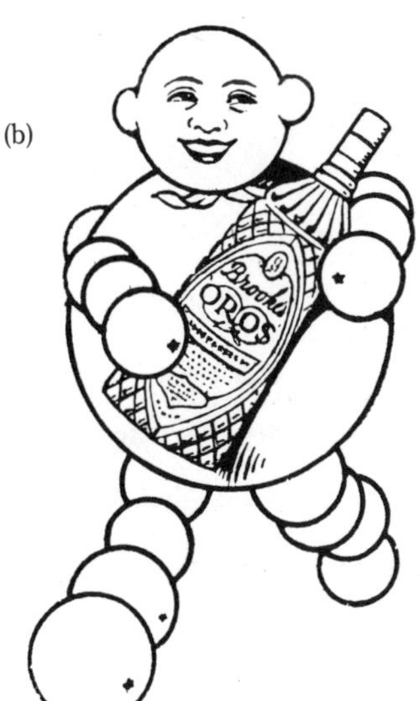

(c)

(d)

(e)

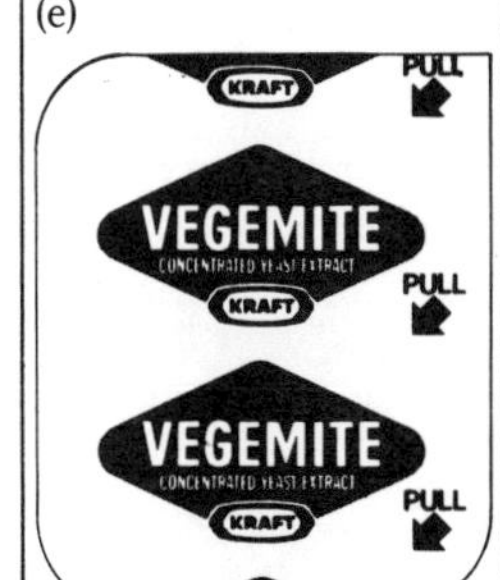

Eatmore

Tea and coffee.

(a) to (d) Billy Tea. James Inglis & Co., tea and coffee merchants, Sydney.
Billy tea was first introduced in 1888. Its unique packaging capitalised on the Gold Rush spirit. The *Swagaroo*, with its bedroll and billy tin, quickly became an institution that eventually made the transition into life (d), replacing the crescent moon and oriental temple as the trademark for Billy Tea.
(a) Wrapper; 1892, (b) 1896, (c) a sample tin of Billy Tea shown actual size, (d) wrapper; c. 1900.

(a)

(b)

(c)

(d)

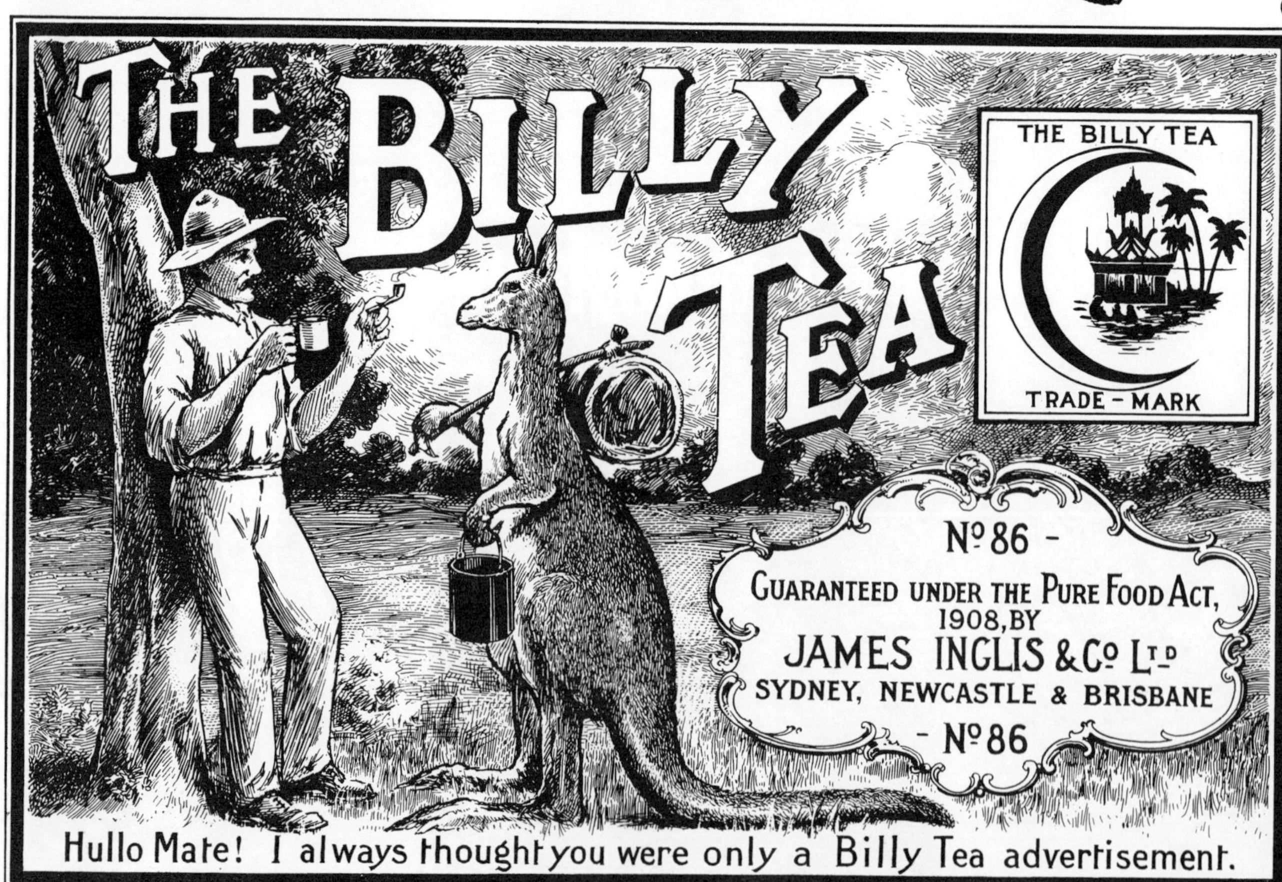

Eatmore

Tea and coffee.

(a) Robur Tea. Hawthorn, Rhodes & Co. Melbourne; 1891.
(b) In 1883, Alfred Bushell commenced selling tea and coffee in Brisbane. His sons, Phillip and Walter, moved to Sydney, and by 1899 Bushell & Co. – *The Tea Men*, were supplying all the major states. In 1912 the company became Bushells Ltd.; the mark shown here depicts Mr Bushell Senior sipping tea and was taken from a label registered in 1920.
(c) (d) Griffiths' Signal Tea was made famous with an advertising campaign of enamelled signs along railway lines, advising travellers of how many miles there were to the next major town and Griffiths Tea. Griffiths Brothers started their tea and coffee operation in the early 1890s in Melbourne. The signature panel (c) was in use by the early 1900s, while Signal Brand (d) had made its appearance by the mid-1920s.
(e) Pasha. Clifford Love & Co. Brisbane. Coffee; 1890.
(f) J. H. Cheetham, Adelaide. Pure Indian teas; 1890.
(g) The Eiffel Tower Blend of Tea. J. A. Bull & Co., Sydney; 1893.
(h) A. M. Bickford & Sons Ltd, Adelaide. Coffee and chicory essence; 1931.

(a)

(b)

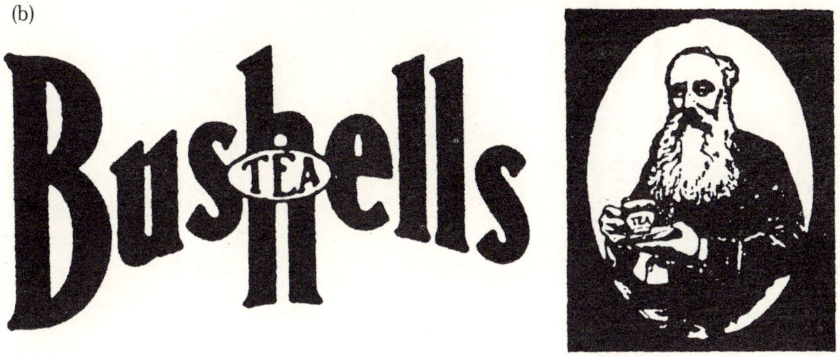

(c)

(d)

(e)

(f)

(g)

(h)

Eatmore

Tea and Coffee.

(a) Pannikin Blend Tea.
The Ceylon Tea Co.
Perth; 1903.
(b) Mutual Tea.
The Austral Ceylon Mutual Tea Co. Ltd, Perth; 1903.
(c) Kinkara Tea.
J. R. Love & Co. Sydney; 1906.
(d) Sun Brand.
Stephen King & Son, Melbourne.
Tea; 1913.
(e) The Invigorating Cup.
J.A. Booth & Co., Sydney.
Tea, coffee, cocoa; 1913.
(f) Zebra Coffee.
The Warren Tea Co. Ltd., Brisbane; 1919.
(g) N. McLeod, Sydney.
Tea, coffee, cocoa; 1920.
(h) C. M. Brooke & Sons, Melbourne.
Coffee; 1926.
(i) Ivan Repin, Sydney.
Coffee and tea; 1932.
The Repin brothers came from Russia to Sydney in 1926 and started their first coffee shop in King St., Sydney, opposite the Supreme Court.

(a)

(b)

(c)

(d)

(e)

(f)

(g)

(h)

(i)

(a)

(b)

(c)

(d)

(e)

Eatmore

Biscuits.

(a) to (d) Swallow & Ariell, Melbourne. Founded by Thomas Swallow in 1854 to manufacture ships' biscuits, Swallow & Ariell is the oldest biscuit manufacturer in Australia. Thomas Ariell joined the business as a partner in 1859 but died in 1875. In 1879 his position was filled by Frederic Derham, Swallow's son-in-law. The business was renamed Swallow & Derham's until 1890 when Swallow died. Derham, for phonetic reasons, changed the name back to Swallow & Ariell. By this stage the Swallow symbol had already gained public acceptance. The Derhams continued to run the company until its takeover in 1965 by Arnott-Brockhoff-Guest Pty Ltd.
(a) From a 1935 price list, (b) c. 1955, (c) c. 1962, (d) 1966.
(e) Arnott's.
In 1865 William Arnott opened a shop in Newcastle to manufacture and sell ships' biscuits to the coal ships. The story goes that one of the captains gave him a parrot for his shop. This parrot became the famous Arnott's symbol. The version shown here was registered by William Arnott Ltd, Newcastle, in 1907, a year before they moved to Sydney.
(f) Long's Cream Cracker.
James Long & Co. Pty Ltd, Ballarat, Vic.; 1906.

(f)

Eatmore

Biscuits.

(a) (b) (c) Aulsebrook & Sons Ltd, Sydney.
(a) 1896, (b) (c) 1897.
Although Aulsebrook were New Zealand biscuit manufacturers, they registered these designs in Sydney.
(d) (Teddy bear shape).
Peek, Frean & Co. Ltd, London.
Biscuits; 1909.
The word *Teddy Bear* has been applied to a variety of biscuits. But the most popular and lasting shape was first registered by Peek, Frean & Co. Ltd, in Australia, in 1909, two years after the term was created as a nickname for Theodore Roosevelt, president of the United States of America, 1901-9. The same biscuit shape was popularised in the post-war period by Guests and is currently marketed by Arnott's.
(e) Swallow & Ariell's round Teddy Bear biscuits; from a 1947 tin label.
(f) Herbert Adams.
Caterer and pastry cook, Prahran, Vic.; 1910.
(g) (h) A. F. Brockhoff & Co. Pty Ltd, Melbourne;
(d) 1934, (e) from a 1937 price list.

(a)

(b)

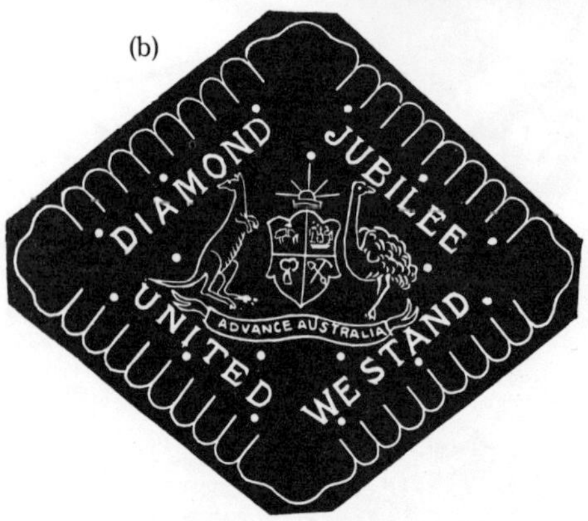

(c)

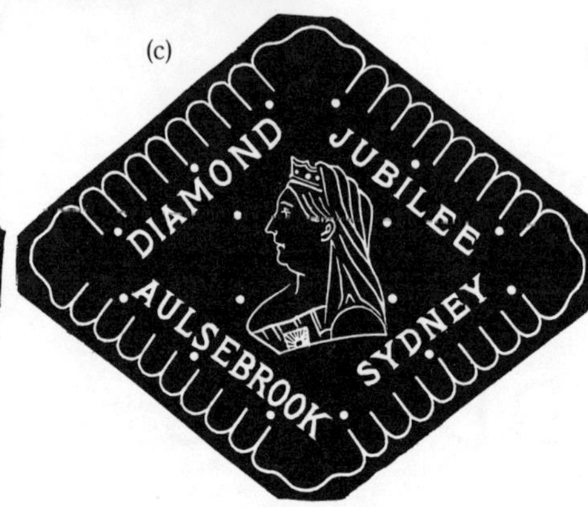

(d)

(e)

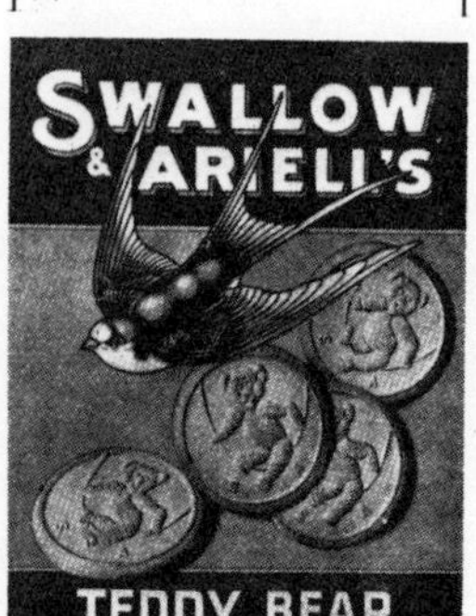

(f)

(g)

(h)

Eatmore

Drinks and cordials.

The Australian summer has always created a large thirst.
(a) Charles Oertel, Sydney.
Aerated waters; 1893.
(b) Marchant & Co.
Aerated waters; 1893.
The symbol of the sliced orange is unusually simple for its time.
(c) Kolazone.
The N.S.W. Aerated Water & Co. Ltd, Newcastle; 1897.
(d) Ding-Dong.
Schramm & Co. Ltd, Medindie, SA.
Mineral and aerated waters; 1903.
(e) Sharpe Bros., Sydney.
Soft drinks; 1907.
(f) Boomerang Tonic.
F. Humphris & Sons Ltd, Jamestown and Adelaide; c. 1910
(g) Kiz.
The Palatine Mfg. Co. Pty Ltd.
Cordials and non-alcoholic beverages; 1910.
(h) American Cream Soda.
Frankston Springs Co., Melbourne.
Soft drinks; 1910.
(i) W. T. Adams, Qld.
Mineral water; 1911.
(j) H. G. H. Miniken, Laverton, WA.
Soft drinks; 1912.
(k) Football Punch.
Clare Mineral Waters Co., SA; c. 1900.

(a)

(b)

(c)

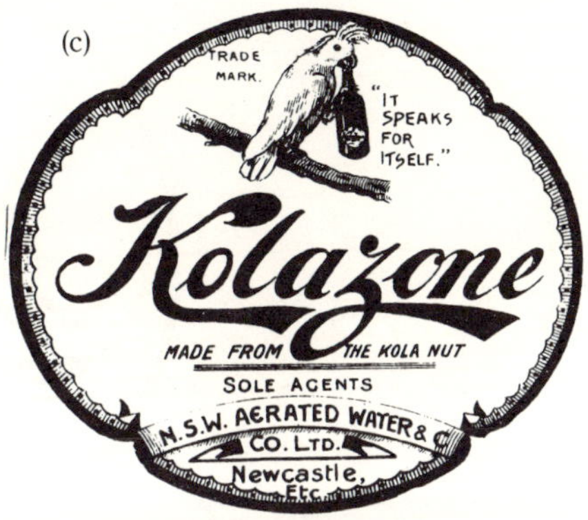

(d)

(e)

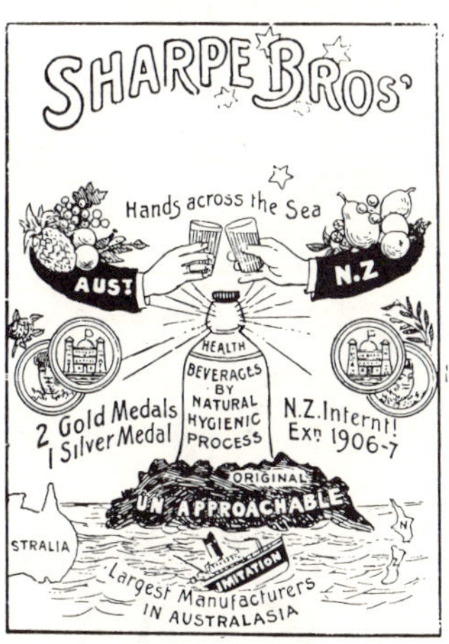

(f)

(g)

(h)

(i)

(j)

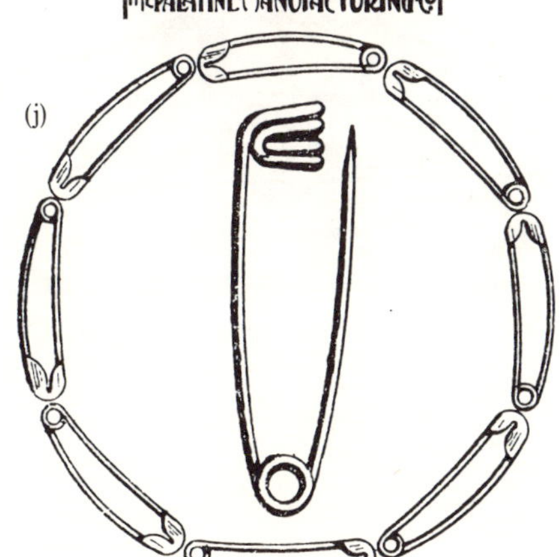

(k)

Eatmore

Drinks and cordials.

(a) The Quencher.
H. A. Grant & Co., Gympie, Qld.
Soft drinks; 1914.
(b) (c) Ecks.
Murray Breweries Pty Ltd, Beechworth, Vic.
Non-alcoholic beer; (b) 1916, (c) from an advertisement appearing 1926.
(d) Coo-ee Brand.
The Coo-ee Mfg. Co. Ltd, Brisbane.
Sparkling non-alcoholic drinks; 1924.
(e) Passiona.
Spencer Milton Cottee, Arondale, Lismore, NSW; 1925.
A drink made from passionfruit.
(f) Lemos.
C. M. Brooke & Sons, Melbourne.
Lemon squash; 1925.
(g) Dinkum Snowee.
L. J. Lush, Mt Gambier, SA.
Mineral and aerated waters; 1925.
(h) Crows Nest.
Cascade Cordials Ltd. Naremburn, NSW.
Soft drinks and cordials; 1931.
(i) Boomerang.
H. Thomson, Sydney.
Mineral and aerated waters.
H. Thomson attempted to register this design in 1934 but abandoned the application 3 years later.

(a)

(b)

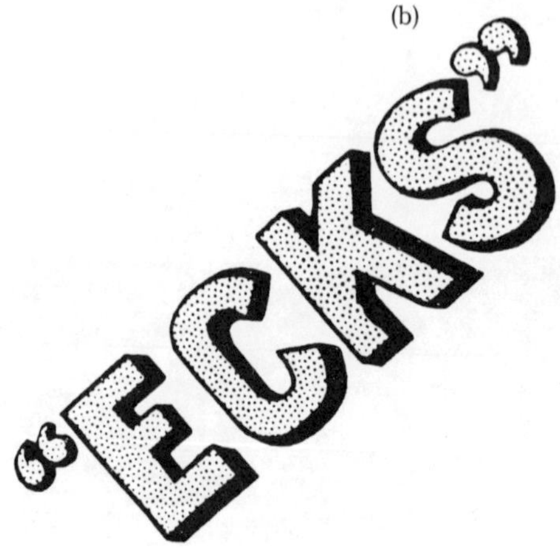

(d)

(e)

(f)

(g)

(c)

(h)

(i)

Eatmore

Drinks and cordials.

(a) Half-Time.
H. Pike & Co., Oakbank, SA.
Non-alcoholic drink; 1930s.
(b) T. Ashby, Cordial Factory, Kyneton, Vic; 1930s.
The *Annythink* label was supposedly used for a drink mixed from anything and everything left over at the end of the day.
(c) Letchfords Aussie Cola; 1930s.
(d) LBW.
O. T. Limited, Melbourne.
Cordials; 1936.
(e) Mac's Cyder & Fruit Juices Pty Ltd, Melbourne.
Non-alcoholic cider and fruit juices; 1939.
(f) Farbest Products Pty Ltd, Sydney.
Fruit juices; 1939.
(g) Hubbly Bubbly.
Motyer & Clement Pty Ltd.
Mineral and aerated waters; 1954.
(h)(i) Taraxale Brewing Co., Melbourne.
Mineral and aerated water; established 1899.
(h) An early label, (i) logo in use since the 1950s, but now almost phased out.
(j) Big Fella.
Murray Breweries Pty Ltd, Beechworth, Vic.
Soft drinks; current.

(a)

(b)

(c)

(d)

(e)

(f)

(g)

(i)

(h)

(j)

Eatmore

Wine.

Australian wine is currently enjoying a boom period. But, for the best part of a century it barely trickled along in the shadow of the national drink – beer. Not even the beautiful Margaret Mildara could charm it into popularity.
(a) H. W. H. Irvine, Great Western Vineyard, Vic; 1906.
(b) Excelsior Vineyard. T. Darveniza, Mooroopna, Vic; 1911.
(c) Orlando Wines. G. Gramp & Sons Ltd, Barossa Valley, SA. The Gramp cellars and vineyards are situated at Rowland Flat, SA. When searching for a brand name for his wine, G. Gramp decided on the Italian translation of Rowland – *Orlando*. This brand name was first registered in 1921 and the script has been featured on stationery, labels, packaging and advertising since that date.
(d) Romalo. Australian Sparkling Wines Ltd; 1922.
(e) Kangaroo Vineyards. J. J. McWilliam & Sons, Sydney; 1923.
(f) Auldana Ltd, Adelaide. Wines; 1920.
(g) Coo-ee Wines. Matteo Fiorelli, Sydney; 1925.
(h) Margaret Mildara. Mildura Winery Ltd, Merbein, Vic; 1955.
(i) Another trademark from Mildura Winery; 1952.
(j) Federal Cask Co. Pty Ltd, Melbourne; Casks and barrels; 1916.

(a)

(b)

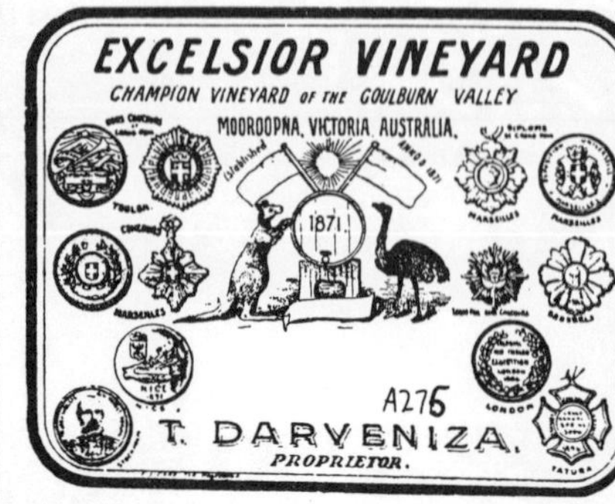

(c)

(d)

(e)

(f)

(g)

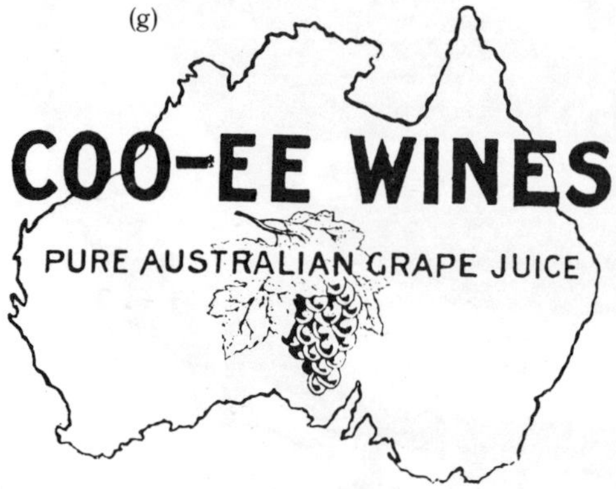

(h)

(i)

(j)

(a)

(b)

(c)

(d)

(e)

(f)

(g)

(h)

(i)

Eatmore

Beer.

Beer drinking has long been a great Australian pastime. As early as 1856, for example, Melbourne had 136 hotels, inns and taverns, and seven breweries. Most of these breweries suffered from the ups and downs of the post-gold rush economy, and in 1907 amalgamated into the Carlton & United Breweries.

(a) Superior Dandelion Ale; 1880s.
(b) Canterbury Extra Stout.
Australasian Breweries Ltd, Sydney; c. 1886.
(c) Carlton First Prize Ale.
Carlton & West End Breweries Ltd, Melbourne; c. 1887.
(d) The Foster Brewing Co. Ltd, Melbourne; 1895.
(e) (f) (g) Three labels registered by McCracken's Brewery Ltd, Melbourne; 1899.
(h) Federal Hop Beer.
J. Prosser & Son, Melbourne; 1899.
(i) Carlton.
Carlton Brewery Ltd, Melbourne; 1906.
(j) Carlton & United Breweries Ltd, Melbourne.
Current corporate logo introduced 1967.
(k) Tooth & Co. Ltd, Sydney.
Brewers, hoteliers and distributors of wines and spirits.
Symbol designed by Huveneers Pty Ltd, in 1978.

(j)

(k)

Eatmore

Beer.

(a) Standard Double Stout.
Tooheys Ltd, Sydney; 1906.
(b) Alliance Temperance Ale.
The S.A. Brewing Co. Ltd, Adelaide; mid-1920s.
(c) (d) Castlemaine Fourex.
The Castlemaine Brewery and Quinlan Gray & Co., Brisbane; (c) 1928, (d) current.
(e) (f) Ballarat Bertie.
Ballarat Brewing Co., Vic.
These two illustrations are from an advertising campaign of the 1930s. In 1926, while on a train trip, the manager of the Ballarat Brewery, Mr Coglan, and an advertising representative conceived of *Ballarat Bertie*. Bertie appeared on the label up until 1971 when the new owners of the Ballarat Brewery, Carlton & United Breweries, removed him for their own corporate logo. The public outcry was so great that Bertie was quickly reinstated.
(g) Nathan Ale.
Geo. F. Shand. Hindmarsh, SA; late 1920s.
(h) Fourex Swan Stout.
The Swan Brewery Co. Ltd, Perth; late 1920s.
(i) Palmerston Dinner Ale.
Ellis & Kells Brewery (Darwin) Ltd; early 1950s.
(j) Grafton Lager.
Grafton Brewing Co. Ltd, NSW; late 1950s.

(a)

(b)

(c)

(d)

(e)

(f)

(g)

(h)

(i)

(j)

Eatmore

Flour.

The basic, simple nature of flour and the lack of product differentiation has led to a large, discursive range of product names and packaging.
(a) Aerial.
S. Thomas & Co., Melbourne; 1908.
(b) The Adelaide Milling Co. Ltd, SA.; 1908.
(c) The Swift.
A. H. Hattersley, Sydney; 1909.
(d) G.P.O.
F. Remfry, Melbourne; 1911.
(e) (f) J. McAlpin & Sons, Melbourne; (e) 1915, (f) 1908.
(g) Featherweight.
Thomas Hayward & Son Ltd, Bunbury, WA; 1916.
(h) Bluebell Brand.
Mitsui, Bussan, Kaisha Ltd, Sydney; 1917.
(i) Gollin & Co. Pty Ltd, Sydney; 1917.
(j) Cafe Brand.
J. J. Sullivan Ltd, Sydney; 1918.

(a)

(b)

(c)

(d)

(e)

(g)

(h)

(i)

(j)

(f)

Eatmore

Flour.

(a) Tank Brand.
Stratton & Co. Pty Ltd, Melbourne; 1918.
(b) Wagga Lily.
The Murrumbidgee Co-op. Flour Milling Co. Ltd, Wagga Wagga, NSW; 1919.
(c) Fielder.
The Regan Palace Roller Flour Mills Ltd, Tamworth, NSW; 1920.
(d) Digger Brand.
Andrews & Son; 1922.
(e) Big G.
Victoria District Co-op. Flour Milling Ltd, Geraldton, WA; 1922.
(f) Calendar Brand.
S. Allen & Sons; 1923.
(g) Oh Boy Brand.
McCorquodale Bros., Sydney; 1932.
(h) Happy Family Brand.
Mungo Scott Ltd, Sydney; 1934.
(i) Aeroplane Brand.
Great Southern Roller Flour Mills Ltd, Fremantle, WA; 1938.
(j) Manu.
Jules Bros. Pty Ltd, Sydney; 1939.

(a)

(b)

(c)

(d)

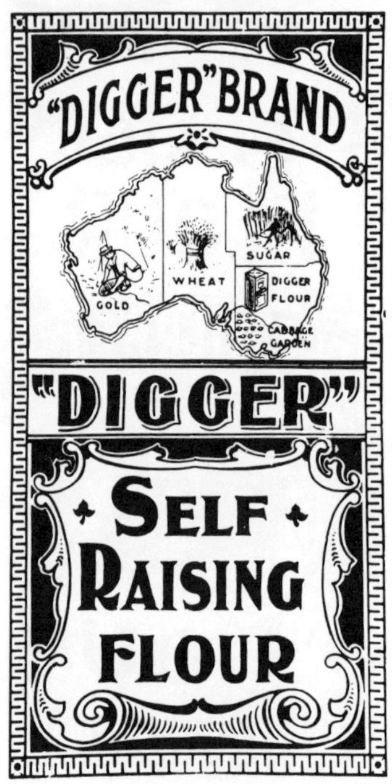

(e)

(f)

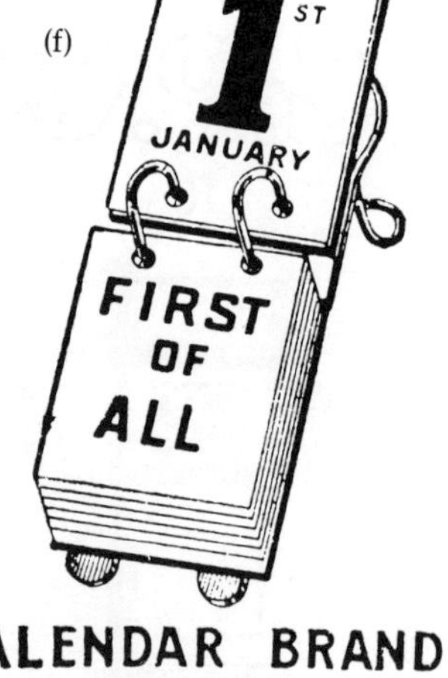

(g)

(h)

(i)

(j)

(a)

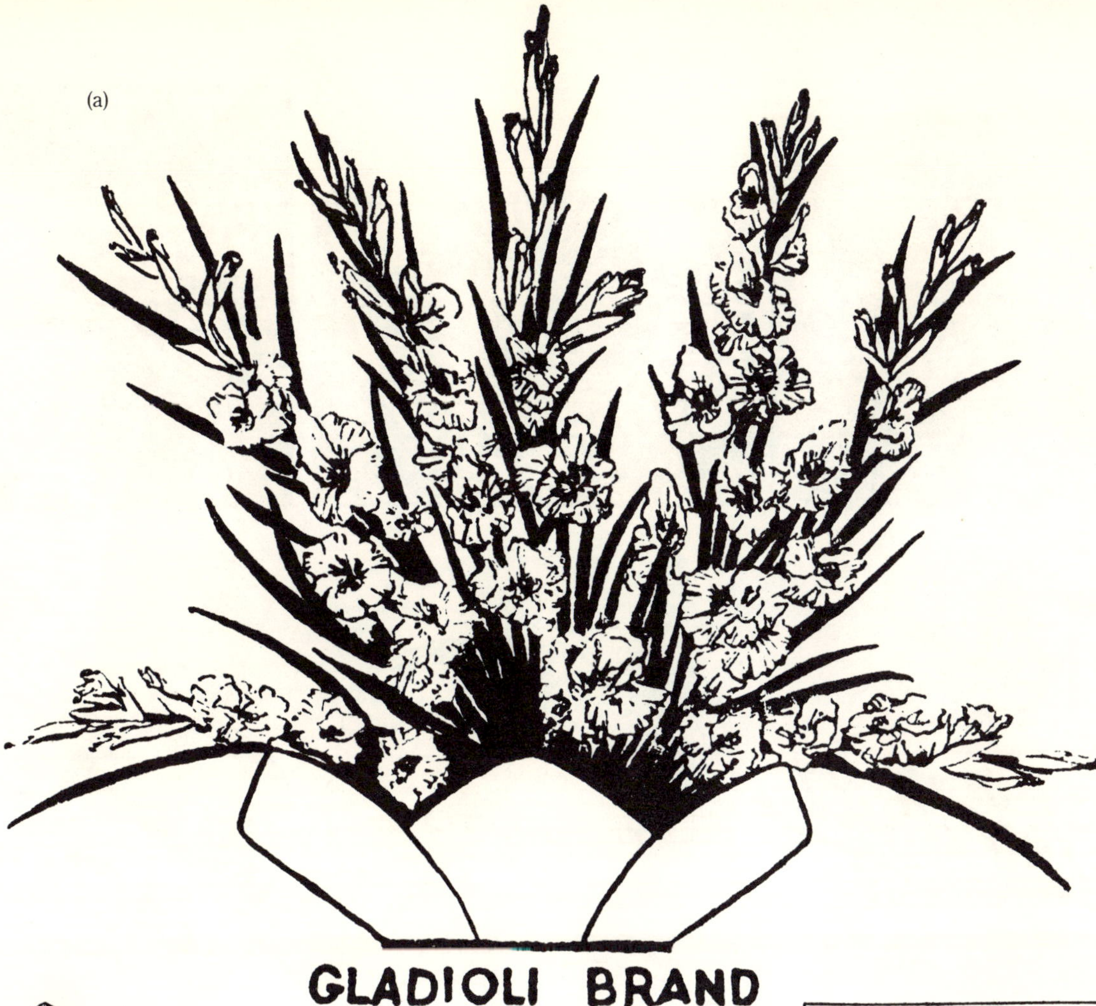

(b)

(c)

(d)

(e)

(f)

(g)

Eatmore

Flour.

(a) Gladioli Brand.
Corowa Milling Co. Ltd, NSW; 1954.
(b) Toucan Brand.
E. Benson & Co., Perth; 1951.
(c) Australian Pacific Traders Pty Ltd, Fremantle, WA; 1953.
(d) Hi-Lift.
William Farber Pty Ltd, Sydney; 1954.
(e) Horse and Sulky Brand.
Corowa Milling Co. Ltd, NSW; 1954.
(f) Betjak.
John Darling & Son Pty Ltd, Melbourne; 1954.
(g) Taxi Brand.
John Darling & Son Pty Ltd, Melbourne; 1957.

Eatmore

Dough.

(a) Good Shot.
D. Mitchell & Co., Sydney.
Baking powder; 1898.
(b) Golden Fleece.
Barter & Co., Sydney.
Baking powder; 1908.
(c) T.B.F. – The Baker's Friend.
A. H. Hattersley, Sydney.
Yeast; 1911.
(d) Peptomalt.
Smith, Mitchell & Co., Brisbane; 1913.
(e) Auto.
Automatic Bakeries Ltd, Brisbane.
Bread; 1914.
(f) Lactaloaf.
Allied Food Industries, Melbourne.
Bread; 1954.
(g) Golden Crust Baking Co., Melbourne.
Bread; 1940.

(a)

(b)

(c)

(d)

(e)

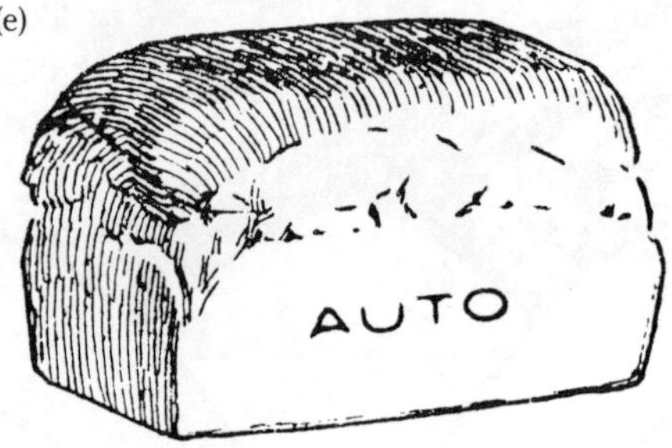

(f)

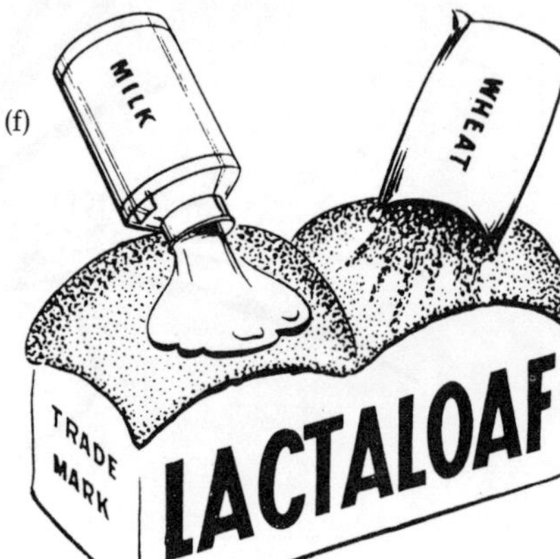

(g)

(a)

(b)

(c)

(d)

(e)

(f)

(g)

(h)

(i)

(j)

Eatmore

Cereal and macaroni.

(a) (b) Scotch, McNabs.
Parsons Bros. & Co., Sydney.
Oatmeal; 1895.
(c) Breakfast D. Light.
W. C. Douglass, Sydney; 1902.
(d) Crem-Ogran.
W. Leslie, Sydney.
Cereals; 1910.
(e) John Bull.
Parsons Bros. & Co. Pty Ltd, Melbourne.
Cereals; 1912.
(f) Grain-O.
F. & C. Piesse, Katanning, WA.
Cereals; 1914.
(g) Bulls-Eye Brand.
Cereal Foods Pty Ltd; 1916.
(h) Vita-Seald.
Frank Leo Marcy, Sydney; 1939.
(i) Kookaburra Brand.
Hancock's Golden Crust Pty Ltd, Melbourne.
Cut macaroni; 1928.
(j) Giant Brand.
Atlas Macaroni Mfg. Co., A. J. Bussola, direttore.
Perth; 1932.

Eatmore

General foods.

(a) Help me through the world.
Brennan & Geragh, Maryborough, Qld; 1900.
(b) Banquet.
Sam War Lee, Uralla, NSW; 1901.
(c) Life-Boat.
The Geelong Harbor Trust Commissioners (trading as Corio Freezing Works), Geelong, Vic; 1909.
(d) Billows Little Pty Ltd, Melbourne; 1911.
(e) Umbrella Brand.
Fred Walker & Co., Melbourne; 1911.
(f) Week-End Brand.
P. W. Heyman, Melbourne; 1913.
(g) Seraf.
Barnes & Co. Ltd, Brisbane; 1923.
(h) Eta.
Marrickville Margarine Ltd, Sydney.
Peanut butter; 1927.
(i) Surf.
H. C. Pannifex & Co., Melbourne; 1931.
(j) Uncle Osbro.
O'Sullivan Bros., Sydney; 1948.
(k) Spud's Potato Products, Sydney; 1938.

(a)

(b)

(c)

(d)

(e)

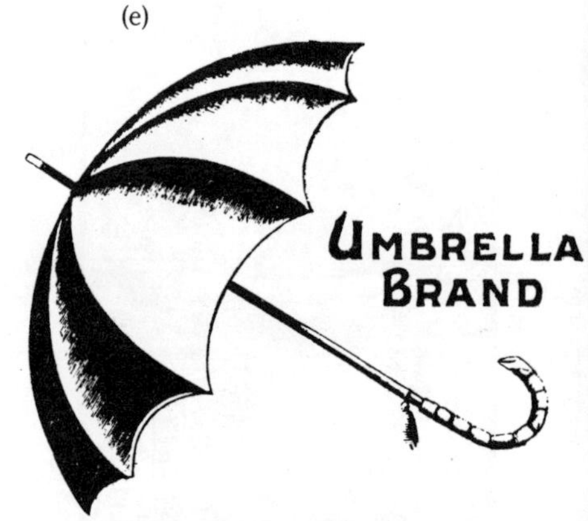

(f)

(g)

(h)

(i)

(j)

(k)

Eatmore

Salt and seafood.

(a) The Bushman.
Brisbane Salt Co., Brisbane; 1902.
(b) The Emu Brand.
The Castle Salt Co-op. Co. Ltd, Adelaide; 1906.
(c) Mermaid.
The Cheetham Salt Pty Ltd. Geelong, Vic; 1913.
(d) Shake-o.
Austral Salt Producers Pty Ltd, Melbourne; 1931.
(e) Kangaroo Table Salt Pty Ltd, Sydney; 1931.
(f) Marine Brand.
Solar Salt Ltd, Adelaide; 1959.
(g) J. & L. Hunt, Sydney. Preserved prawns; 1909.
(h) Schnapper Brand.
John Reid, Newcastle, NSW; 1910.
(i) Westwater Crayfish.
Russel Export Agency Pty Ltd, Perth; 1947.
(j) Sharkol.
The Producers' Co-op. Distributing Society Ltd, Sydney.
Fish oil; 1941.
(k) Kooka Cooking Salt.
Salpak Pty Ltd, Melbourne; current.

(a)

(b)

(c)

(d)

(e)

(f)

(g)

(h)

(i)

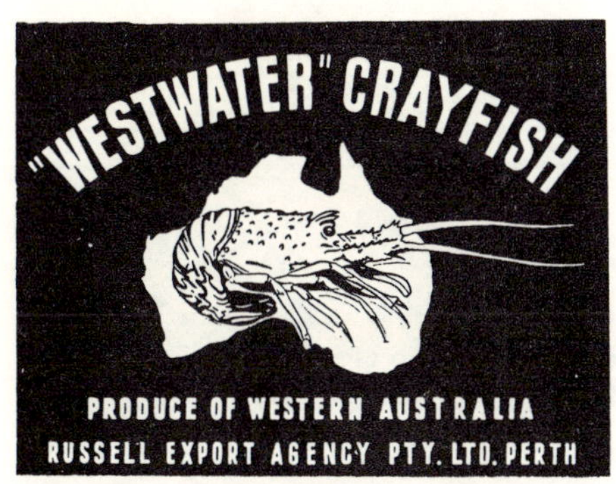

(j)

(k)

Eatmore

Pork.

(a) Yorick.
Vetch & Stokvis, Melbourne; 1900.
(b) Cation & Hilton, Melbourne; 1900.
(c) Castle Brand.
W. P. Hill, SA; 1909.
(d) Farmhouse.
Darling Downs Co-op. Bacon Co. Ltd, Qld; 1912.
(e) Sausagina.
J. J. Corden & Co., Melbourne.
Meat and preservatives; 1913.
(f) Home on the Pig's Back.
A. W. Anderson, Sydney; 1938.
(g) Best's Continental Smallgoods, Sydney; 1939.
(h) Presto Smallgoods, Sydney; 1970s.

(a)

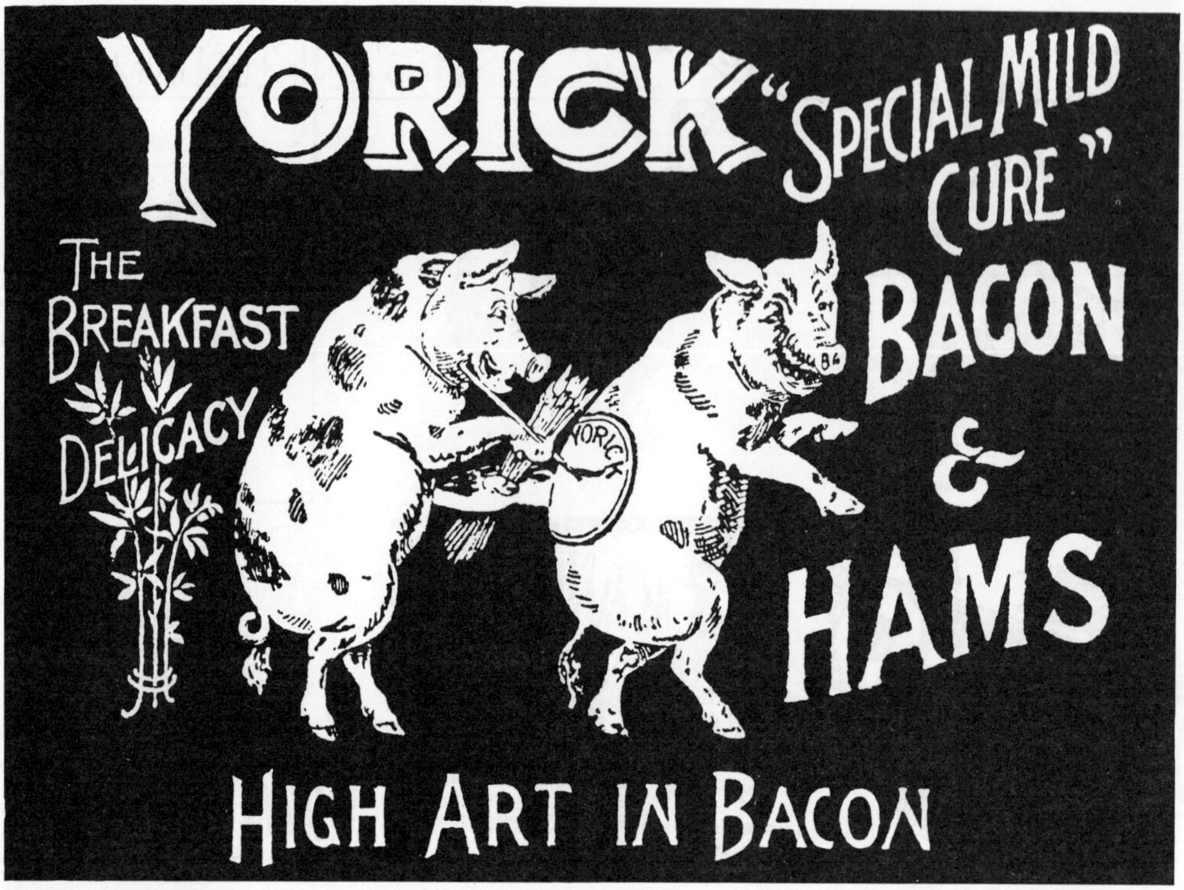

(b)

(c)

(d)

(e)

(f)

(g)

(h)

a)

(b)

(c)

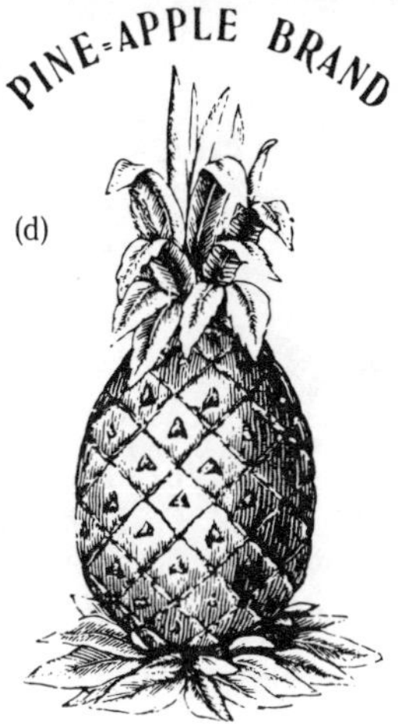

(d)

(e)

(f)

Eatmore

Nothing to argue about.

Mel. B. Spurr (c) was an English comedian and monologist who toured Australia in 1903-4. He arrived from England via South Africa. His shows received rave reviews and capacity audiences. The tour covered Hobart, Melbourne, Sydney and New Zealand – providing Spurr with a great personal income. In late 1904, he returned to Melbourne for a second season. He produced two handbills (a) (b) with himself featured in one of them. During the Australian tour Spurr suffered from glycosuria, a form of diabetes. This was complicated by an attack of influenza in New Zealand. In Melbourne the travel-tired and sick Spurr continued with his nightly one-man shows. On Monday, 19 September, 1904, his manager forced him to bed. By the following Sunday Mel. B. Spurr had died.

He was buried at the St Kilda cemetery, Melbourne, two days later. His popularity with Australian audiences was reflected in a public subscription conducted by the *Argus* to erect a headstone over his grave.

The same year Mel. B. Spurr arrived in Australia, J. C. Hutton registered Pine-apple Brand (d). Some time after his death they adopted the *Don't argue – Hutton's is best* slogan (e) – an adaptation of Spurr's 'Don't argue' handbill featuring himself. This trademark gained instant popularity and has been maintained ever since; (f) current.

Mel. B. Spurr, in an interview with *New Idea*, just before his death, stated these to be the best four lines ever written:

Trust no future, howe'er pleasant;
Let the dead past bury its dead:
Act, act, in the living present,
Heart within and God o'erhead.

Could he have known that he would be immortalised on a pack of bacon?

Source: *Mel. B. Spurr – His Life, Work, Writings and Recitations* by Harry A. Spurr, A. Brown & Sons Ltd, London.

Eatmore

Dairy and poultry produce.

(a) Nursery.
Gowrie Dairy Supply, Qld.
Condensed milk; 1909.
(b) Table Brand.
Thompson, Thomas & Co., Melbourne.
Butter and dripping; 1914.
(c) Happy Day.
Graham Chain Dairies; 1931.
(d) The Austral Canning Co. Pty Ltd, Melbourne.
Butter; 1933.
(e) Moo-Moon.
United Vendors Pty Ltd, Brisbane.
Milk; 1938.
(f) H. Playford, Melbourne.
Eggs; 1894.
(g) Thomas S. Fox.
Fish, poultry and game; 1910.
(h) Valentine's Restaurant, Sydney.
Chicken in the basket; 1955.
(i) Tex Turkey Farm, Frankston, Vic.
Dressed turkeys; 1954.

(a)

(b)

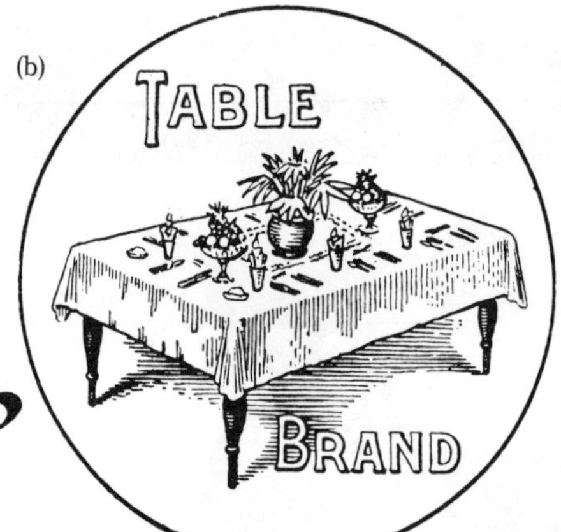

(c)

(d)

(e)

(g)

(f)

(h)

(i)

(a)

Eatmore

Rosella – the Saucy Bird.

Although it was not registered until 1899, the Rosella trademark appeared on company letterheads as early as 1897. The name was adopted in 1894 by Messrs H. R. McCracken and T. J. Press as a brand-name for their jams and preserved fruits. When they went into liquidation in late 1895, the business was acquired by Messrs F. J. Cato, B. Jenkins, C. F. Guthridge and E. Burke and the Rosella Preserving Company Limited was formed.

The rosella, referred to in an early poster as the *Saucy Bird* was, by the 1930s and 1940s, gradually used less and less until it was almost phased out in favour of the distinctive script. In the 1970s, possibly as a result of renewed interest in corporate memorabilia, the rosella was reinstated onto company packaging.

(a) The Rosella Preserving Co. Pty Ltd, Melbourne; 1899,

(b) 1905, (c) from an advertisement appearing 1927 and (d) 1957.

(e) In 1894, a year before McCracken and Press used the rosella for their jams and preserves, it was registered by R. Leech of Brighton, Vic., for eucalyptus oil.

(b)

(c)

(d)

(e)

Eatmore

Sauce, pickles and soup.

(a) V & S Brand.
R. C. Verney & Sons, Brisbane.
Tomato sauce; 1897.
(b) Moa Sauce Co.; 1908.
(c) Wattle Tree Brand.
Wattle Preserving Co., Melbourne.
Tomato sauce; 1910.
(d) White Crow.
Francis Longmore & Co., Melbourne; 1912.
(e) W. R. A. Crane, Adelaide.
Sauces and pickles; 1912.
(f) Skipping Girl.
The Vinegar Co. of Australia, Melbourne; 1913.
An advertisement appearing in 1916 simply showed the trademark and posed the question: *Why does she look so happy?* Then answered: *Because she knows everybody likes her*.
In the mid-thirties the skipping girl acquired the name 'Little Audrey' as plans were under way to erect a neon sign of her – the first animated neon in Melbourne. She skipped on and on to become a Melbourne landmark, providing free entertainment for children and adults alike, until 1968 when the vinegar company decided to move to Altona. At the new site Little Audrey was deemed a traffic hazard and could not be installed. She was sold to a panel beater. There was a public outcry. Two years later, due to the enterprise of John Benjamin, governing director of the Crusader Plate Company, and in response to the many requests from her 'fans', Little Audrey was reinstated to her former glory on the roof of John Benjamin's factory in Abbotsford, two doors down from her original position. She has skipped on ever since. Thank you John Benjamin!
(g) (h) H. M. Leggo & Co., Bendigo, Vic.
Sauces, pickles, soups; (g) 1913, (h) 1925.
(i) (j) Tom Piper.
Sidney Brown & Co. Pty Ltd, Melbourne.
Canned foods; (i) 1937, (j) 1960s.

(a)

(b)

(c)

(d)

(e)

(f)

(g)

(h)

(i)

(j)

(a)

(b)

(c)

(d)

(e)

(f)

(g)

(h)

(i)

(j)

(k)

Eatmore

Jam, jelly and honey.

(a) Tasmanian Jam & Preserved Fruit Co., Launceston, Tas.; 1878.
(b) All the rage. John Connell & Co. Ltd, Sydney. Jam; 1894.
(c) O.K. The Australian Jam Co.; 1906.
(d) Laver Bros & Co., Collingwood, Vic. Preserved fruit and vegetables; 1909.
(e) (f) (g) Aeroplane Jelly. Traders Ltd, Sydney. Jellies, jelly crystal, custard powders; (e) mid 1930s, (f) early 1950s and still current, (g) current. Although the plane was their registered trademark the *I like Aeroplane Jelly* song, first recorded in 1930, has become the company's real trademark:

I've got a song that won't take very long,
Quite a good sort of note if I strike it.
It is something we eat, and I think it's quite sweet,
And I know you are going to like it.
I like Aeroplane Jelly, Aeroplane Jelly for me.
I like it for dinner, I like it for tea.
A little each day is a good recipe.
The quality is high as the name will imply
And it's made from pure fruits, one more good reason why.
I like Aeroplane Jelly, Aeroplane Jelly for me.

(h) Peter Pumpkin & Co., Sydney. Jam, jellies; 1950.
(i) Hiv-Alu. G. Wood Son & Co., Adelaide. Honey; 1920.
(j) Sunbeem. Australian Honey Producers Co-op. Society Ltd, Adelaide; 1940.
(k) Golden Bee Honey. R. Stephens, Mole Creek, Tas.; 1955.
(l) Q.C.T. Queensland Country Traders Ltd, Brisbane. Arrowroot, jam, pickles; 1934.

(l)

Eatmore

Fruit.

(a) Soccer Brand.
Paterson & Co. Ltd, Perth.
Apples; 1934.
(b) Excello.
The Griffith Co-op. Society Ltd, NSW.
Oranges; 1921.
(c) Ark Brand.
The Renmark Fruit Growers Co-op. Ltd, SA.
Dried fruits; 1921.
(d) Help us to Health you.
Harcourt Fruit Supply Co., Vic.
Fresh fruit; 1923.
(e) Sunfed Brand.
Peninsula Co-op. Fruitgrowers Association Ltd, Melbourne.
Fresh fruit; 1930.
(f) Yonga.
N. H. Malcom, Melbourne.
Oranges; 1931.
(g) Atlas Brand.
W. H. Beauchamp & Co. Pty Ltd, Hobart.
Apples; 1931.
(h) (i) Paterson & Co. Ltd, Perth.
Apples; 1934.
(j) Digger Brand Apples.
Cudlee Creek, SA; 1936.
(k) The lovely 'Chiquita (little girl) Banana'.
A trademark of United Fruit Co., Boston, USA.
She made this appearance in a Melbourne *Better Food Exhibition* catalogue in 1955.

(a)

(b)

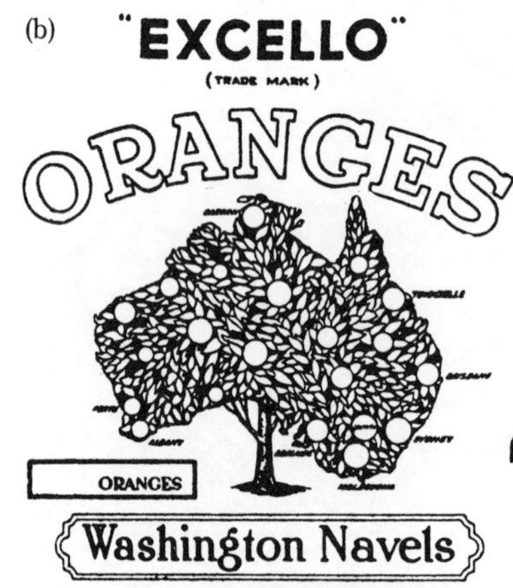

(c)

(d)

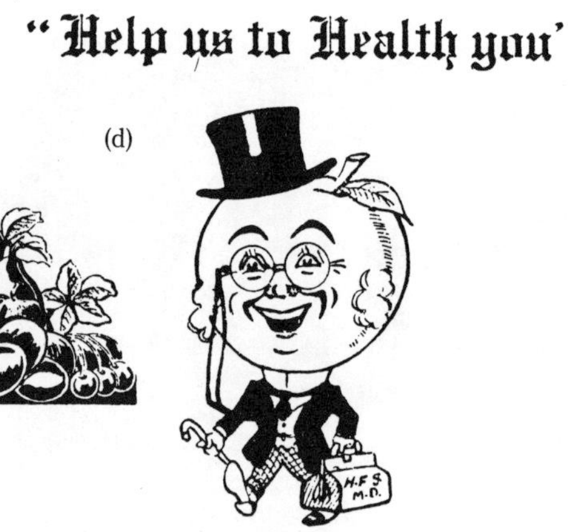

(e)

(f)

(g)

(k)

(h)

(i)

(j)

(a)

(b)

Eatmore

Ice cream.

(a) Pick-a-niny Freeze. H. Augustus Gray, Sydney; 1922.
(b) Jok-Meg Dainties. Parisian Delicacies and Biscuit Co., Sydney; 1925.
(c) (d) Peters Ice Cream. Peters American Delicacy (Victoria) Ltd, established 1929.
(c) From an advertisement appearing 1934.
(d) Current Peters Ice Cream logo.
From the mid 1950s Peters Ice Cream outlets were identified by a large, three dimensional ice cream cone. This has now become their popular symbol.

(c)

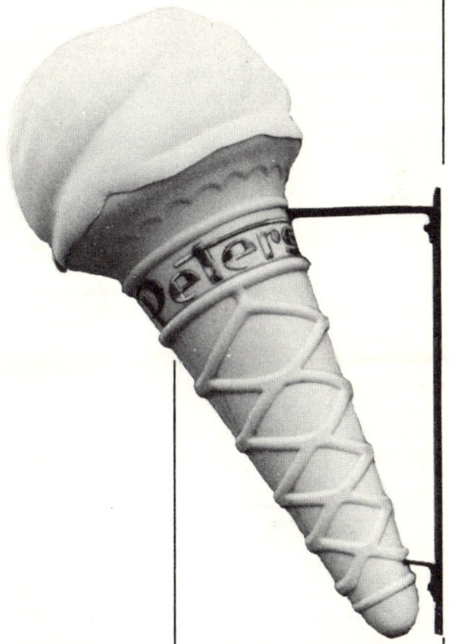

(e)

(e) Sennitt's Ice Cream. J. P. Sennitt & Son Pty Ltd, Melbourne; 1951.
(f) Toppy Toppa. Toppa Ice Creams Ltd, Melbourne; 1952.
(g) Tommy Swallow. Swallow & Ariell Ltd, Melbourne; 1956.
(h) Zig and Zag. Peters Ice Cream (Victoria) Ltd, Melbourne; 1957.
Zig and Zag (Jack Perry and Doug McKenzie) were created with the commencement of Australian television in 1956. Their original thirteen week contract was extended over thirteen years. Promoting Peters Ice Cream as *The Health Food of a Nation*, they became a Melbourne institution.

(f)

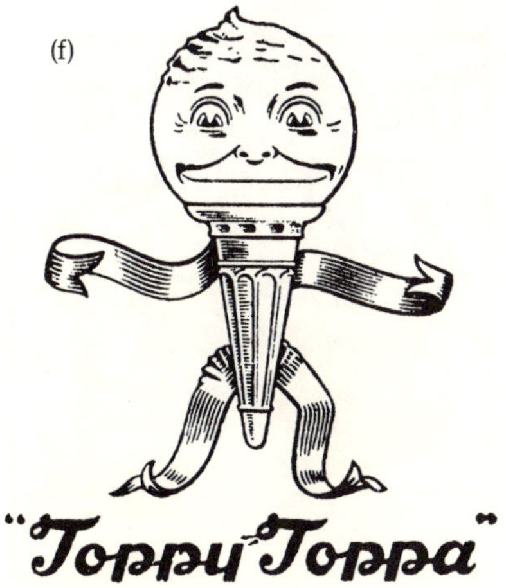

(g)

(h)

(d)

Peters

Eatmore

Lollies.

Sweets: for children, they are a purpose for existence; for adults, one of life's more inexpensive luxuries. In Australia, the confectionery industry started in small backyard factories. Their success or failure lay in their ability to create a flavoured sensation to tickle the taste buds of the populace. Those who succeeded in creating a popular brand, were then faced with amalgamations and takeovers. But, through all this corporate turmoil, the popular brands have survived.

(a) to (f) James Stedman-Henderson's Sweets, Sweetacres, Rosebery, Sydney.
(a) A series of brand cards for loose confectionery; 1930s.
(b) Minties; introduced 1922.
(c) A Minties advertisement appearing 1926.
(d) Jaffa; introduced c. 1931.
(e) Throaties; introduced 1929. This illustration is from an advertisement appearing 1940.
(f) Fantales; introduced 1940. This illustration is from an advertisement appearing 1946.

(a)

(b)

(d)

(c)

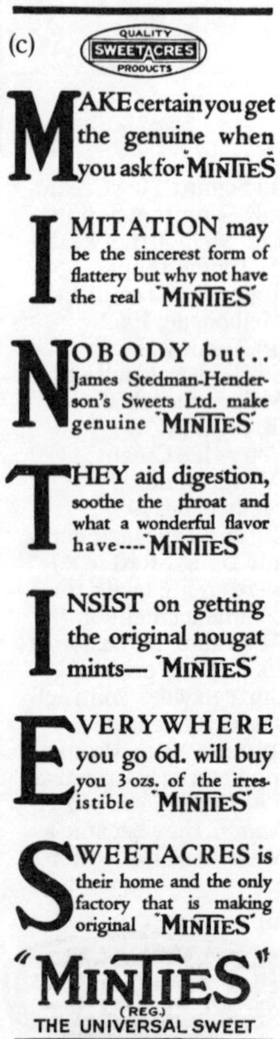

(e)

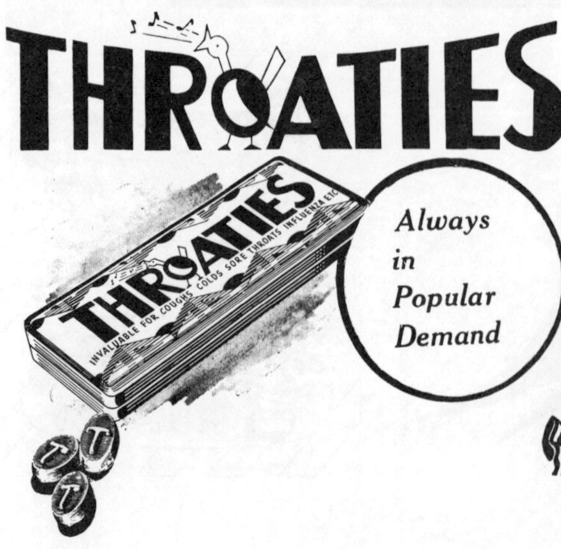

(f)

(a)

(b)

(c)

(d)

(e)

(f)

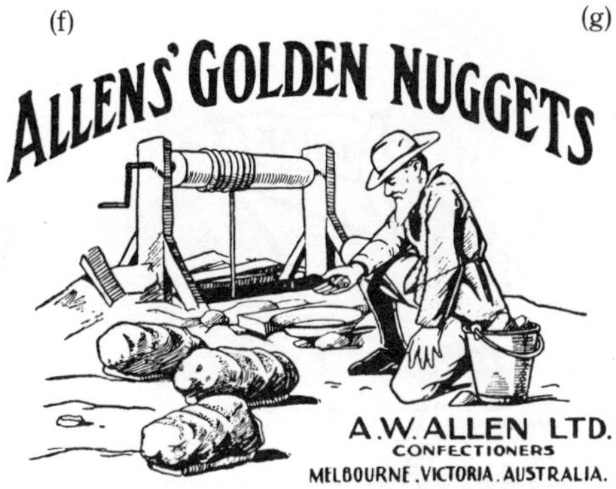

(g)

(h)

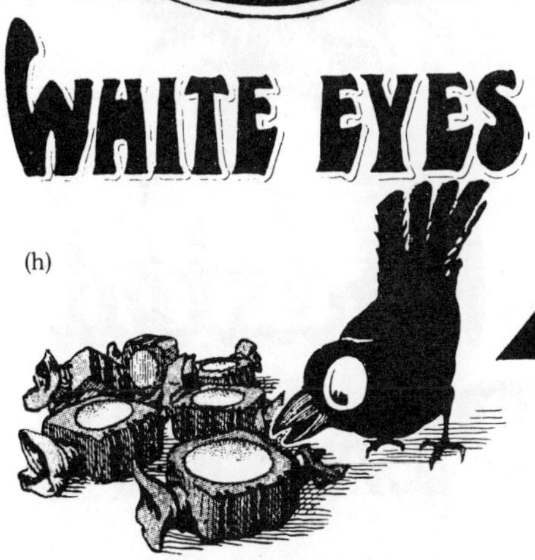

(i)

(j)

(k)

(l)

(m)

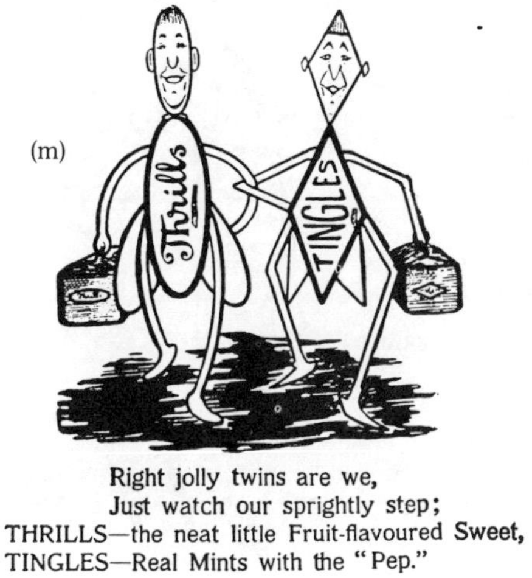

(n)

Eatmore

Lollies.

(a) to (d) Mac Robertson, Melbourne.
(a) Macpherson David Robertson's signature. He started the business in 1880. By the turn of the century the stylized signature trademark
(b) was being applied to an enormous range of confectionery as well as signage and vehicles.
(c) MacRobertson Freddo Frogs; 1939, (d) current.
(e) to (i) A. W. Allen Ltd, Confectionery Works, North Melbourne; 1906. At the age of 20, A. W. Allen commenced manufacturing confectionery in 1891. Within 18 years his was claimed to be the third largest confectionery company in Victoria.
(f) Golden Nuggets; 1922.
(g) Steam Rollers; 1932.
(h) White Eyes; 1934.
(i) Trademark; 1956.
(j) Kool Mints.
Griffith Sweets Pty Ltd, Melbourne; 1939.
Griffith Sweets was acquired by Allens in 1965.
(k) (l) Right-o, Good-o.
J. Walton, Adelaide; 1922.
(m) Thrills and Tingles.
Newblades Ltd; 1922.
(n) The Lucky Cat Confectionery Co., Melbourne; 1923.
(o) Biddell's Young Australia.
Biddell Bros. Ltd, NSW; 1914.
Young Australia or *the Little Boy from Manly*. In 1885, when the New South Wales Corp returned victoriously from the Sudan, a small boy burst from the crowd and threw them a penny. This event was captured by Hop – a *Bulletin* cartoonist of the day. The Little Boy character was adopted by other cartoonists and used as a symbol of the young, emerging spirit of Australia.

Eatmore

Nuts.

(a) Zee-Nut.
The Pacific Candy Co.; 1914.
(b) (c) Peanut Pete, Kernel Cashew.
Vita Foods Supply Co. Pty Ltd, Sydney; 1947.
(d) Admiral Peanuts.
Eric Silvers, Melbourne; 1949.
(e) Kingaroy Kid.
N. G. Scales, Sydney; 1949.
(f) Planters Nut & Chocolate Co., USA; 1920.
The Planters *Mr Peanut* originated in the USA in 1916, arriving in Australia four years later. It wasn't long before he had Australian look-alikes to contend with:
(g) Auto Brand.
Automatic Traders Pty Ltd; 1925.
(h) Peanut Twins.
Sym Choon & Co., Adelaide; 1927.
(i) Mr Peanut.
Teds Peanuts, Melbourne; 1938.

(a)

(b)

(c)

(d)
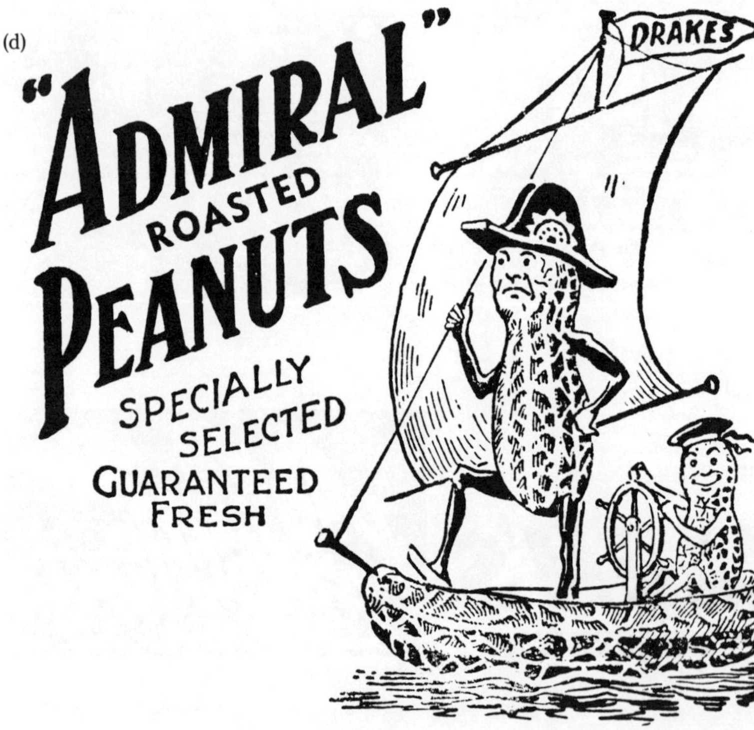

(e)

(f)

(g)

(h)

(i)

12. THEY FIT.

The best known advertising figure in Australia.
In 1906, J. K. Pearson and J. L. G. Law formed a partnership to manufacture shirts. In 1911 they converted it to a company and combined the first two letters of their surnames to create the corporate name: Pe-La-Co. Mulga Fred, an actual aboriginal from the Geelong area, and the line *My tinkit they fit* were adopted as the new company's advertising promotion. Mulga Fred or Pelaco Bill as he became known, was featured on posters, point of sale and in press advertisements. The original portrait of him by A. T. Mockridge, still hangs in the company's head office in Melbourne.
Ken Doe, of Paton Advertising, replaced Mulga Fred with Bambi Shmith and the new advertising slogan *It is indeed a lovely shirt sir!*
(a) Mulga Fred.
Pelaco Limited, Richmond, Vic.
Shirts and other clothing; from the 1941 Pelaco Annual Report.
(b) (c) Pelaco trade cuts featuring Mulga Fred; 1940s.
(d) Bambi Shmith; 1950s.
(e) Chief.
E. E. Whitmont, Sydney.
Shirts and other clothing; 1921.
It is possible that this trademark was created in an attempt to capitalise on Mulga Fred's outstanding success.

(a)

(b)

(c)

(d)

(e)

They fit

Hats and umbrellas.

The Hat King. The Commonwealth Umbrellarian. Shoes worth an Encore. Australians kept up with the fashions from top to bottom.

(a) The straw without a flaw.
A. M. & G. Fischer, Sydney.
Straw hats; 1907.
(b) The Hat King.
Thomas Trevena, Melbourne; 1912.
(c) K9.
G. Shrimpton & Sons, Sydney.
Hats; 1922.
(d) Your Hat Sir!
United Felt Hats Pty Ltd, Melbourne; 1930.
(e) Webster & Co., Melbourne.
Umbrellas; 1898.
(f) The Commonwealth Umbrellarian.
Christie, Sydney; 1904.
(g) Famous all over the States.
Paterson, Laing & Bruce Ltd, Melbourne.
Umbrellas; 1907.
(h) H. Porter & Co., Sydney.
Leather goods; 1912.

(h)

(a)

(b)

(c)

(d)

(e)

(f)

(g)
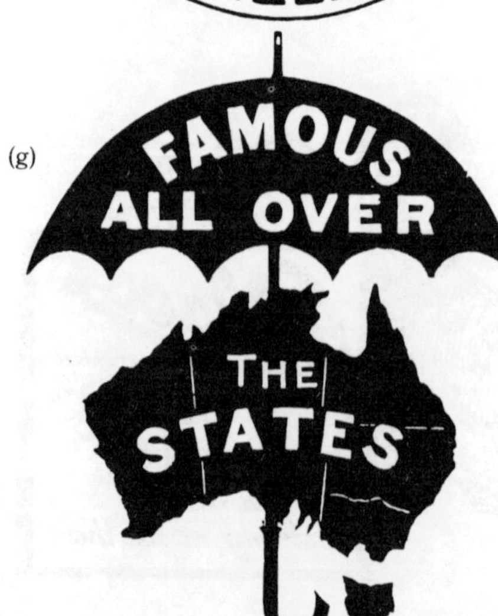

They fit

Boots and shoes.

(a) J. H. Abbott & Co., Bendigo, Vic. Boots and shoes; 1900.
(b) Kangaratta. Bedgood & Co., Melbourne. Boots and shoes. An advertisement appearing 1901.
(c) The Encore Shoe. Joseph Florey, Adelaide; 1906.
(d) Ironbark. Alex Cunningham, Brisbane; 1907.
(e) T. C. Jackson, Melbourne. Leather goods; 1908.

(a)

(b)

(c)

(d)

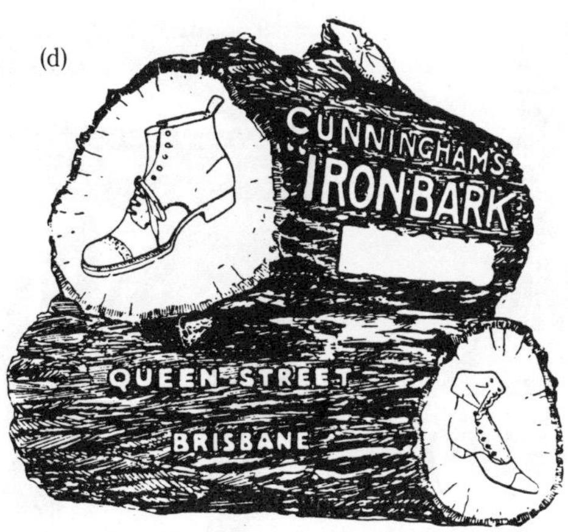

(e)

They fit

Boots and shoes.

(a) W. Leeming.
Great Colonnade Boot Bazaar. Cnr. Errol St. and Victoria St., North Melbourne; c. 1893.
(b) The one star of the Southern Cross.
Christensen & Co., Brisbane.
Boots and shoes; 1912.
(c) Paddle Brand.
Paddle Bros., Melbourne.
Boots and shoes; 1912.
(d) Pyramid Girl.
Knowlman & Son, Goulburn, NSW.
Footwear; 1915.
(e) The S.N. Boot.
S. Niness, NSW; 1923.
(f) Hapytoz Pty Ltd, Melbourne.
Shoes; 1926.
(g) Walkabout.
R. White Pty Ltd, Melbourne.
Shoes; 1936.
(h) Rondon Shoes, Sydney; 1954.
(i) Julius Marlow Pty Ltd, Melbourne.
Footwear; 1955.
(j) Even Keel.
Specialised Heels Ltd, Melbourne.
Snap heels; 1933.

(a)

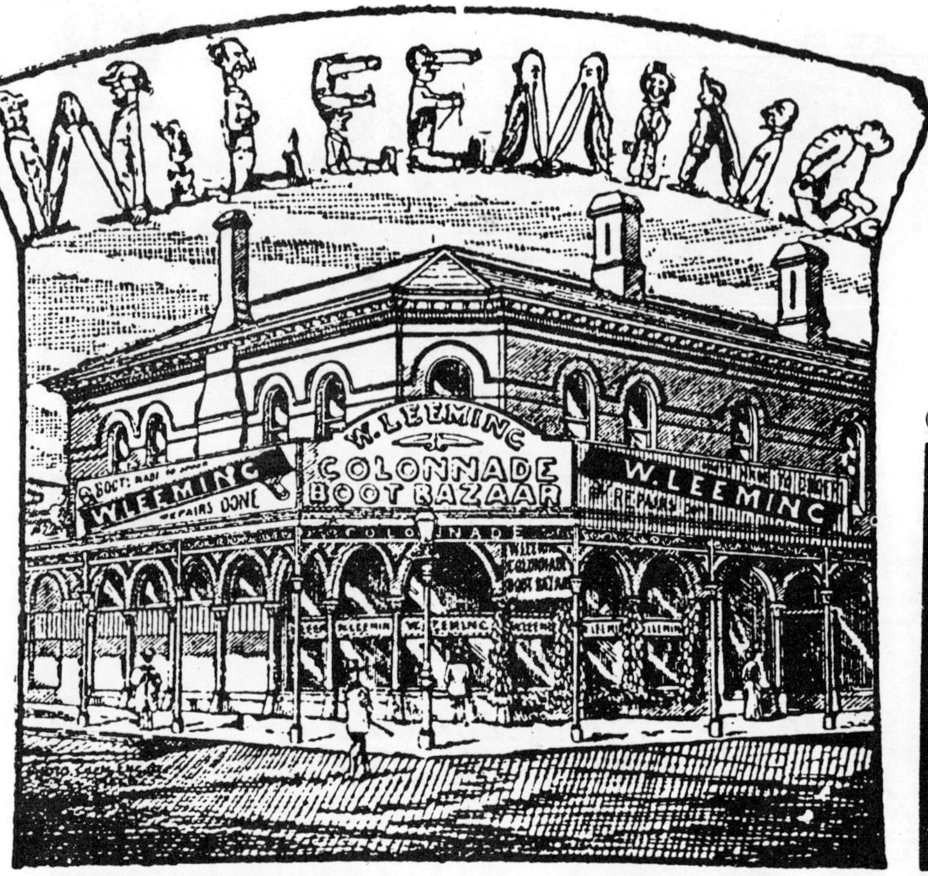

(b)

(c)

(d)

(e)

(f)

(g)

(h)

(i)

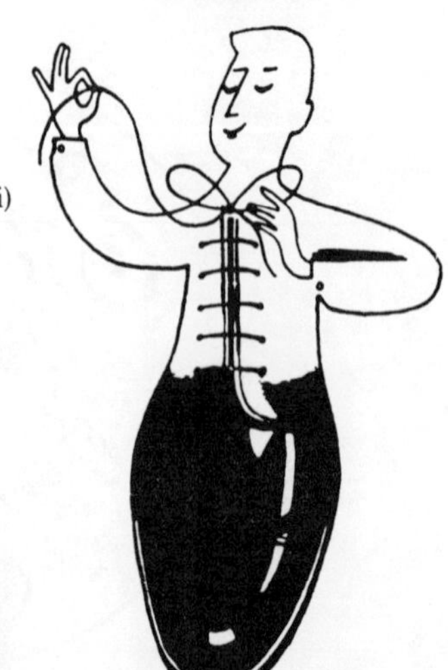

(j)

(a)

(b)

(c)

(d)

(e)

(f)

(g)

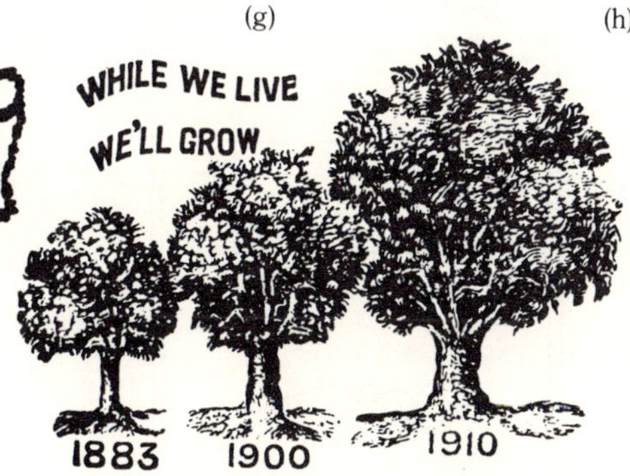

(h)

(i)

(j)

(k)

(l)

They fit

All over.

(a) Genuine Parramatta Tweed.
Murray Bros., Parramatta, NSW; 1892.
(b) Yarmouth.
R. A. Bradbury & Co., New Zealand.
Oil clothing; 1899.
(c) Kan-Ka.
Marshall & Co., Melbourne.
Articles of clothing; 1901.
(d) Given Away.
Frank Samuel Meters, Melbourne; 1903.
To prolong the life of a suit, a spare pair of trousers were sometimes given away as part of the purchase.
(e) Moon Brand.
J. McEvoy & Sons.
Articles of clothing; 1907.
(f) Golden Fleece.
Thomas Murray & Co., Vic.
Hosiery; 1908.
(g) While we live we'll grow.
W. J. Overell & Son Ltd.
Draper; 1909.
(h) Shearwool.
Sargood Bros., Melbourne.
Underwear; 1910.
(i) The Eagley Co. Pty Ltd, Melbourne.
Clothing; 1910.
(j) Ergon Brace & Leather Goods Mfg. Co., Melbourne; 1911.
(k) Konfidence.
Leviathan Clothing Co., Melbourne; 1912.
(l) Buckley & Nunn, Melbourne.
Merchants and importers; 1915.

They fit

All over.

(a) The test of our shirts is in the wash tub.
C. Gilbert Ltd, Brisbane; 1912.
(b) Tug of War.
Sargood Bros., Sydney.
Clothing; 1915.
(c) The Pioneer Handkerchief Co., Sydney; 1917.
(d) The Bank Bell Brand.
Banks Bell & Co., Melbourne.
Clothing; 1917.
(e) The Favourite Brand.
Freedman & Co., Brisbane.
Clothing; 1922.
(f) Adelaide on Wheels.
Southern Australian Portable Outfitting Co., Adelaide; 1912.
(g) G. J. Plenty, Son & Co., tailors and mercers; 1925.
(h) O.B.
K. S. & H. R. Nettheim, Sydney.
Clothing; 1926.
(i) Non-Tayr.
Murdochs in Park St. Pty Ltd, Sydney.
Clothing; 1927.
(j) Cheerio.
Lewisco Mfg. Co., Melbourne.
Handkerchiefs; 1927.
(k) Write to PA about it!
S. G. Gould, Brisbane.
Clothing; 1929.
(l) Delilah.
The Baker Knitting Mills Pty Ltd, Melbourne; 1930.
(m) Gibsonia.
Foy & Gibson Pty Ltd, Smith St., Collingwood, Vic.
Clothing; 1918.

(a)

(b)

(c)

(d)

(e)

(f)

(g)

(h)

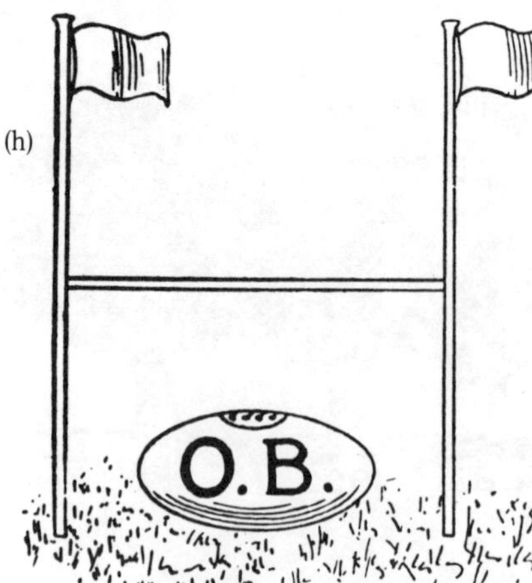

(i)

(m)

(j)

(k)

(l)

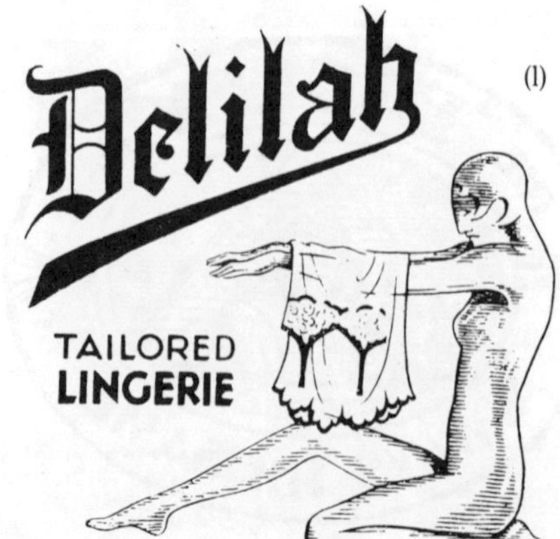

(a)

(b)

(c)

(d)

(e)

(f)

(g)

(h)

(i)

(j)

(k)

(l)

(m)

They fit

All over.

(a) Twin Tie.
Myers & Co., Melbourne; 1931.
(b) Speede.
Macrae Knitting Mills Ltd, Sydney.
Bathing and athletic costumes; 1931.
(c) Babnaps.
Farmer & Co., Sydney.
Infants' squares; 1936.
(d) T. Curtis Ltd, Sydney.
Neckties; 1935.
(e) Heavy Duty.
David Solomon & Sons Ltd, Sydney.
Working trousers; 1935.
(f) Neva-Rip.
The Herald Clothing Co., Adelaide.
Work clothes; 1938.
(g) Tradesman.
The Herald Trading Co., Adelaide.
Work clothes; 1938.
(h) The Vital 'V'.
Pelaco Ltd, Melbourne.
Shirts; 1938.
(i) Tiger Tim.
F. S. Walton & Co., Melbourne.
Outwear; 1939.
(j) Noveltie.
Novelta Textiles Pty Ltd, Sydney.
Neckties; 1942.
(k) Wilga Productions Pty Ltd, Sydney.
Clothing; 1949.
(l) Blue Bird Hosiery Mills Pty Ltd, Melbourne; 1950.
(m) Koala.
Pure wool scarf label.
(n) (o) (p) The Myer Emporium Ltd, Melbourne. (n) Imprint on an early paper bag, (o) (p) elements of the current corporate identity designed by Huveneers Pty Ltd in 1972.

(n)

(o)

M

(p)

MYER

They fit
All over.

(a) Collegian.
Pero Clothing Co. Pty Ltd, Melbourne.
Youths' outwear; 1950.
(b) Bell's.
Bellcraft Knitting Mills Pty Ltd, Melbourne.
Underwear; 1951.
(c) Stayput Trousers.
Cox & Sons, Brisbane; 1952.
(d) E. E. Whitmont & Sons Pty Ltd, Sydney.
Clothing; 1954.
(e) Embassy.
G. J. Coles & Coy Limited, Melbourne.
The Embassy Brand was first used on stationery lines in 1929. Today it has been extended to practically every product line sold by Coles.
(f) Prettymiss.
Elliss & Sytton Pty Ltd, Sydney.
Girls' frocks; 1954.
(g) to (l) Chesty Bond.
Bond's Wear Pty Ltd, Sydney.
Chesty Bond was created in 1938 by Sid Miller and Ted Moloney of J. Walter Thompson Advertising. As well as appearing in stores as a life-sized shop dummy, Chesty was the hero of a weekly comic strip. A number of companies attempted to mimic the comic strip approach to advertising, but none achieved the success of Chesty Bond. Since its inception, the simple Bond's singlet hasn't changed in concept or appearance. Chesty, on the other hand, has been updated to blend with the fashions of the day.
(g) Cartoon strip; 1954, (h) 1938, (i) 1956, (j) (k) current, (l) Chesty Bond Junior; 1956.

(a)

(b)

(c)

(d)

(e)

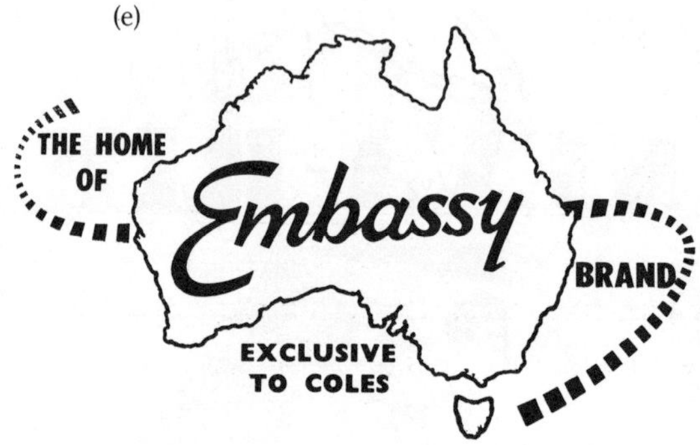

(f)

(g)

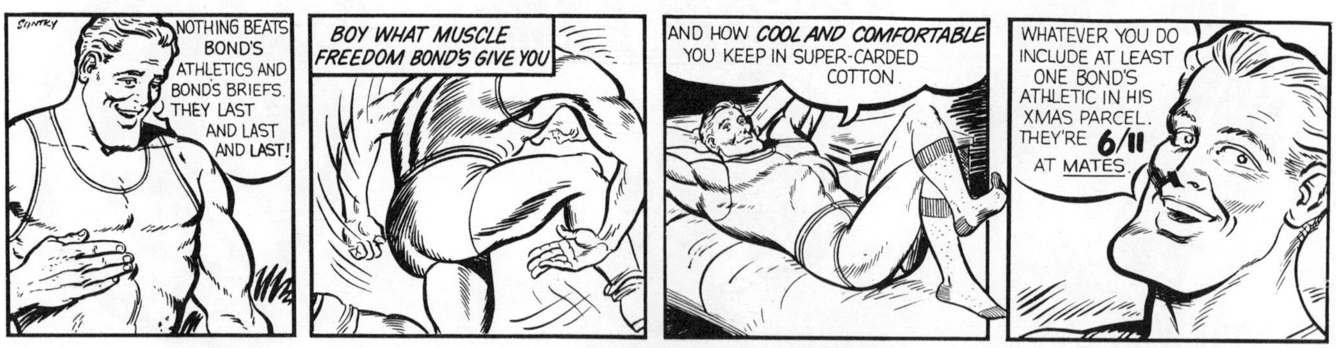

(h)

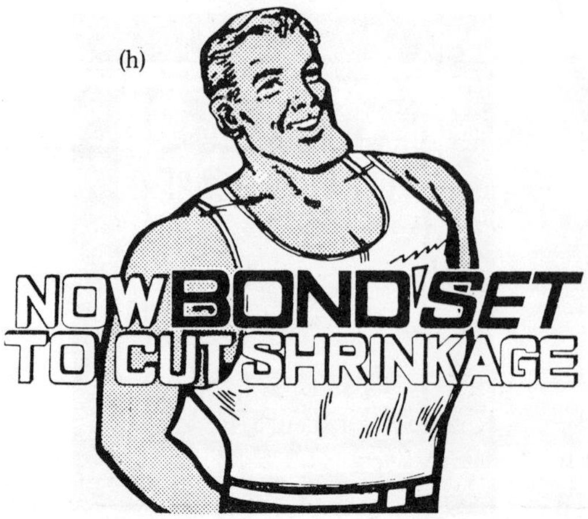

(i)

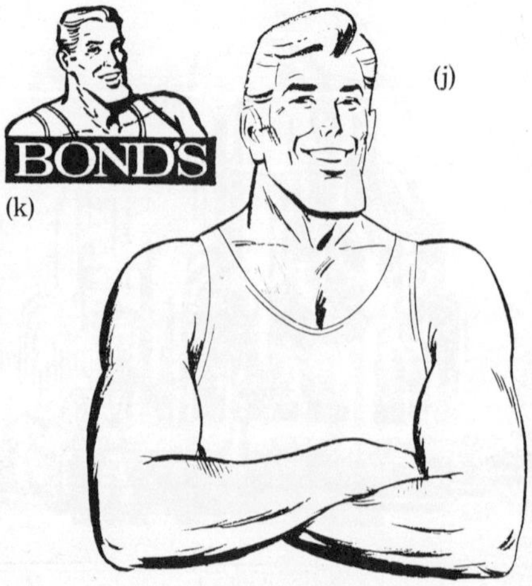

(k)

(j)

(l)

(a)

13. MARSOAPIAL VIEWS.

Cleaning is a daily ritual. But, via advertising, it has been promoted to the point of becoming an insidious addiction. Soaps and polishes claim to save work when their very existence creates it. Australians, like the rest of the modern world, have bathed in the 20th century fixation with hygiene, developing their own *marsoapial views* for these products of routine.
(a) Parry & Co., Sydney. Soap; 1886.
(b) Jinnie-Wash Clomobeal.
H. M. Roope, Ingleburn, NSW; 1929.

(b)

Marsoapial views

Of cleaning and candles.

Soap and candles were both made from tallow (melted animal fat) and they were traditionally manufactured by the same companies.
(a) Starlight.
Lever Bros. Ltd, Sydney.
Soap; 1906.
(b) Velvet.
J. Kitchen & Sons Ltd, Melbourne.
Soap; 1906.
(c) Torfol.
Hansen & Co., Melbourne.
Disinfectant; 1908.
(d) Stormlight.
Lever Bros. Ltd, Sydney.
Soaps; 1909.
(e) Preservene.
James Henty & Co. Mfg. Dept. Pty Ltd, Melbourne.
Candles, soap; 1910.
(f) Mylius Bros. – Eclipse Soap & Candle Co. Melbourne.
Soap; 1910.
(g) Handy Ann.
Lever Bros. Ltd, Sydney.
Perfumed soap; 1910.
(h) Gnome.
J. Kitchen & Sons Ltd, Melbourne.
Candles, soap; 1911.
(i) Rinso.
Lever Bros. Ltd, Sydney.
Washing powder; 1911.
(j) Kill Smell.
J. I. Tiefenbeck, Sydney.
Disinfectant; 1908.

(a)

(b)

(c)

(d)

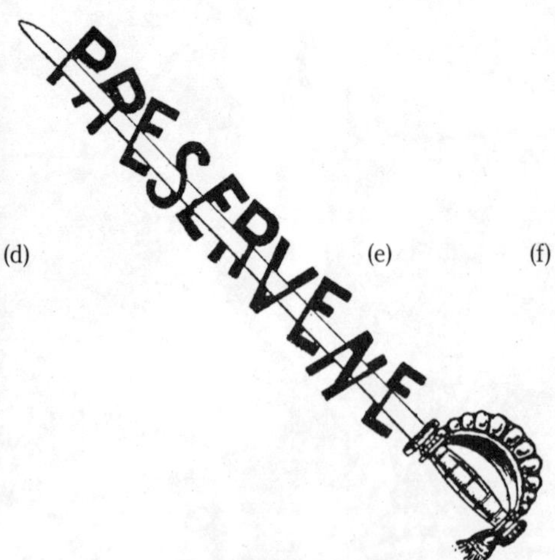

(e)

(f)

(j)

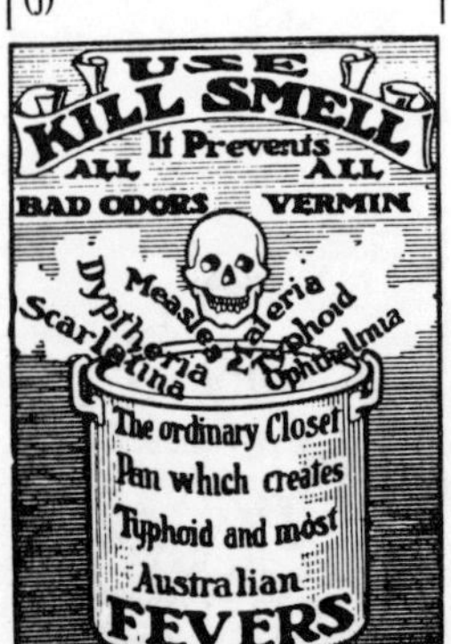

(g)

(h)

(i)

Marsoapial views

Of cleaning and candles.

(a) Triplets.
W. H. Burford & Sons, Adelaide.
Candles, soap; 1912.
(b) Witch.
J. Kitchen & Sons Ltd, Melbourne.
Candles, soap; 1912.
(c) Su-Tall.
Campbell Bros. Ltd, Brisbane.
Soap; 1912.
(d) Chloro Naptholeum.
United Distributing Companies Ltd, Sydney.
Disinfectant; 1912.
(e) Lever Bros. Ltd, Sydney.
Soaps; 1912.
(f) Saturn.
Lever Bros. Ltd, Sydney.
Soap; 1914.
(g) Handy Jack.
Stanmare Mfg. Co., Sydney.
Soap; 1915.
(h) Solvol.
J. Kitchen & Sons Pty Ltd, Melbourne.
Soap; 1915.
(i) The Digger Brand 'Washo' Soap.
W. H. Carwardine; 1916.
(j) Occo.
Emily Hilton, Sydney.
Soap; 1916.
(k) The Brisbane Soap Co. Ltd; 1918.
(l) Clean All Cleanser.
A. C. Webster, Torrensville, SA; 1923.
(m) Laundrena.
Clifford Love & Co. Ltd, Sydney; from the 1926 *Commonwealth Trades Alphabet.*

(a)

(b)

(c)

(d)

(e)

(f)

(g)

(h)

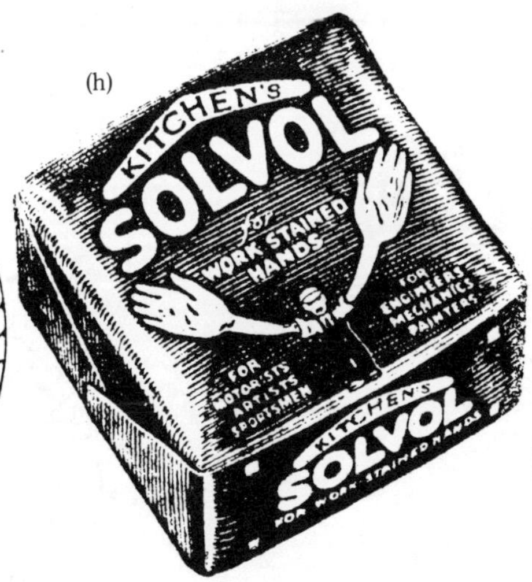

(i)

(j)

(k)

(l)

(m)

Marsoapial views

Cleaning and candles.

(a) Even a man can do it. The Bunyip Soap Co. Ltd, Adelaide; 1923.
(b) Reel Brand. Williams Trading Co., Sydney. Candles, soap; 1923.
(c) (d) Pearson Soap Co. Pty Ltd, Melbourne; (c) 1926, (d) 1927.
(e) Timid Joe. A. Tilley, Melbourne. Dog soap; 1927.
(f) Disho. The Bunyip Soap Co. Ltd, Adelaide; 1940.
(g) Glo-White Products, Sydney. Detergent; 1956.
(h) Velvet Shaving Stick. J. Kitchen & Sons Pty Ltd, Melbourne; from an advertisement appearing 1926.

(a)

(b)

(c)

(d)

(h)

(e)

(f)

(g)

Marsoapial views

Of toiletries.

With the money left over from the housekeeping, the housewife could enjoy small selfish pleasures like a splash of *Eau de Queensland* on a *Depilatoned* armpit.
(a) Eau de Queensland. Taylors & Elliotts Ltd, Brisbane. Perfumery; 1927.
(b) The Four Sevens Mfg. Co., Sydney. Perfumery; 1915.
(c) Campbell's Marguerite. The Brisbane Soap Co. Ltd. Perfumery; 1918.
(d) Garrod & Roberts Ltd, Sydney. Perfumery; 1920.
(e) Lady Olive. E. W. Kitchen, Sydney. Perfumery; 1922.
(f) Bridestowe Estate, Lilydale, Tas. Perfumery; 1926.
(g) Welcome to a good town. Sheldon Drug Co. Ltd, Sydney. Perfumery; 1928. The design elements of this trademark are outweighed by its mystery.
(h) Depil-A-Tone. H. J. Williams, Sydney. A depilatory; 1933.
(i) Sheer. The Myer Emporium Ltd, Melbourne; 1941.
(j) Satanic. W. M. F. Drever, Melbourne. Perfumery; 1946.
(k) René Henry, Melbourne. Perfumery; 1956.
(l) The Master Ladies Hairdressers Association of N.S.W.; c. 1927.
(m) The Master Ladies Hairdressers & Cosmeticians Association of Victoria; c. 1927.

(a)

(b)

(c)

(d)

(e)

(f)

(g)

(h)

(i)

(j)

(k)

(l)

(m)

Marsoapial views

Of polishes.

Housework made easy.

Phoebe, the Queen of Shines, reclined on the moon with the promise: 'Lightens work and leaves you leisure for recreation.' Unfortunately for the housewife there were enough different polishes to keep her polishing forever.
(a) Electric Polish.
H. G. Walker,
Melbourne.
Plate powder; 1893.
(b) Furline.
Henry McEvoy, Vic.
Fur cleaner; 1907.
(c) Phoebe Polish.
A. M. Bickford & Sons
Ltd, Adelaide; 1908.
(d) Yankee Mfg. Co.,
Sydney.
Polishes; 1908.
(e) (f) Monkey Brand.
Lever Bros. Ltd, Sydney.
Polish; (e) 1910, (f) 1944.
(g) Simple Simon.
A. Alexander & Co.,
Melbourne.
Polish; 1912.
(h) Lustro Mfg. Co.
Dry stove polish; 1919.
(i) Kwick and Easie.
Wiltshire's Pty Ltd,
Melbourne.
Cleansing and polishing
preparations; 1926.
(j) Milky Way.
A. McLeod Paterson,
Melbourne.
Floor polish; 1939.
(k) Slick.
L. T. Wilkinson,
Melbourne.
Polish; 1943.
(l) Kan Kleen.
The Kay Chemical Co.
Polishing compound;
1922.

(a)

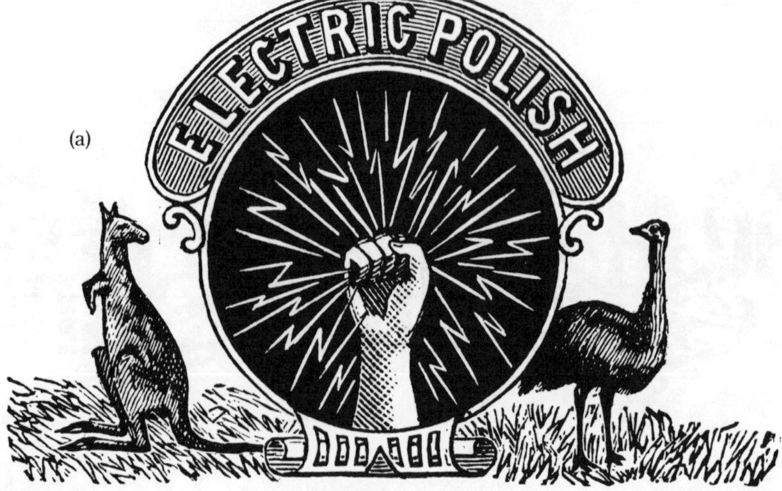

(b)

(c)

(d)

(e)

(f)

(g)

(h)

(i)

(j)

(k)

(l)

(a)

(b)

Marsoapial views

Of boot and shoe polish.

In the huge variety of boot and shoe polishes the only visible difference between brands was the design that graced the humble 7 cm can.
(a) (b) Gazeka.
William Leeming, Melbourne.
Shoe paste; 1906.
The Gazeka appears to have been created for the William Leeming Boot Stores – see page 132(a), by Jessie Dyson.
Appearing on hoardings and advertisements, it became a popular mythical creature of the time – also see page 51(d).
(c) Pacific.
Joseph Durham, Sydney; 1907.
(d) Bunyip.
Alfred Montague de Ruisset, Sydney; 1910.
(e) Navy.
George Townsend Erry, Melbourne; 1912.
(f) Emu.
D. Kennedy, Sydney; 1914.
(g) Roo.
A. F. & P. White; 1920.
(h) Koala.
A. Keillor; 1920.
(i) Meltonian (Australia) Pty Ltd, Melbourne; 1937.

(c)

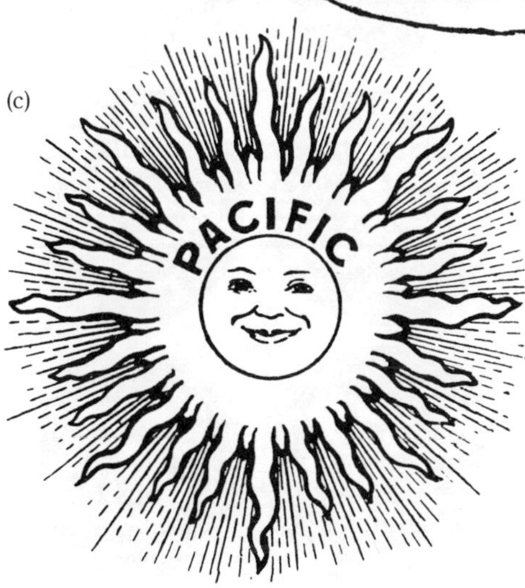

(d)

(e)

(f)

(g)

(h)

(i)

Marsoapial views

Of boot and shoe polish.

(a) to (u) Kiwi Boot Polish.
W. Ramsay, Melbourne;
(a) original can, 1906,
(b) symbol, c. 1920;
(c) current symbol introduced 1972.
Internationally, Kiwi Boot Polish is possibly Australia's most successful product. Created by William Ramsay in 1906, Kiwi was named after the symbol of his wife's homeland – New Zealand. In 1912, William's father, John, took the product to England and aggressively marketed it to the British Army. With the help of World War I, sales soared and Kiwi polish gained world wide acceptance. Today it is sold in 173 countries – a success that has led to a multitude of imitations:
(d) to (g) Japan.
(h) (i) India.
(j) Taiwan.
(k) Singapore.
(l) to (o) Vietnam.
(p) Israel.
(q) Finland.
(r) Unidentified.
(s) (t) (u) Korea.
(v) Sparkling Wine.
Blakeys Boot Protectors Ltd; 1921.
(w) Jacko.
W. K. Burnside Pty Ltd, Melbourne; 1930.
(x) Gay Boy.
Shyne Mfg. Co.; 1935.
(y) Tuff Tips.
E. G. Falls, Adelaide.
Shoe tips; 1929.

(b)

(a)

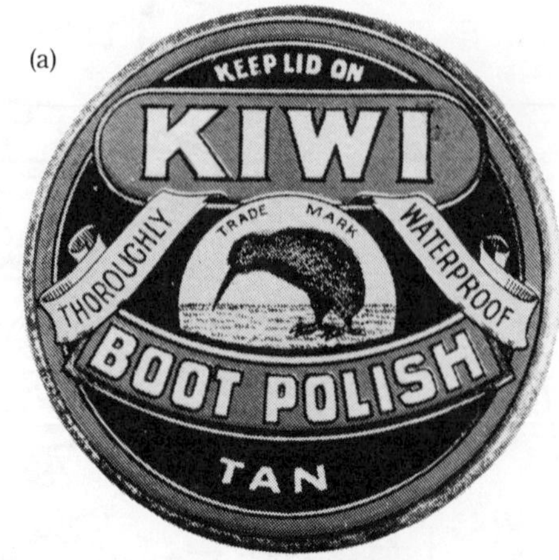

(c)

(d)

(e)

(f)

(g)

(h)

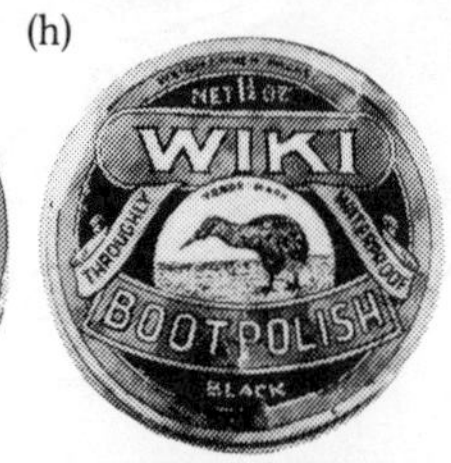

(i)

(j)

(k)

(l)

(m)

(n)

(o)

(p)

(q)

(r)

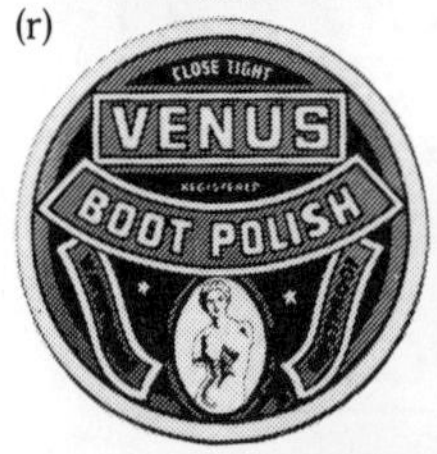

(s)

(t)

(u)

(v)

(w)

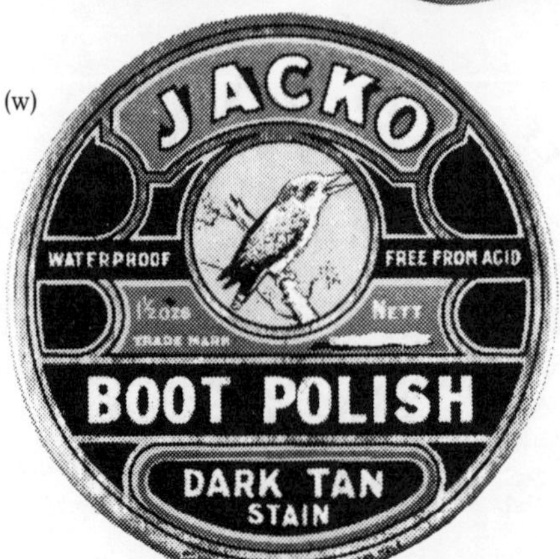

(x)

(y)

(a)

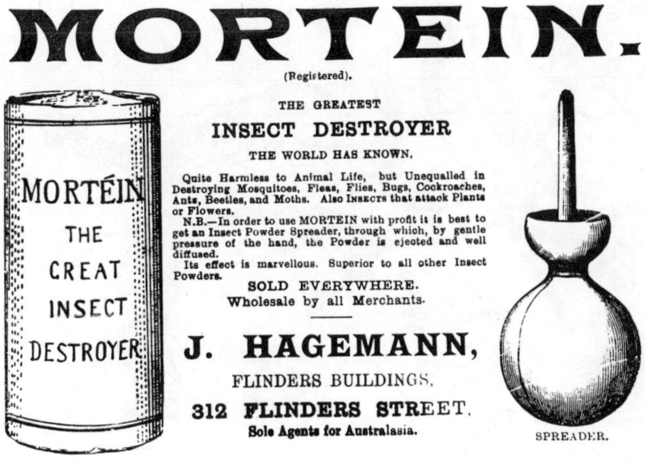

(b)

(c)

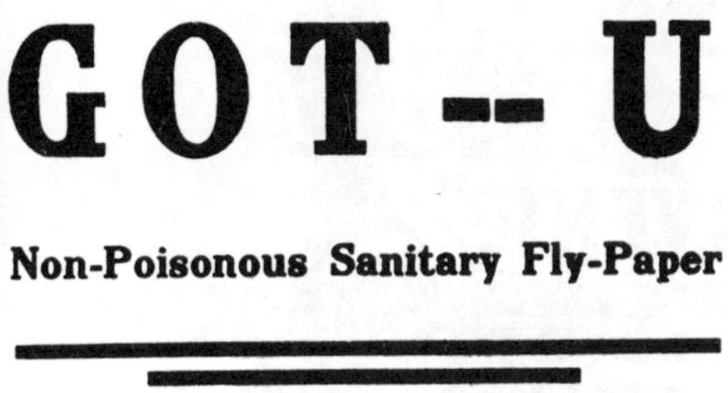

(d)

(e)

(f)

(g)

(h)

(i)

(j)

(k)

(l)

Marsoapial views
Of insecticides.

Musca domestica – the common housefly and scourge of every Australian home. Early this century it was responsible for spreading infantile diarrhoea, dysentery, typhoid, cholera, yaws and anthrax. Boomerang Fly Paper promised to catch the germs with the fly, but straight-out mortality was far more popular. Mortein built their reputation on the motto *Kills 'em stone dead*.

(a) (b) Mortein; from advertisements appearing (a) 1893, (b) 1960. Around 1880 John Hagemann began importing a Pyrethrum Powder from Germany and marketing it under the brandname *Mortein*. He appointed Samuel Taylor as wholesale distributors. In 1942 they took over complete ownership of the product. It is believed the famous *When you're on a good thing stick to it* visual of a dog and a mosquito was created specifically to promote Mortein. There is evidence, however, of its use to promote other products – see page 82 (h) – and of its appearance in newspaper cartoons.

(c) Got-U.
Florence Walters.
Fly-paper; 1919.

(d) The Aussie-Catchy-Foot.
W. Ellix, Perth.
Fly-paper; 1921.

(e) Boomerang.
W. A. Amor, Melbourne.
Fly-paper; 1922.

(f) Crasho.
J. S. Steele, Melbourne.
Insecticide; 1924.

(g) Fly Cop.
R. R. Pritchard, Sydney.
Insecticide spray; 1926.

Continued on page 179

(m)

Marsoapial views

Of pest control.

Rats, mice, snails, slugs, birds, cockroaches and ants were also given the domestic death penalty.
(a) Larter's Common Sense Rat Exterminator. From an advertisement appearing 1908.
(b) Pitt's Wheat. W. C. Kernot, Geelong, Vic. Poisoned wheat; 1909.
(c) Solvento. The Cockroach & Black-beetle Extermination Co., Sydney; 1921.
(d) The Bugs' Funeral Insecsterminator. The Bargain Shop; 1922.
(e) Leeks Cockroach Expeller. W. Rumsey-Williams; 1923.
(f) I'm Powellised! H. W. Powell & Co. Pty Ltd, Sydney. White ant, borer and vermin destroyers; 1951. In a letter to us, H. W. Powell wrote of his trade-mark: 'I sought something with a touch of humour but with simplicity. The final design fulfilled that idea to the letter, particularly the woebegone expression of the termite on his back.'
(g) Slug-Go. Thomas James Mannion, Vic.; 1924.
(h) Defender Co., Sydney. Snail and slug killer; 1938. The design shown here is an advertisement which appeared in 1979.
(i) Slug-Em. M.A.M. Marlow, Wembley, WA. Snail and slug killer; 1960.
(j) Fumarat. Lance Le Souef Pty Ltd, Melbourne. Rat fumigators; 1936.

(j)

(a)

(b)

(c)

(d)

(e)

(f)

(g)

(h)

(i)

(a)

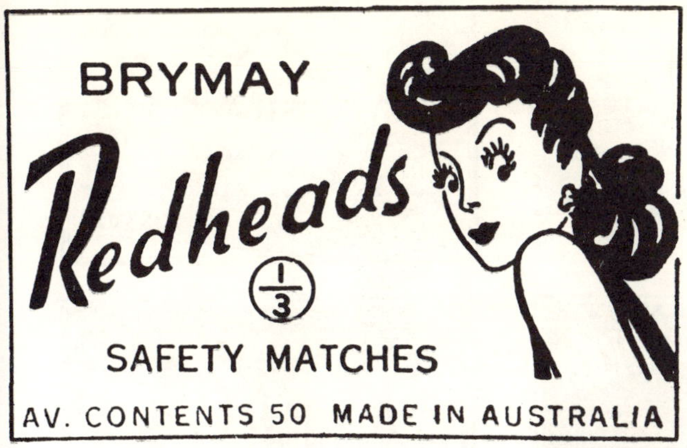

(b)

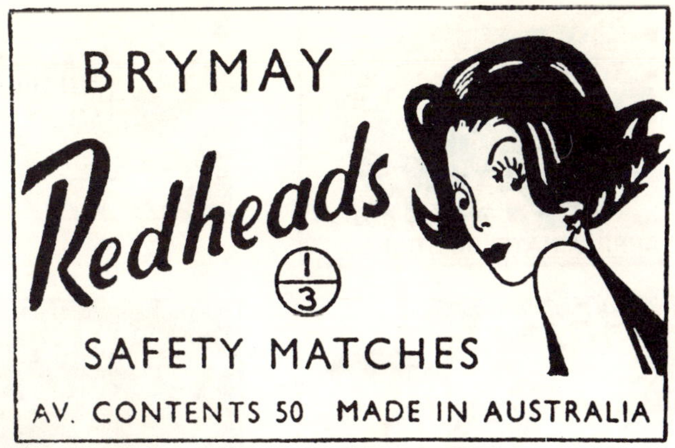

(c)

(d)

(e)

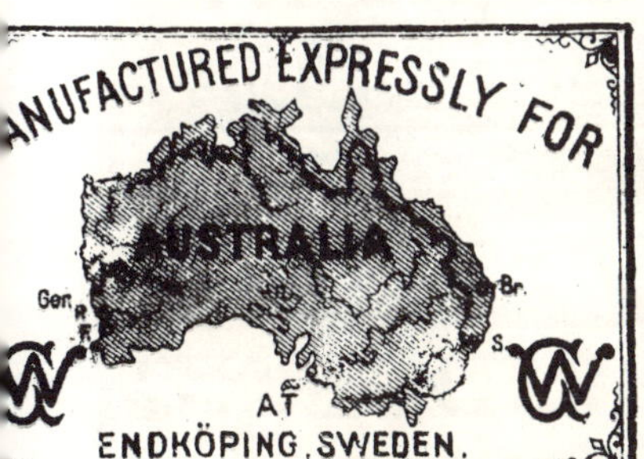

(g)

(h)

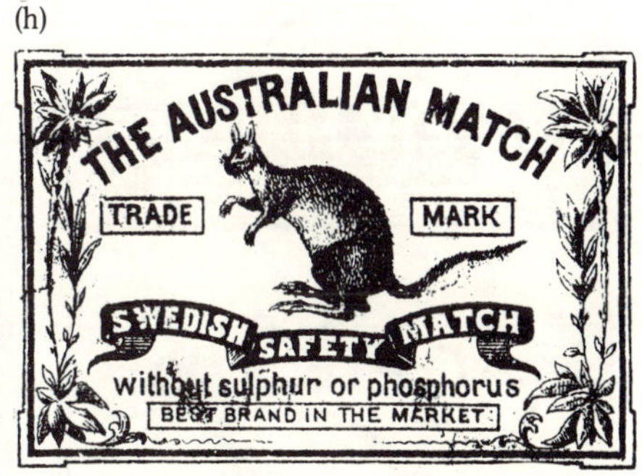

(i)

(j)

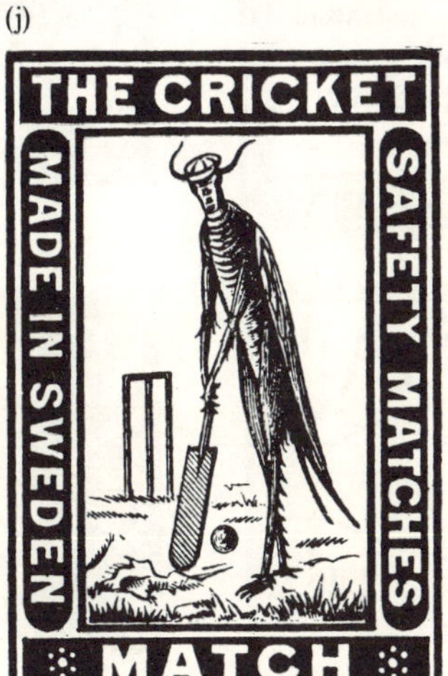

(k)

(l)

Marsoapial views

Of matches.

(a) to (d) Redheads. Bryant & May Pty Ltd, Melbourne. Matches; (a) 1946, (b) 1958, (c) c. 1971, (d) 1979. Redheads matches derive their name from the red striking head on the match. Since its introduction in 1946, the pack design has gone through three basic changes. It is interesting to note that the first change (1958) was one of hairstyle only. The subsequent change (1971) by Melbourne designer Brian Sadgrove and the current design (1979) were purely graphic revamps which maintained the 1958 hairstyle regardless of the changes that had taken place in the real world of women's hair design. The bar-room practice of converting the Redhead's shoulder to a penis, as an explanation of what she is looking at, can be performed on all four designs and is probably as old as the 1946 design. (e) Redheads. Riesa Match Factory, East Germany; a contemporary imitation of Bryant & May's Redheads.

The early Australian match market was dominated by imported brands. The few small Australian match manufacturers were slowly taken over by the English based company, Bryant & May. With the Government ban on imported matches in the late 1920s, Bryant & May developed into Australia's largest match manufacturer. (f) Manufactured Expressly for Australia. Sweden; c. 1898.

Continued on page 179

(m)

Marsoapial views

Of matches.

(a) Ram Brand.
Japan; c. 1905.
(b) Kangaroo.
A. S. Haik Adam.
Japan; c. 1905.
(c) Australia.
Mitsui Bussan Kaisha,
Japan; c. 1905.
(d) Kangaroo Brand.
Masudaya & Co., Japan;
c. 1905.
(e) The Federal Taend-stikker.
Norway; 1905.
(f) Kangaroo.
Japan; c. 1905.
(g) The Dingo Taend-stikker.
Norway; c. 1905.
(h) The Southern Cross.
Bryant & May Ltd,
London; c. 1908.
(i) The Nugget of the
Southern Seas.
Austria; c. 1910.
(j) Platypus.
E. L. Bell & Co. Pty Ltd,
Melbourne; c. 1911.
(k) (l) Australian Flag,
Coo-ee.
Australian Match Works
(E. L. Bell & Co.)
Melbourne; c. 1920.
(m) Magpie.
Bryant & May,
Melbourne; c. 1920.
(n) Melbourne Cup
Brand.
J. X. Rowan; 1923.
(o) Bridge.
The Federal Match Co.,
Sydney; c. 1926.
(p) Black Swan.
The W. A. Match Co.,
Perth; c. 1932.
(q) Federal Match Co. of
Australia Pty Ltd,
Sydney; c. 1937.
(r) Matches packed by
Brymay for the
Australian Army; 1979.
(s) Dingo.
A contemporary brand
made and sold in
Holland.
(t) Austral Matches Ltd,
Sydney; c. 1926.

(t)

(a)

(b)

(c)

(d)

(e)

(f)

(g)
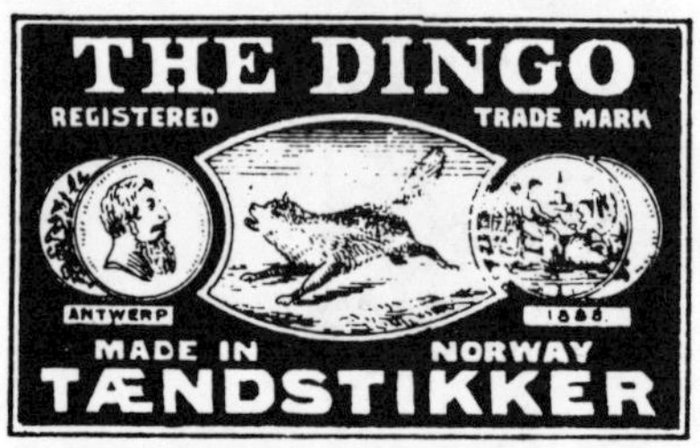

(h)

(i)

(j)

(k)

(l)

(m)

(n)
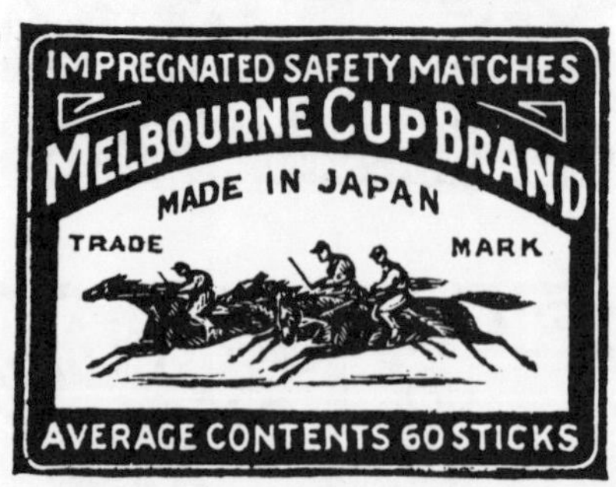

(o)

(p)

(q)

(r)

(s)

Marsoapial views

Of sewing and stewing.

(a) The Australian Sewing Machine.
A. Macrow & Sons Pty Ltd, Melbourne; 1908.
(b) The A.N.A. Sewing Machine.
Ward Bros. Melbourne; 1908.
(c) Austral Sewing Machine.
F. A. Bergmann, Melbourne; 1927.
(d) Emu.
J. Juleff & Sons, Sydney. Gas and fuel stoves; 1922.
(e) Chu-Chin-Chow.
O. Asche, Sydney. Cooking stoves; 1923.
(f) Albion Koala Cooker.
United Metal Industries Ltd, Brisbane.
Stoves and cooking ranges; 1928.
(g) Early Kooka.
Metters Ltd, Sydney.
Stoves; Early Kooka appears to have first been registered in 1920 although this design is from a later period.
(h) Potmend.
S. Cohen Sons & Co., Melbourne.
Cement; 1915.

(a)

(c)

(b)

(d)

(e)

(f)

(g)

(h)

Marsoapial views

All around the house.

(a) Empire Beds. Newlands Bros., Sydney; 1914.
(b) the Acme Beds Co. Ltd, Sydney; 1914.
(c) Jonchair. Johnston's Pty Ltd, Melbourne. Furniture and upholstery; 1928.
(d) Sno-Man Serv-ice. J. B. Chandler & Co., Brisbane. Refrigerators; 1933.
(e) Savaday. A. J. Veall Pty Ltd, Melbourne. Washing machines; 1938.
(f) Orchard's Pty Ltd, Sydney. Clocks and watches; 1939.
(g) Restinese. The Myer Emporium Ltd, Melbourne. Furniture; 1938.
(h) Wagon-Lit. Mark Foys Ltd, Sydney. Mattresses; 1941.
(i) Stilbetta. Stilwells, Bendigo, Vic. Furniture and upholstery; 1945.
(j) Hecla Electrics Pty Ltd, Melbourne. Appliances; 1950.
(k) BBB. Buesst & Bills Bros. Pty Ltd, Melbourne. Mattresses; 1953.
(l) Tecnico Limited, Sydney. Lawn mowers; 1959.
(m) Burge's Bros & Co. Ltd, Inverell, NSW. Emporium; 1913.

(a)

(b)

(c)

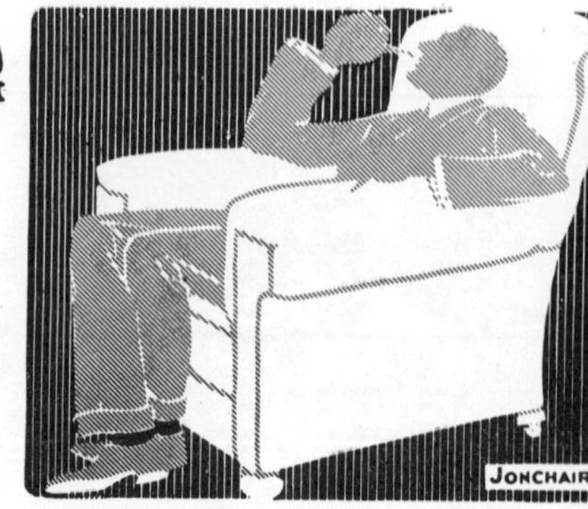

(d)

(e)

(f)

(g)

(h)

(i)

(j)

(k)

(l)

(m)

(a)

(b)

14. BE IN IT.

Australia has the shortest annual working hours in the world, or inversely, the most recreation time in the world. Time to spend on sport, music, reading, or just about anything – as long as there is a need to *be in it*.

(a) Luna Park, Sydney; 1970s and earlier.

(b) Life. Be in it. Department of Youth Sport and Recreation, Victoria.

In 1975, Alex Stitt created the 'Life. Be in it' family for an animated television campaign commissioned by the Victorian Department of Youth Sport and Recreation, through their advertising agency, Monahan Dayman Adams. Amidst controversy as to its worth, the campaign went national and the Government declared December 2nd, 'Life. Be in it' Day.

(c) Life. Be out of it. The alternate society's answer to 'Life. Be in it'.

(c)

Be in it

Toys and sports gear.

(a) Santa Claus.
H. S. Chipman.
Games and sporting articles; 1886.
(b) Kangy Brand.
P. L. Ransom, Melbourne.
Toys; 1922.
(c) Boomaroo Toys.
Artlay Mfg. Co., Sydney; 1945.
(d) Racer.
Mick Simmons, Sydney.
Sporting goods; 1907.
(e) W. Plant & Co. Ltd, Sydney.
Tennis and gut strings; 1925.
(f) Seniorgut.
Senior Gut Mfg. Co. Ltd, Sydney.
Tennis and gut strings; 1932.
(g) C. & G. Miller, Ballarat, Vic.
Hairdressing salon, tobacconist and fishing tackle; from an advertisement appearing 1911.
(h) The Ark Brand.
Jarke Pty Ltd, Melbourne.
Sporting goods, fishing tackle and nets; 1934.
(i) The Gotcher.
Edward Bentley & Sons Pty Ltd, Sydney.
Fishing line and tackle; 1940.
(j) Sydney Sports Stores.
L. W. Dodge & Co., Sydney; 1912.

(a)

(b)

(c)

(d)

(e)

(f)

(g)

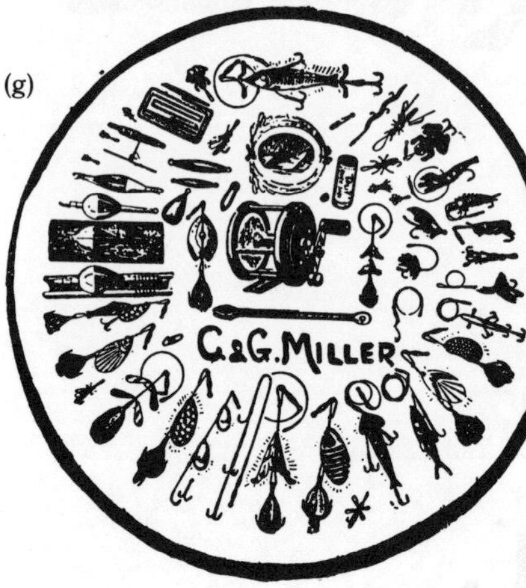

(h)

(i)

(j)

(a)

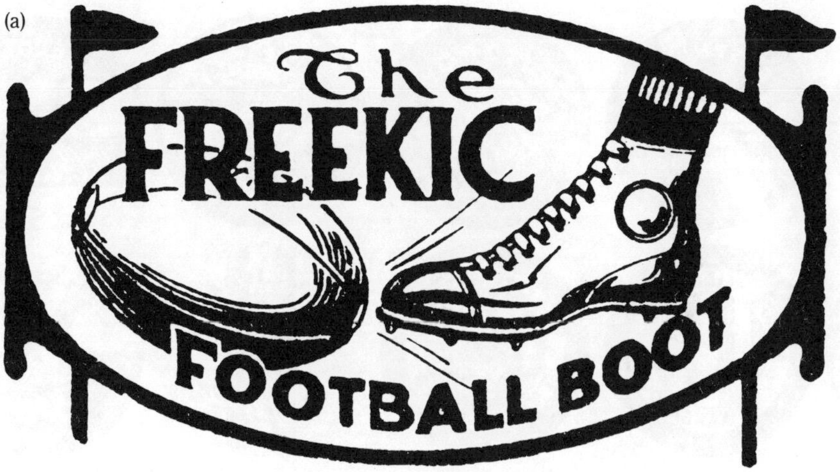

(b)

(c)

(d)

(e)

(g)

(f)

(h)

(i)

(j)

(k)

Be in it

Footy gear.

Sport is Australia's major recreational pastime. And in the sporting heart of Australians, football has kicked the biggest goal.
(a) The Freekic Football Boot.
J. Hunter & Son Ltd, Sydney; 1913.
(b) The Forward Football Boot.
J. Hunter & Son Ltd. Sydney; 1911.
(c) Play-On.
The Harold Shop Co. Pty Ltd, Melbourne.
Football boots; 1950.
(d) (e) Kangaroo Brand.
T. W. Sherrin, Melbourne.
Footballs; (d) 1906, (e) advertisement showing current trademark.
(f) (g) (h) Native Brand.
Ross Faulkner Pty Ltd, Melbourne.
Footballs; (f) c. 1927, (g) modernization used until 1979, (h) current.
Sherrin have been making footballs in Australia since 1879. After the Spalding takeover of Sherrin, their major opposition, Ross Faulkner, claim to be the only wholly Australian owned football maker. However, both companies are now under threat with the introduction of cheap Indian footballs which, in Western and South Australia, have already made their way into League matches.
(i) Lyre Bird.
Nutting and Young, Melbourne.
Footballs; 1930s.
(j) Westralia.
H. Fischer Ltd, Perth.
Footballs; 1923.
(k) Goal Finder.
Overell's Limited. Brisbane.
Footballs; 1929.

Be in it

Footy.

Australian Rules Football was founded in Victoria by T. W. Wills and his brother-in-law H. C. A. Harrison, after Wills concluded that rugby was 'unsuitable for grown men engaged in a living'. He formed the first clubs in the Geelong area in 1856 and the first Melbourne club in 1859. While researching football club symbology we found a sad lack of information on the development of club emblems, but many variations in their representations. Top two rows, page 154: Melbourne *Herald*; c. 1960. Bottom three rows, page 154: Weg (William Ellis Green), cartoonist with the Melbourne *Herald*; current. *Courtesy The Herald and Weekly Times Limited*. Page 155: official VFL Properties Club emblems; 1975. *Courtesy VFL Properties*.

(m)

(a)

(b)

(c)

(d)

(e)

(f)

(g)

(h)

(i)

(j)

(k)

(l)

(a) The Carlton Blues.
(b) The Collingwood Magpies.
(c) The Essendon Bombers.
(d) The Fitzroy Lions.
(e) The Footscray Bulldogs.
(f) The Geelong Cats.
(g) The Hawthorn Hawks.
(h) The Melbourne Demons.
(i) The North Melbourne Kangaroos.
(j) The Richmond Tigers.
(k) The St Kilda Saints.
(l) The South Melbourne Swans.
(m) the Victorian Football League; 1975.
(n) Anti-Football League. Every religion has its heretics. The almost religious fervour of some football supporters has created a group of football heretics: the Anti-Football League. It was started in 1967 by Keith Dunstan and Douglas Wilkie of the Melbourne *Sun* to raise money for charity. Its membership has reached over 120,000 people. Their symbol is a square football: 'We designed the badge in the shape of a red cube symbolic of something that would not bounce' said Keith Dunstan.

(n)

Be in it

Rugby.

The first Australian Rules club in New South Wales was formed by the University of Sydney in 1864. In the same year they also formed their first rugby club. The latter game went on to dominate the State while Australian Rules has remained the prime footy pastime of the southern States.

The New South Wales Rugby League (m) consists of the following clubs:

(a) The Balmain Tigers.
(b) The Canterbury-Bankstown Bulldogs.
(c) The Cronulla-Sutherland Sharks.
(d) The Eastern Suburbs Roosters.
(e) The Manly-Warringah Sea Eagles.
(f) The Newtown Jets.
(g) The North Sydney Bears.
(h) The Parramatta Eels.
(i) The Penrith Panthers.
(j) The South Sydney Rabbitohs.
(k) The St George Dragons.
(l) The Western Suburbs Magpies.

The designs for the 12 clubs were rationalised in 1979 from existing club symbology. *Courtesy New South Wales Rugby League Properties Division.*

(a)

(b)

(c)

(d)

(e)

(f)

(g)

(h)

(i)

(j)

(k)

(l)

(m)

(a)

(b)

(c)

(d)

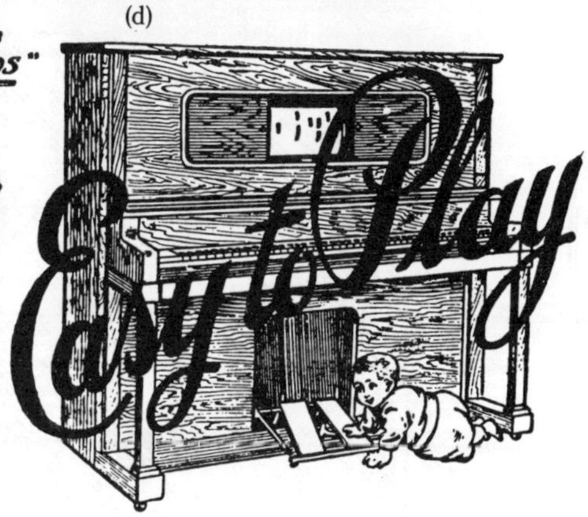

(e)

(f)

(g)

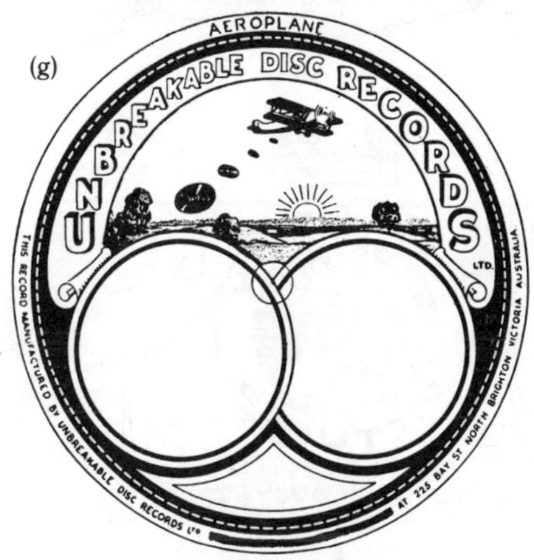

(h)

(i)

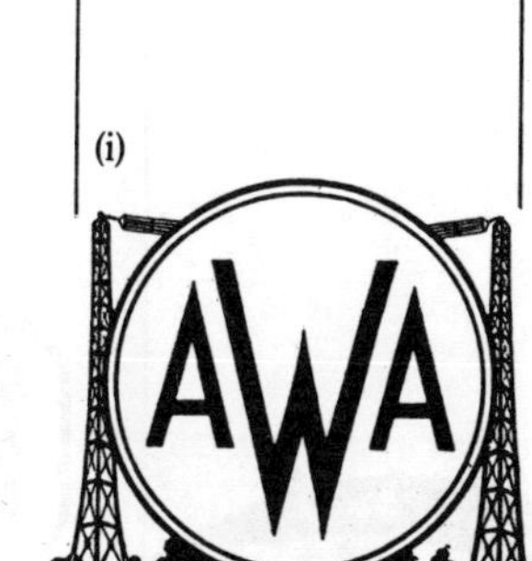

Be in it

Music.

There was a time when every home had a piano. And a musician. Now, instead of a piano that is *easy to play*, there is a TV that is *easier to watch*.

(a) Golden Strad.
Frank Albert, Sydney.
Strings for musical instruments; 1895.
(b) Cookaburra.
N. A. Rubens & Co., Melbourne.
Musical instruments; 1911.
(c) Wright's Pianos.
J. Dixon Wright, Melbourne; 1913.
(d) Easy to Play.
E. F. Wilks & Co. Ltd, Sydney.
Player pianos; 1918.
(e) McCann Bros., Tas.
Piano and other musical instruments; 1922.
(f) Hugo Wertheim Pty Ltd, Melbourne.
Records; 1926.
(g) Aeroplane.
Unbreakable Disc Records Ltd, Melbourne; 1927.
(h) Nicholson's Pty Ltd, Sydney.
Musical instruments; 1937.
(i) AWA.
Amalgamated Wireless Australasia Ltd, Sydney; 1924.

Be in it

Movies.

With the use of a koala in his Efftee Film Productions symbol, Frank Thring Senior created a precedent for film companies in the thirties. Cinesound Productions quickly followed with the kangaroo. The American imported Movietone adopted the kookaburra. And the little known Hawkinsfilm adopted *Peter the Cockatoo*.

(a) Filmads.
Cartoon Filmads Co., Sydney; 1918.
(b) Golden Wattle Films Syndicate, Sydney; 1920.
(c) Union Theatres Ltd; 1920.
(d) Eurythmic.
F. W. Thomas.
Films; 1922.
(e) Sovereign Pictures.
Cinema Motors Publicity Co., Sydney; 1924.
(f) Efftee Film Productions, Melbourne; 1931. *Courtesy National Film Archive, National Library of Australia.*
(g) Cinesound Productions Limited, Sydney; 1932. *Courtesy Cinesound Productions Limited.*
(h) Master Pictures.
Australasian Films Ltd; 1932.
(i) Hawkinsfilm Naturaltone Productions.
S. W. Hawkins, Sydney; 1932.
(j) Galaxy Drive-In Theatre.

(a)

(b)

(c)

(d)

Eurythmic

(f)

(e)

(g)

(h)

(i)

(j)

(a)

(b)

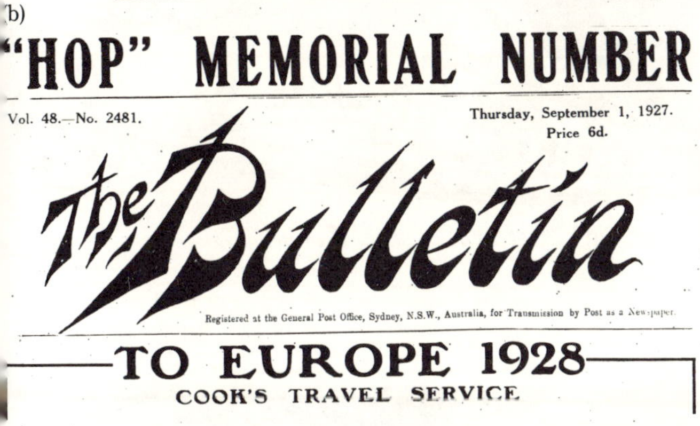

(c)

(d)

(e)

(f)

(g)

Be in it

Reading.

Although not trademarks in the traditional sense, mastheads were originally used to reflect the nature of the publication, a practice that has fallen victim to the simplicity of modern design.

(a) (b) *The Bulletin*. This weekly broadsheet established in 1880 by J. F. Archibald and John Haynes of Sydney became known as the *Bushman's Bible*.

(a) 1880, (b) the simplified script was introduced in 1886. *Courtesy P.B.L. Marketing Pty Ltd.*

(c) *Garden and Field*, Adelaide.

Although this journal was established in 1875, the masthead shown here is from a later period.

(d) *The Australian Brewer's Journal*, Sydney and Melbourne. Established 1881.

(e) *Australasian Hardware and Machinery*, Melbourne. Established 1886.

(f) *The Australian Cordial Maker and Aerated Water Trade Gazette*, Sydney, London, Melbourne. Established 1889.

(g) Gordon & Gotch, established 1853, Sydney. Designs and devices for advertising, stationery and periodicals; press telegrams and press matters of all kinds; 1895.

Be in it

Reading.

(a) *The Australasian Fireman*, Melbourne. Established 1886.
(b) *The Advance Australia Journal*, Melbourne. Established 1897.
(c) *The Australian Agriculturist and Live Stock Journal.* Established 1894.
(d) *The Commonwealth Laundry Journal*: the official organ of the Victorian Laundry Association. Established 1902.
(e) *Smith's Weekly*. Established by Joynton Smith in Sydney; 1919.
(f)(g) *The Sun News Pictorial*, Melbourne. Established 1922;
(f) original masthead,
(g) the rooster was introduced into the masthead in 1926. *Courtesy The Herald and Weekly Times Limited*.
(h) *Pep*: the snappy little mag; from an advertisement appearing 1926.

(a)

(b)

(c)

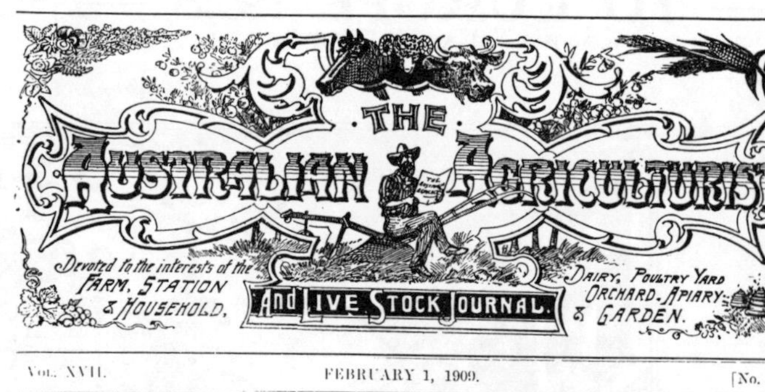

(d)

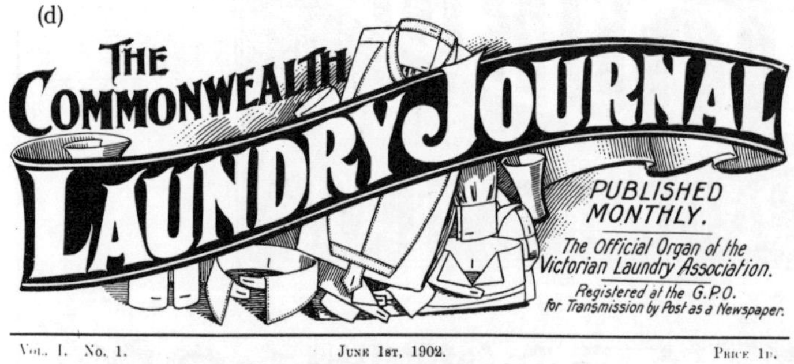

(e)

(f)

(g)

(h)

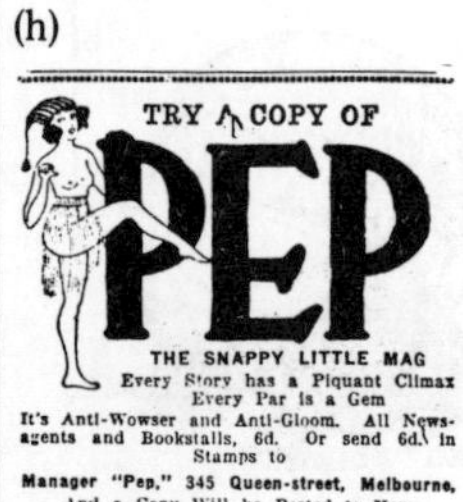

Be in it

Smoking.

At the turn of the century smoking was still a refined pleasure, and small, luxury cigarette companies abounded. Brands were manufactured and sold regionally, sometimes restricted to a single suburb. But slowly these companies and their quaint brands disappeared or sold out to large overseas interests. The new brands were national and international. Smoking was big business.

(a) Chimpanzees. M. Friedlander, Melbourne. Cigars; 1894.
(b) Wattle Cigarettes. The Oriental Cigarette Co. Melbourne; 1909.
(c) Lambs' Porto. (W. Berry) Lamb & Co., Sydney. Tobacco, cigars and cigarettes; 1909.
(d) Aerial Cigarettes. F. P. H. Schroeder. Sydney; 1911.
(e) Early Bird. The British-Australian Co. Pty Ltd, Melbourne. Tobacco; 1911.
(f) (g) Tango, Trafalgar. Mulco, Sydney. Cigars; 1914.
(h) Snap. A. Julies, Vic. Tobacco; 1925.
(i) Pipe Hospital. F. J. Coomber, Brisbane; 1890.

(a)

(b)

(c)

(d)

(e)

(f)

(g)

(h)

(i)

Be in it

Smoking.

(a) Magpie Cigarettes.
J. J. Schuh Tobacco Co. Pty Ltd, Melbourne; 1920s.
(b) (c) Three A's, Bridge.
The Pacific Tobacco Industries Australasia Ltd, Sydney.
Cigarettes and tobacco; 1930.
(d) Kookaburra Cigarette Paper Tube Mfg. Co., Sydney.
Cigarette paper tubes; 1931.
(e) Lifeguard.
The Globe Tobacco Co., Sydney.
Cigarettes and tobacco; 1933.
(f) Gumrice Cigarette Paper.
From a match cover advertisement; c. 1938.
(g) Craven.
Carreras Ltd, Melbourne; 1906. The revised Craven 'A' was registered in 1940. The design shown here is the current one.
(h) Turf.
Alexander Boguslavsky Ltd; 1920. Subsequent proprietors: G. G. Goode Ltd, Melbourne;1931, and Carreras Ltd, Melbourne; 1940.
Craven 'A' and Turf are two of the early international brands still in existence. Over the years they have remained virtually unchanged.

(a)

(b)

(c)

(d)

(e)

(f)

(g)

(h)

15. CURE-EM-QUICK.

Mandrake Salve claimed to cure sore throats, piles, dandruff and rheumatism. Merson had a 'Wonder' cure for epilepsy. And Dr Boxwell provided 'Silent Pills' for females. There was a time when we had a cure for everything. Now, with its fine-tuned diseases and strangely named drugs, modern medicine has convinced us otherwise. But the public's need for a *cure-all* has been slow dying. *Aspro, Vincents* and *a Bex, cup of tea and a good lay down*, have become the cure-alls for those not-so-deadly ailments like the common cold and the fashionable migraine. Whether it's a family favourite or a modern miracle drug, the demand is still the same: *cure-em-quick*.

(a) D. W. Gleeson, Vic. Medicine for human use; 1896.
(b) Aspro. Geo. R. Nicholas & Co., Melbourne. Aspirin or acetyl salicylic acid tablets; 1917.
(c) Bex. Beckers Pty Ltd, Sydney. A medicinal preparation; 1937.
(d) Vincent's Powders and Tablets. From an advertisement appearing 1951.
(e) Cure-em-quick. A. W. Allen Ltd, Melbourne. Confectionery; 1933.
In recent years Cure-em-quick changed its name to *Check-em-quick* as a cure to restrictive legislation.

(a)

(b)

AsPRO

(c)

(d)

(e)

"CURE-EM-QUICK"

Cure-em-quick

For anything.

(a) (b) (c) Bosisto's Parrot Brand Eucalyptus Oil. Joseph Bosisto, Melbourne; (a) c. 1898, (b) from an advertisement appearing 1916. Joseph Bosisto started distilling eucalyptus oil in 1852. This is the first known commercial exploitation of eucalyptus. The brand is still in existence today (c).
(d) Bunyip Brand. Robert Lee, Melbourne. Embrocation; 1893.
(e) Spiderite. W. Hollingsworth & D. Thomson, Launceston, Tas. A cure for consumption; 1900.
(f) Dr Boxwell's Silent Pill for Females. Martin & Co., Perth; 1903.
(g) Euky Bearub. Felton Grimwade & Bickford Pty Ltd, Melbourne. Eucalyptus oil based rub for the relief of colds, coughs, insect bites and muscular aches; current packaging.

(a)

(b)

(c)

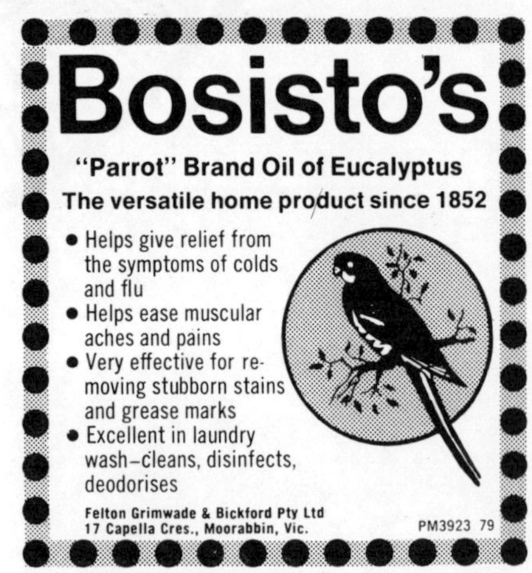

(d)

(Bunyip Brand.)

(e)

(f)

(g)

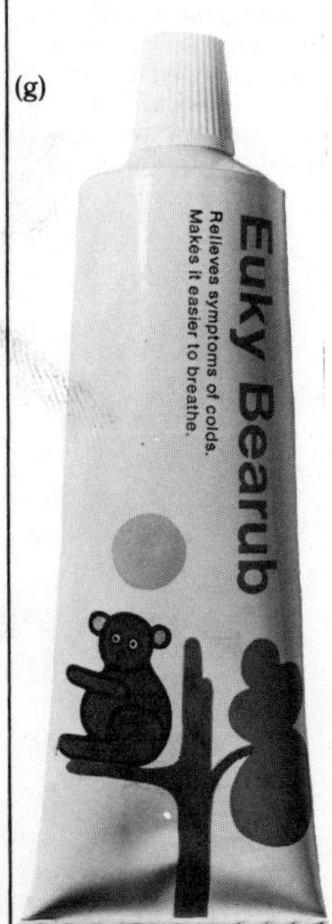

(a)

(b)

(c)

(d)

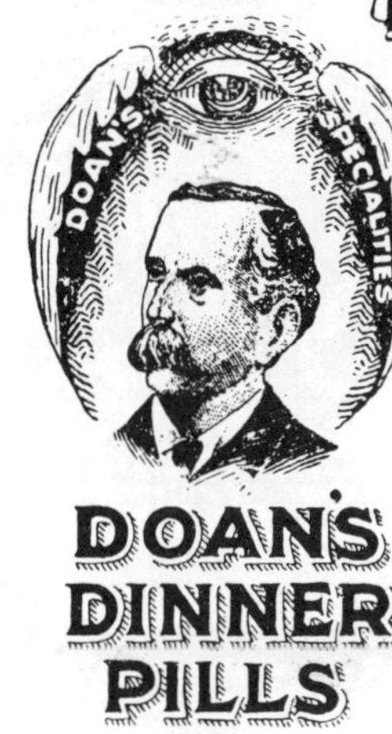

(e)

(f)

(g)

(h)

(i)

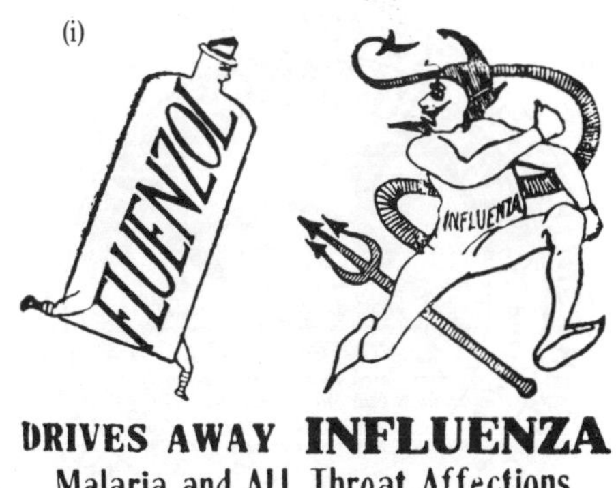

Cure-em-quick

For anything.

(a) Atkin's Quinine Tonic Wine.
Jenny Atkin, widow, Melbourne; 1906.
(b) You Cure.
Wood & Co., Melbourne; 1907.
(c) Stang.
E. Mackenzie, Sydney. Nerve pills; 1907.
(d) Doan's Dinner Pills.
Foster-McLellan Co. Sydney; 1907.
(e) Our Jack Brand.
A. M. Bickford & Sons Ltd, Adelaide.
A trademark used for a wide range of goods; 1908.
(f) Swastic.
Hector Moffat, Dundas, Tas.
Medicine; 1908.
(g) Clavis Rheuma.
Mark Goldman, Adelaide.
Medicinal preparation; 1908.
(h) Shampuna.
Edwin Holland, scalp and hair specialist, Melbourne; 1910.
(i) Fluenzol.
The Fluenzol Pty Ltd, Wellington, New Zealand.
Medicine; 1911.

Cure-em-quick

For anything.

(a) Old Witch Mfg. Co., Sydney.
Salve; 1911.
(b) (c) Palmer's Pink Powders, Palmer's Carrageen Cough Mixture.
A. M. Palmer & Co., Ballarat, Vic.; from two advertisements appearing 1911.
(d) Roseen Sure-Cure.
S. Lazell, Kalgoorlie, WA; 1911.
(e) Mersons 'Wonder' cure for epilepsy.
Thomas H. Merson, Melbourne; 1911.
(f) The Bendigo Digger Brand.
Albert Bush, Vic.
Eucalyptus oil; 1913.
(g) Teslaconi.
W. A. Gray, electrotherapist, Melbourne; 1914.
(h) Heenzo.
G. W. Hean, Sydney.
Cough mixture; 1916.
(i) Mandrake Salve.
B. Herbert, Sydney.
Cure-all; 1919.
(j) A.M.S.
T. A. Dickson, chemist, Geelong, Vic.
Digestion and liver remedy; 1919.
(k) Life Guard.
A. McLintock & Co. Pty Ltd, Melbourne.
Chemical for human use; 1919.

(a)

(b)

(c)

(d)

(e)

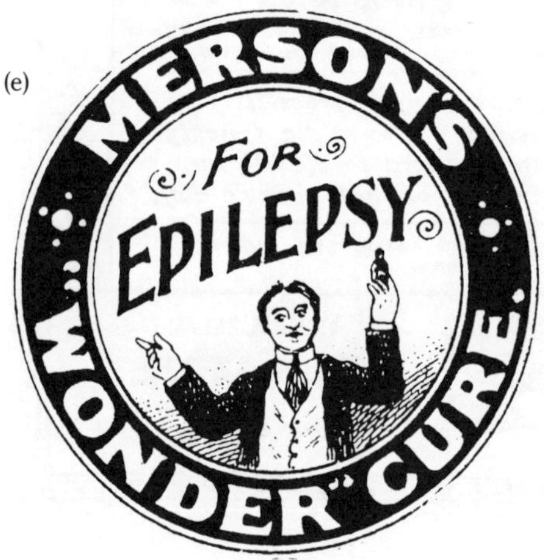

(f)

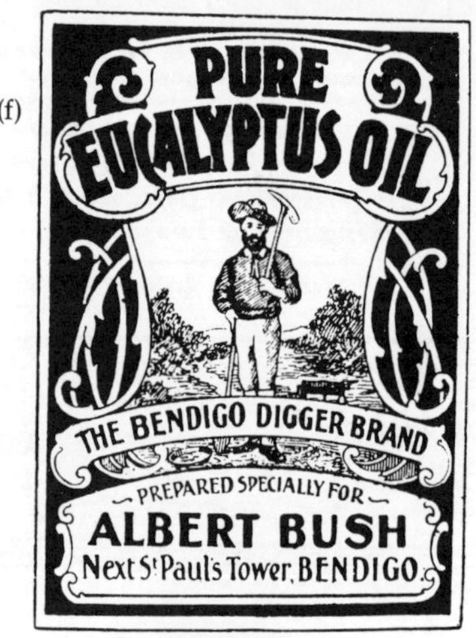

(g)

(h)

(i)

(j)

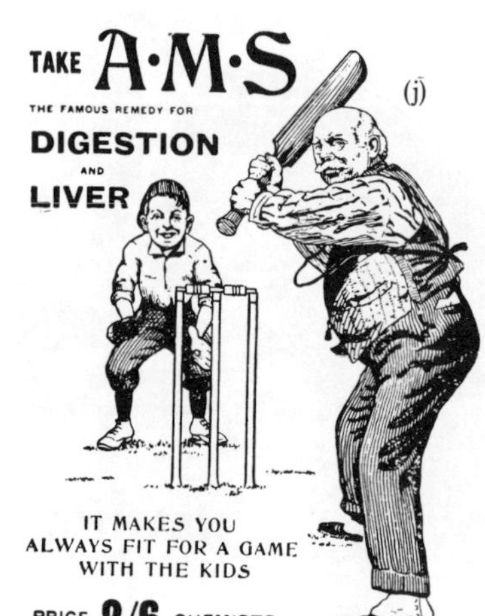

(k)

Cure-em-quick

For anything.

(a) Eazoids.
Pals Pepmintum Chemical Co.; 1919.
(b) Diviner.
J. J. Midson, Qld.
Cough remedy; 1921.
(c) Kiss it and make it better.
A. S. Cohn, Vic.
Medicines; 1921.
(d) Stiffitis Ltd, Melbourne.
Analgesic; 1922.
(e) Goanna Salve.
Jessey Marney, J. C. Marconi, Brisbane.
Cure-all; 1923.
This preparation is still available today.
(f) Kagro.
B. Kay, Sydney.
Scalp preparation; 1924.
(g) Heelsup Buckin.
W. D. Hindmarsh Morris, Mount Barker, SA.
A preparation for skin diseases; 1926.
(h) Hedake Torpedo.
W. Davies, Sydney.
Headache powders; 1929.
(i) Hed-eez.
Pepmintum Chemical Co. Melbourne.
Headache pills; 1919.

(a)

(b)

(c)

(d)

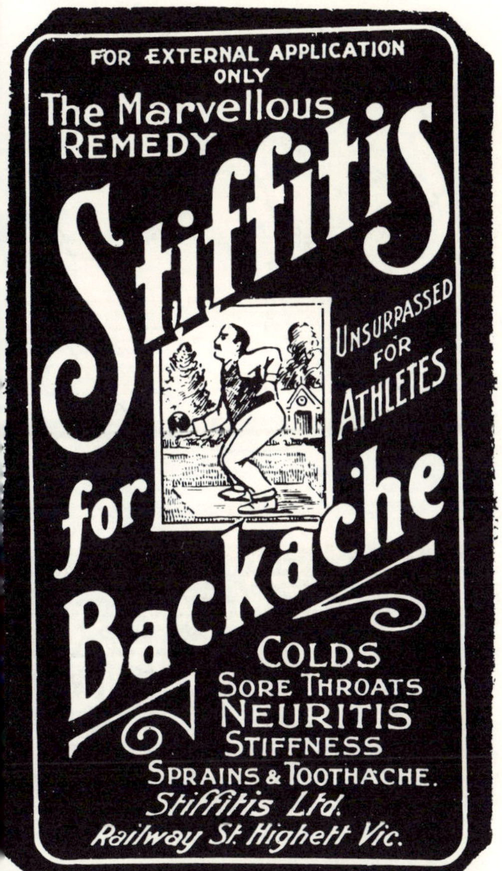

(e)

(f)

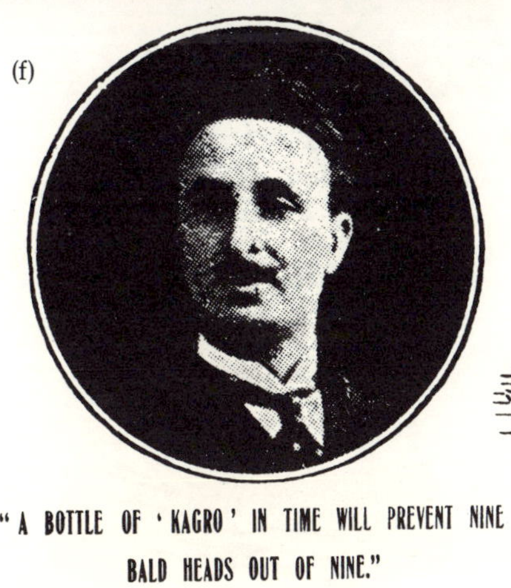

(g)

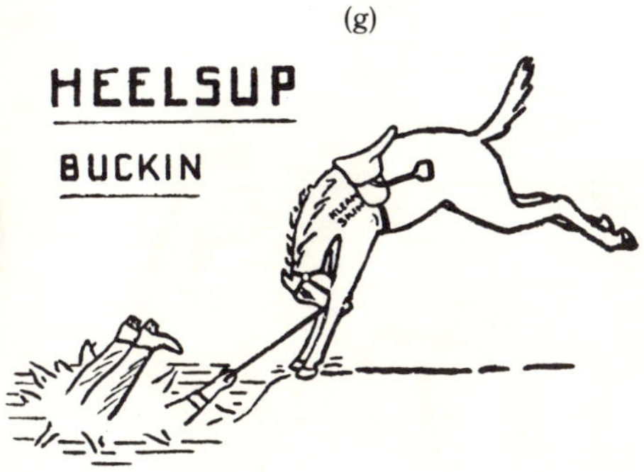

(h)

(i)

Cure-em-quick

For anything.

(a) Wallaby Brand.
Henry B. Smith, Melbourne.
Eucalyptus oil; 1929.
(b) Nu Kik.
W. T. Firmstone, Sydney.
Medicine; 1930.
(c) Tigers.
H. J. Kenne, Sydney.
A preparation for the relief of throat soreness; 1932.
(d) Bronch-o-form.
H. F. Ryan, Melbourne.
Bronchial medication; 1933.
(e) Tummies (Tum-Ease)
A. S. M. Waites, Sydney; 1933.
(f) Kangaroo Pills.
W. J. Ledger, Melbourne; 1941.
(g) Happy Jack.
Alpha Laboratories, Sydney.
Liver saline; 1945.
(h) Sootha-Pain.
T. G. Marsden; 1946.
(i) Medi-Chocs.
H. C. Sleigh Ltd, Melbourne.
Laxative; 1949.
(j) Pinke Zinke.
Am-o-lin Laboratories, Sydney.
Suntan blockout; 1950.
(k) Surfrider Suntan.
Amalgamated Pharmacists Pty Ltd, Sydney; 1954.
(l) DHA.
Drug Houses of Australia; c. 1937.

(a)

(b)

(c)

(d)

(e)

(f)

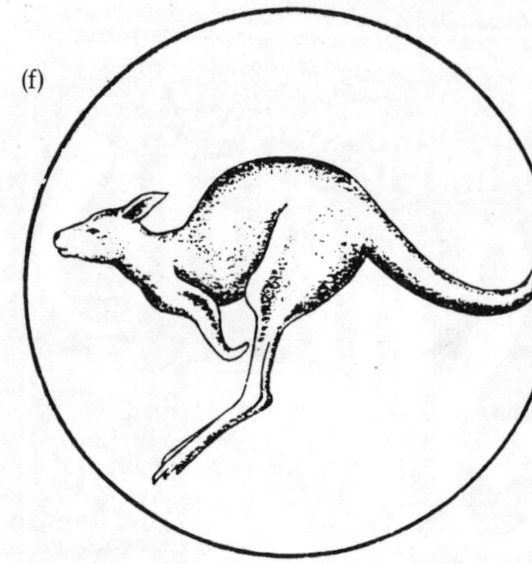

(g)

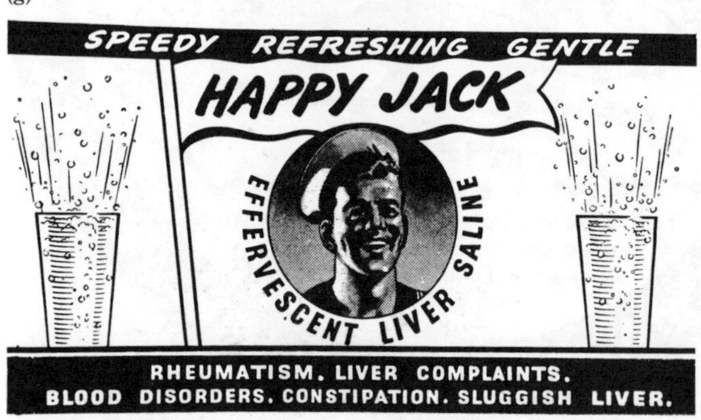

(h)

(i)

(j)

(k)

(l)

Cure-em-quick

For foot care.

As the foot slipped in importance as a means of transport, so did the advertising for its repair and maintenance. Will we ever see smiling feet again?

(a) Trouchet's Corn Cure. A. Trouchet, Kalgoorlie, WA, 1907.
(b) Kiora. A. R. Hibbard, Sydney. Corn ointment; 1908.
(c) Magician. Sylvia Curnow, chiropodist, Sydney. Corn cure; 1913.
(d) Swamp. Z. E. Williams, Brisbane. Corn cure; 1921.
(e) Smiling Feet. B. V. King Pty Ltd, Melbourne; 1938.
(f) U-no. E. R. Knight, Brisbane. Foot powder; 1925.
(g) The Keene Co., London. Corn cure ointment; 1910.
(h) E. Lawrence & Co., Chicago. Corn cure; 1919.

(a)

(b)

(c)

(d)

(e)

(f)

(g)

(h)

Cure-em-quick

For tooth decay.

(a) Pearladenta.
Mary Jane Kinch, NSW.
Tooth paste; 1906.
(b) A. R. Creswick,
dentist, Adelaide.
Artificial teeth; 1906.
(c) Twentieth Century.
Myer Emporium Ltd.
Melbourne.
Tooth brushes; 1932.
(d) Anticary.
R. B. Wolfe, Bellingen,
NSW.
Tonic and mouth wash;
1938.
(e) Mr Decay.
F. H. Faulding & Co. Ltd,
Adelaide.
Preparation for gums and
teeth; 1940.
(f) Purabreth.
Brenco Products,
Brisbane; 1938.
(g) Wirth Laboratory,
Melbourne.
Dentures; 1945.

(a)

(b)

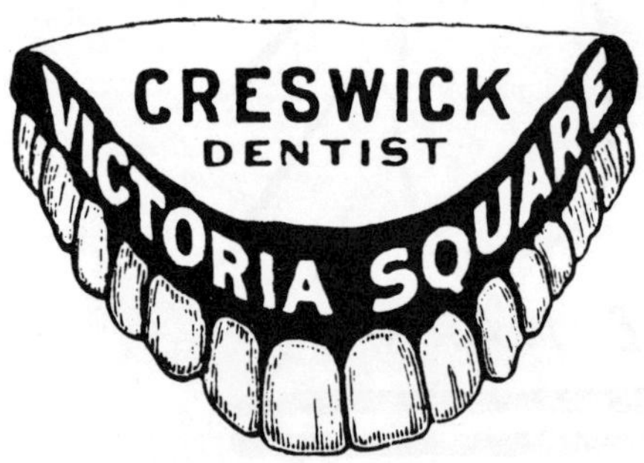

(c)

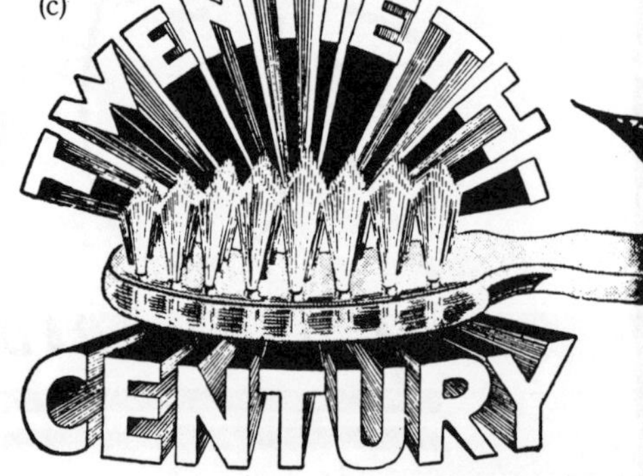

(d)

(e)

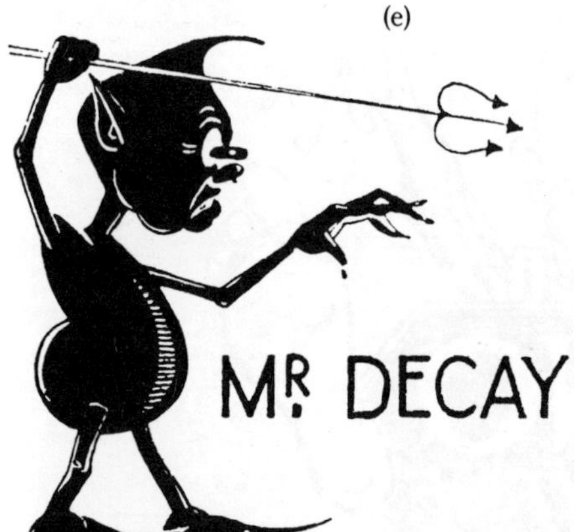

(f)

(g)

Appendix I

Local Government seals and shields.

There are over 860 Local Government bodies in Australia. Each one possesses its own seal or shield which can loosely be described as an operational trademark appearing on letterheads, vehicles, council chambers, etc..

Their symbology is rich in native fauna and flora, Aboriginals, features of local districts and reminders of pioneering days.

Their finish ranges from the foreign formality of The College of Arms, London, to the more parochial style scratched by the local town artist. This selection was made at random covering material from 1940 until the present. Some of these symbols may currently be obsolete or revised.

Row (a) Auburn NSW, Bathurst NSW, Blacktown NSW, Botany NSW, Broken Hill NSW.
Row (b) Buninyong Vic., Burke Qld., Carrathool NSW, Coonamble NSW, Corio Vic., Darwin NT.
Row (c) Drummoyne NSW, Gordon Vic., Gympie Qld., Ipswich Qld., Jemalong NSW, Jerilderie NSW.
Row (d) Kiama NSW, Kowree Vic., Ku-ring-gai NSW, Kyogle NSW, Leichhardt NSW.
Row (e) Manly NSW, Marrickville NSW, Mordialloc Vic., Mirboo Vic., Mudgee NSW.
Row (f) Murrurundi NSW, North Sydney NSW, Parramatta NSW, Portland Vic., Quirindi NSW, Randwick NSW.
Row (g) Ryde NSW, Sarina Qld., Shoalhaven NSW, Sutherland NSW, Swan Hill Vic, Townsville Qld.
Row (h) Traralgon Vic., Wagga Wagga NSW, Willoughby NSW, Wingecarribee NSW, Wonthaggi Vic., Woodburn NSW, The local Government Association of the Northern Territory.

Appendix II

Foreign marks using Australian symbolism.

With a few minor exceptions, this book has concentrated on Australian trademarks used by Australian companies. Here are examples of foreign companies who, for whatever reason, have adopted Australian symbology in their trademarks.

Some, like Collyns and Co. of London (a), completely lacked research. Their trademark for wines depicts Aborigines wearing turbans and feathers, while holding up bunches of grapes to an American Indian style encampment across a river.

Others, like Volkswagen Australia, were created to give the local division an obvious feeling of national belonging.

(a) Coo-ee Brand. Collyns & Co., London. Wines; 1889.
(b) The Southern Cross. The Wolseley Sheep Shearing Machine Co. Ltd, Great Britain; 1898.
(c) I. P. Clarke & Co., Leicester, England. Sewing cotton, cotton yarn; 1902.
(d) The Commonwealth. Doulton & Co. Ltd, Lambeth, England. Sanitary wares; 1902.
(e) Kangaroo Brand. Parkes & Gnosill Ltd, England. Draft hames of metal; 1906.
(f) Emu Brand. Wolverhampton Corrugated Iron Co. Ltd, England; 1906.
(g) Kangaroo Brand. J. R. Thompson & Co., London. Composition for the manufacture of printers' rollers; 1908.
(h) Kangaroo. C. A. Rickards Ltd, Manchester, England. Silk; 1908.
(i) Welcome Nugget. T. C. Williams Co., New York. Tobacco; 1908.
(j) Emu Brand. J. E. Duffield & Co., USA. Hickory tool handles; 1910.
(k) Volkswagen Australia; 1960s.

(a)

(b)

(c)

(d)

(e)

(f)

(g)

(h)

(i)

(j)

(k)

(a)

(b)

(c)

(d)

(e)

(f)

(g)

(h)

(i)

(j)

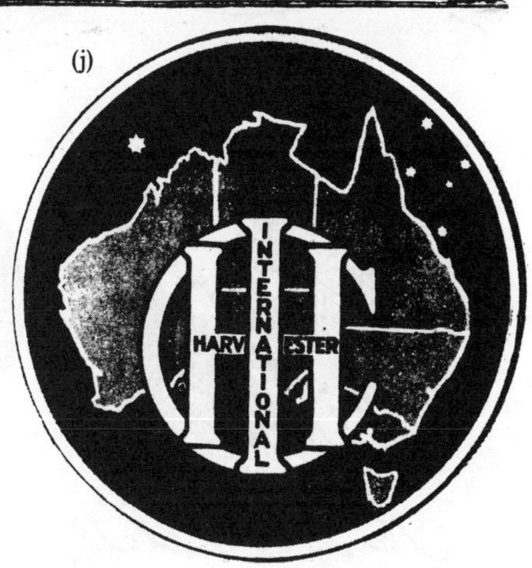

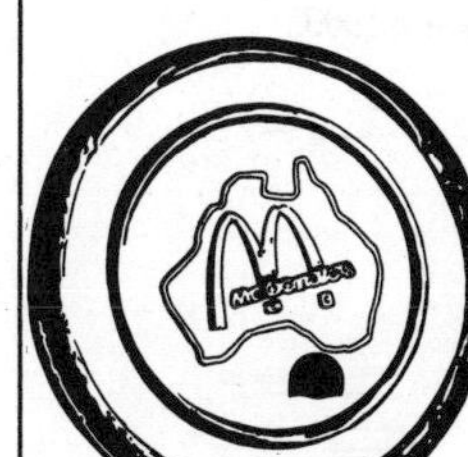

(k)

Appendix II

Foreign marks using Australian symbolism.

(a) Jonathan Dearden & Co. Ltd, England. Cotton piece goods; 1910.
(b) G. & J. Zair, England. Whips; 1911.
(c) Syddo. W. Oddy, England. Cloths and stuffs of wool, worsted or hair; 1912.
(d) The British Australian Oil Co. Ltd, England; 1914.
(e) The Union Bag & Paper Co., USA. Paper bags; 1914.
(f) Emu Twist. David Dunlop, Petersburg, USA. Tobacco; 1916.
(g) M. W. Gloag & Son, Scotland. Wines and spirits; 1919.
(h) Cockatoo Cigarettes. Reed Tobacco Co., Richmond, USA; 1923.
(i) Einrich Matejka. Czechoslovakia. Glass; 1929.
(j) International Harvester Co. of Australia Pty Ltd. Agricultural machinery; 1939.
(k) McDonald's Family Restaurants. American system family restaurant chain. Take away cup lid; collected c. 1978.

Appendix III

Multi-nationals before it was a dirty word.

Some of the world's current multi-nationals were arriving in Australia as early as the 1860s. In 1876, Singer Sewing Machines of New York claimed the honour of being the first trade-mark registered in Victoria. Coca-Cola arrived in 1905. Evinrude boat motors in 1913. Kellogg's Snap Crackle Pop in 1942. The invasion steadily continued. From England, Europe, USA and more recently Japan, their arrival was always welcomed.
With every new foreign product Australians felt part of the world so far away. But, with the shrinking of the globe, the welcome is wearing thin.
(a) Singer's Sewing Machines. Singer Mfg. Co., New York; 1876.
(b) Bull's Head. J. & J. Colman, London; 1893.
(c) Quaker. The American Cereal Co., Chicago; 1899.
(d) Milo. Henri Nestle, London; 1903.
(e) General Electric Co. of Schenectady, New York; 1906.
(f) Mercedes. Daimler Motoren Gesellschaft, Germany; 1906.
(g) The Shell Transport & Trading Co., London. Lubricants and fuels; 1906.
(h) King C. Gillette. Gillette Safety Razor Co. USA; 1906.
(i) His Master's Voice. The Gramophone & Typewriter Ltd, England; 1906. The mark shown here is from a 1939 advertisement and, like today's mark, has changed little from Francis Barrand's painting *Nipper* on which the original was based in 1900.
(j) A. & F. Pears Ltd, London. Soap; 1909.

(a)

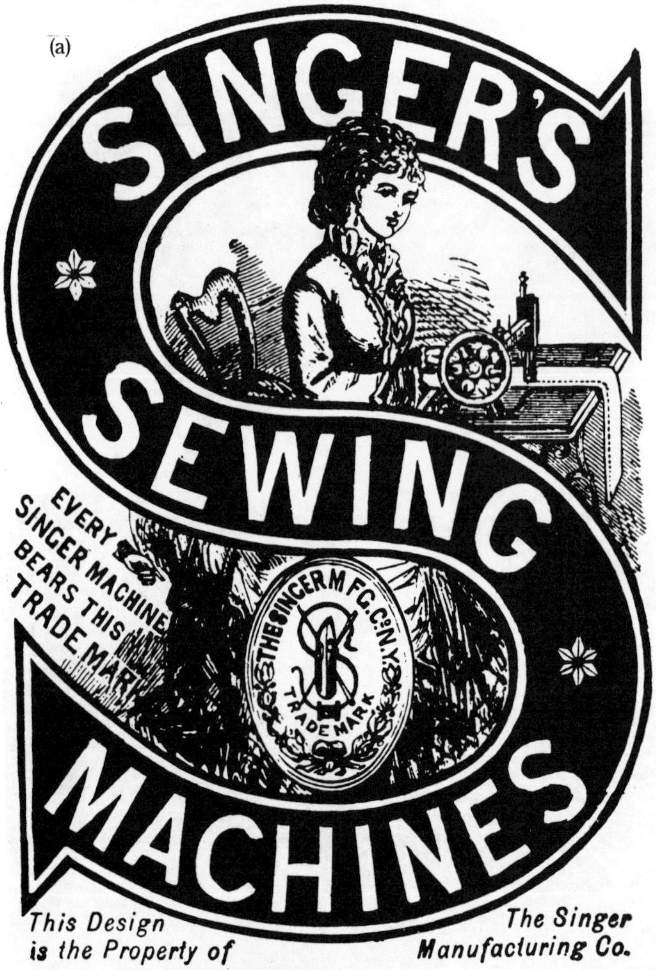

(b)

(c)

(d)

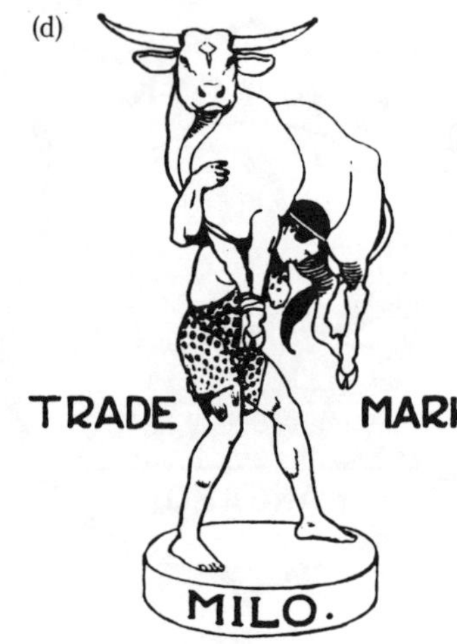

(e)

(f)

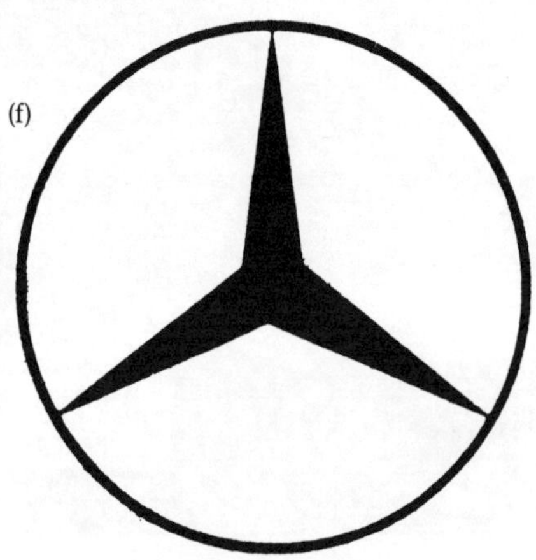

(g)

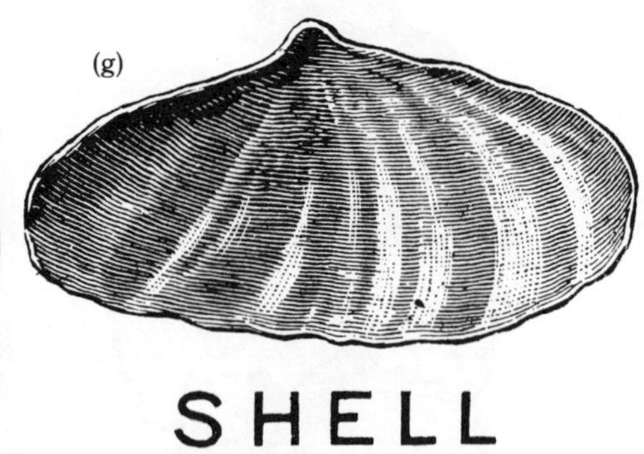

(h)

(i)

(j)

(a)

(b)

(c)

(d)

(e)

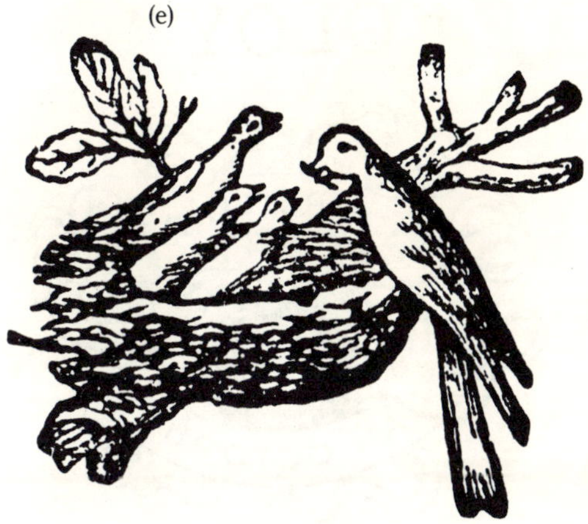

(f)

(g)

(h)

(i)

(j)

(k)

(l)

(m)

Appendix III

Multi-nationals before it was a dirty word.

(a) Daimler Co. Ltd, England.
Motor cars; 1911.
(b) H. J. Heinz & Co., Pittsburgh, USA.
Foods, pickles and preserves; 1911.
(c) Austin Motor Co. Ltd, England.
Motor cars; 1911.
(d) Pegasus Brand. Standard Oil Co., USA; 1911.
Later to become Mobil.
(e) Nestle & Anglo-Swiss Condensed Milk Co., Swizterland; 1912.
(f) Columbia Graphophone Co., USA. Dictaphone; 1913.
(g) Chubb & Sons Lock & Safe Co., London; 1915.
(h) John Mackintosh Ltd, England.
Confectionery; 1917.
(i) Levi Strauss & Co., San Francisco.
Copper riveted clothing; 1917.
(j) Ilford Ltd, England.
Film; 1918.
(k) Michelin Tyres, France.
The Michelin character *Bibendum* was created by Andre Michelin in 1898. In 1919 Bibendum appeared in the first advertisement for Michelin Tyres in Australia.
(l) Jantzen Knitting Mills, Oregon, USA; 1925.
(m) Penguin Books, England.
Paperback books; 1935.
Penguin was established in Australia (Melbourne) in 1946.

Appendix IV

Foreign thoughts.

A great number of the trademarks in this book can be described as nothing short of bizarre. To prove that in this respect Australians were not alone in the world, here are some marks registered in Australia by foreign companies.

(a) B. Muratti Sons & Co. Ltd, England.
Tobacco manufacturers; 1897.
(b) George Craddock & Co., England.
Unwrought and partly wrought metals; 1906.
(c) The British Xylonite Co. Ltd, England.
Combs and brushes; 1907.
(d) The Gloy Mfg. Co., England.
Adhesives; 1909.
(e) Jacques Schiesser, Germany.
Knitted underwear; 1906.
(f) The Max Milking Machine Co., Denmark; 1911.
(g) Comica.
H. Danzer, France.
Films; 1911.
(h) Wonder.
The Watson Co., USA.
Fly killer; 1912.
(i) W. Radam, USA.
Medicine; 1913.
(j) The Welsbach Light Co. of Australia Ltd; 1913.
(k) The Polack Tyre & Rubber Co. Ltd, England; 1913.
(l) Moline Plow Co., USA.
Agricultural machinery; 1912.

(a)

(b)

(c)

(d)

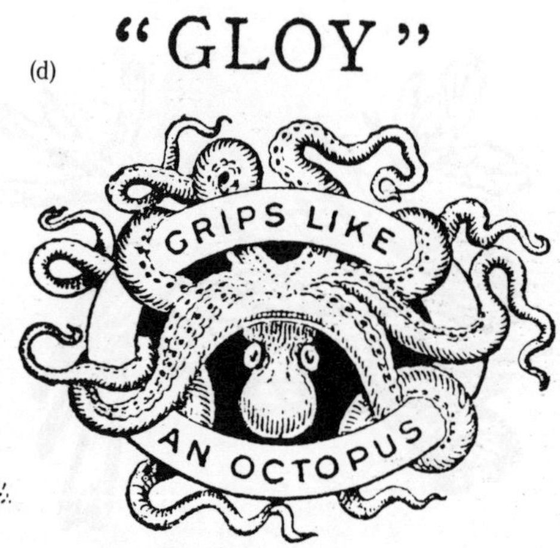

(e)

(f)

(g)

(h)

(i)

(j)

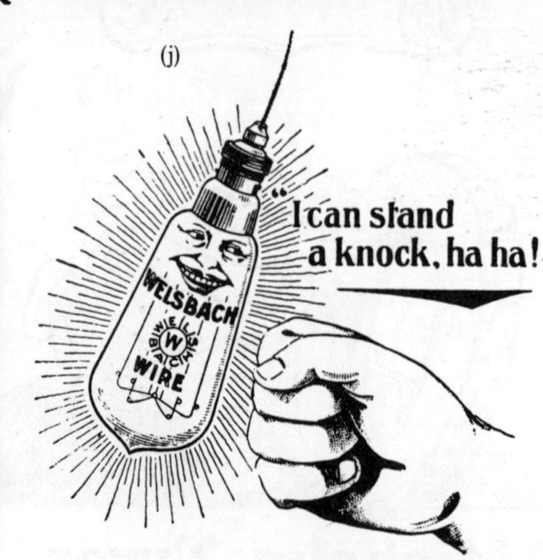

(k)

(l)

Appendix IV

Foreign thoughts.

(a) 20 Mule Team Brand. Borax Consolidated Ltd, England; 1916.
(b) The Boyshform Brassier Co., USA; 1921.
(c) P. D. Carnegie & Sons Ltd, England. Whisky; 1926.
(d) W. J. Myatt & Co., England. Shaving blades; 1934.
(e) Knightwear. Schoefield Preston & Co. Ltd, England. Piece goods mainly or wholly cotton; 1935.
(f) Puck. New York Hamburger Gummi-Waaren Co., Germany. Combs; 1937.
(g) S. Hubbard Ltd, England. Women's hats; 1944.
(h) Autophone Ltd, England; 1949.
(i) Horn. Sun Chemical Corporation, USA; 1950.
(j) Porcupine. Richard Johnson & Nephew Ltd, England. Barbed wire; 1952.
(k) Soren Skifter, Denmark. Ties; 1945.

(a)

(b)

(c)

(d)

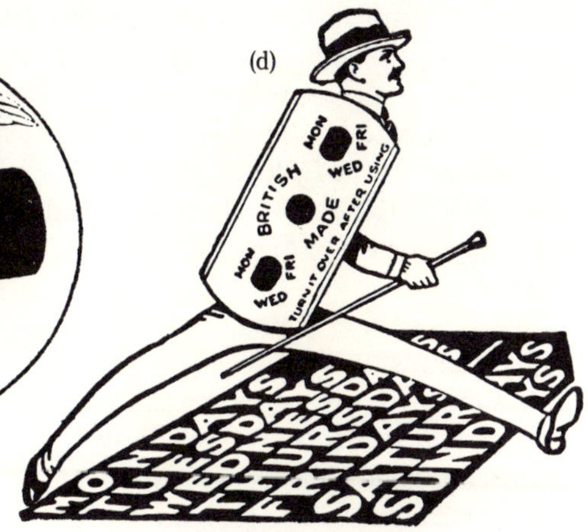

(e)

(f)

(g)

(h)

(i)

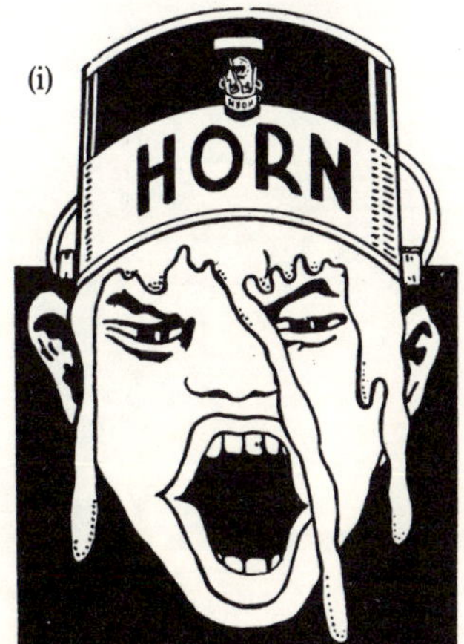

(j)

(k)

Appendix V

Being there.

Mark Lewis was born in St Kilda, Victoria, on May 15, 1908. Now, at the age of 72, he reminisces about the fields and hedges of Brighton, of open air theatres and moonlight ferry rides on the Bay. But his real love was the early advertising on railway hoardings: 'I suppose it was corny but it was honest. Not like today, where everything is so utterly distorted. And it follows you home and chases you inside.'

Dear Sirs, 13 May 1976

It was with great interest that I read Don Petersen's write-up of your activities. I have had a long interest in Australian advertising and, from my standpoint of 68 years, may offer a suggestion or two unfamiliar to you.

On my wall I have posters for that once ubiquitous feature of the local scene – *Dr Morse's Indian Root Pills* (for the liver) – and one less-known, *Golden Sparks Tea* distributed by James Service & Co. of Melbourne. However, one item which vividly struck my imagination as a child, on railway hoardings, was for *Leeming's Boots and Shoes*. A large mythical beast – the Gazeeka – occupied most of the space – attired in Leeming's boots and a wide grin. The period would be pre-1914 War. Leeming's had shops in Bourke Street, near Tivoli, and Chapel Street, Prahran. Also worthy of rescuing from oblivion is *Cobra Boot Polish*. Around that same period, full page ads in the *Bulletin* revolved around a comic Indian fakir attended by a Kangaroo and a Koala, accompanied by a jingle, commencing *Chunda Loo from Akim Foo*.

Speaking of jingles, you are probably familiar with the amusing rhymes in press classified ads proclaiming the virtues of *Woods Great Peppermint Cure*. On the subject of classifieds, two regular inserts always appealed to my sense of humor. One read: 'Aunty – the conductor was quite right: two fares if you occupy two seats. Why not take Formettes and again be slender?' The other ran: 'Madam Ghurka (not a crystal gazer): better to be told the cold, hard truth by experts than to be flattered by fools!'

During the thirties, one product depicted on hoardings announced: *Bovite for me. I'm a sandwich!*

Soap ads are a rich field – *Monkey Brand* (Won't wash clothes) and *Old Dutch Cleanser* (Chases dirt) will be familiar. *Witch Soap* had ads in the saloon cars of trams. A witch's head had movable eyeballs which revolved with the tram's motion. You will have encountered *Dandy Starch*, *Lewis & Whitty's Blue* (What are the wild waves saying?) and *Reckitt's Blue* (Out of the blue comes the whitest wash). *Wellington's Knife Polish* (Graced by a profile of the Duke) was essential in the home.

Who could forget *Boyproof* watches (4/6d I think) dispensed by such firms as *Edments*? A weatherboard shop demolished several years ago, opposite South Melbourne Market, had on the wall facing the rail-line a bold notice for *The wonder of the age – Koopman's Lotion*.

Early breakfast foods I remember are *Purina Crispies* and *Ha Va Oats*. Then there was *Aerial* self-raising flour, illustrated by a boy, airborne, hanging onto the tail of a kite.

One graphic poster in the 1920 period on St Kilda station was advertising a seasonal beach show. A surprised matron with upraised hands and hairpins flying out of her hair-do, cried: 'Good gracious! Haven't you seen the *Ideals*?'

Two slogans worthy of salvage are *Always fit for a game with the kids* – a bat-wielding oldster illustrating some tonic – three letters which elude me. The other – *Even a man can do it* was attached to some laundry product – perhaps a soap powder. On the topic of soap, there was a rising sun with chanticleer crowing and the jingle:

Early to bed, early to rise
Early Morn Soap, a pleasant surprise.

Then we come to tobacco – *Lucy Hinton* and *Happy Thoughts*. (A nostalgic picture of the latter showed a young man leaning against a log cabin – the smoke cloud he is blowing contains a picture of his beloved.) Movies – back around 1920 there was a fluttering in the dovecotes when a film tentatively dealing with (hush) *social* diseases appeared – *The Sin Woman* – with the caption *Bold but clean!*

Hoping this is of some interest.

Cordially,
Mark Lewis.

PS: Do try and rescue the Gazeeka and Chunda Loo from oblivion!

Bombala, NSW, August 1978. Photograph © Richard Tipping.

Continued from page 23
(v) Alpha Engineering Co. Ltd, Sydney. Metal goods; 1929.
(w) Super Speed. Mick Simmons Ltd, Sydney. Sporting equipment; 1931.
(x) Spear Point Brand. Australian Tack Mfg. Co., Girraween, NSW; 1937.
(y) Hi-Fi. K. C. J. Nicoll, Elsternwick, SA. Recording needles; 1942.
(z) Slick. L. T. Wilkinson, Melbourne. Patching material; 1943.
(aa) Landliner. Dyson's Peninsular Motors Pty Ltd, Frankston, Vic.; 1946.
(ab) Ever-Clear. E. Lufft & Son Pty Ltd, Sydney; 1953.
(ac) Australian Anodisers, Mortlake, NSW; 1954.
(ad) Agserv. Agricultural Services Pty Ltd, Sydney; 1955.
(ae) Symbol of an Italian music festival held in Australia sometime during the 1970s.

Continued from page 32
League of Australia (R.S.L.) was formed out of various State bodies. The original badge (i) contained only a soldier and a sailor as the RAAF had not yet come into existence. (j) The current badge, adopted 1941, is coloured red, white and blue. The red represents the blood bond of war with fellow members. The white represents the purity of motive for membership. And the blue indicates willingness to serve a fellow member anywhere under the blue sky. Neither wealth, nor influence, nor social standing can purchase the badge.

Continued from page 36
(m) Mae Vest. J. & L. M. Brandon. Inflatable plastic water vest worn around the chest. Used for learning to swim and as a life saver; 1950.
(n) Abbo-Liter. Abbott Laboratories, USA. Preparations and solutions for intravenous injection; 1951. This tradename demonstrates the pitfalls of entering a foreign market without consideration for the local language.
(o) Strip-Teasies. Login Corporation Pty Ltd, Sydney. Cellulose sausage casings; 1951.
(p) Chickemite. C. H. Mylles, Walkerville, SA. Processed food; 1952. Application abandoned.
(q) Ute. Commonwealth Metallic Pty Ltd, Sydney. Wheelbarrows; 1952.
(r) Diminuentoe. ® The Myer Emporium Ltd, Melbourne. Boots, shoes and slippers; 1953.
(s) Go-Poof. Freshness Ltd. Deodorants for personal use; 1954.
(t) Olitalia. Ieraci Bros., Carlton, Vic. Olive oil; 1955.
(u) Calfeteria. New Zealand Pasture Implement Co. Pty Ltd, Melbourne. Animal feeding devices; 1957.
(v) Car-B-Que. Cratchley Advertising Agency Pty Ltd, Sydney. Portable car griller/cooker; 1957.
(w) Downunda. Glenford Clothing Co. Pty Ltd, Sydney. Articles of clothing for men and boys; 1957.
(x) Moo-Vellous. American Traders (Adelaide) Ltd, Dairy products; 1958.
(y) Jelicious Jelly Crystals. Clarence Mfg. Co., Sydney; current packaging.

Continued from page 56
(o) The Maisie Chocolate Co., Sydney. Confectionery; 1917.
(p) Kangaroo Oilstone. F. H. Dallison; 1919.
(q) Roo Motors. W. B. Foulis, Sydney; 1921.
(r) A. E. Otway. Chemical substances; 1921.
(s) Austral Reinforcement System. C. F. Whiffen, Sydney; 1921.
(t) Grown in Australia. Victorian Central Citrus Association, Melbourne; 1922.
(u) Malleys Ltd, Sydney. Sheet iron; 1923.
(v) Orna. Hanro (Australia) Bendigo Knitting Mills Pty Ltd, Vic. Underwear; 1927.
(w) Kanga Brand. The Castlemaine Woollen Co. Ltd; 1930.
(x) Sans Equa. The Sherington Co., Orange, NSW. Polish; 1930.
(y) *Die Brücke.* German-Australian Publication, Sydney; 1933.
(z) Preservol. D. J. Caute & Son, Mackay, Qld. Polish; 1934.
(aa) Australia's Best. Vincenzo Oriti, fruit merchant, Toowoomba, Qld.; 1943.
(ab) Commonwealth of Australia. Axeheads; 1945.
(ac) Durham Chemicals (Australia) Pty Ltd, Sydney. Zinc oxide and other chemicals; 1948.
(ad) Clem's Cordials. Broken Hill, NSW. Soft drinks; contemporary, collected 1977.

Continued from page 92
(h) (i) (j) State Savings Bank of Victoria.
(h) Common seal; 1853.
(i) Symbol; 1958.
(j) Current symbol designed by Les Mason; 1975.
(k) to (o) Australia and New Zealand Banking Group Ltd.
(k) (l) (m) Company seals showing amalgamation of predecessor banks to form the A.N.Z. Bank in 1951.
(n) Symbol; 1951.
(o) Current symbol introduced 1971.
(p) (q) The National Bank of Australasia Ltd.
(p) Early badge; from a document dated 1926.
(q) Current symbol introduced 1968.
(r) (s) The Commercial Bank of Australia Ltd.
(r) Early seal; date unknown.
(s) The current symbol, a stylized magnet and keeper representing safety and security, was introduced in 1958.
(t) Bankcard. Charge Card Services Ltd, Sydney; 1974. As plastic cards replace paper money, the Bankcard symbol is becoming the new dollar sign.

Continued from page 145
(h) Nok-Out Mfg. Co. Sydney. Insect killer; 1930.
(i) Pest-Ax. G. Watson, Sydney. Insect destroyer; 1931.
(j) Dethblo. Julius Cohn, Adelaide. Insect destroyer; 1932.
(k) (l) Two foreign imports to help fight the war:
(k) Flit. Stanco (Australia) Pty Ltd, Sydney. Insecticides; 1940.
(l) De-Fly-Er. Insecticide vaporiser; c. 1954.
(m) Peter Panda. Pura Chemicals Pty Ltd, Sydney. Fly killer; 1949.

Continued from page 147
(g) Australian Safety Matches, Sweden; c. 1898.
(h) The Australian Match. Sweden; c. 1898.
(i) The Kookaburra Safety Match. Uddevalla Tandsticks Fabriks Aktiebolag, Sweden; 1898.
(j) The Cricket Match. Sweden; c. 1903.
(k) Platypus Safety Matches. Nam Sang Woo, Samarang, Java; pre-World War I.
(l) Lyre Bird Brand. Holland; c. 1910.
(m) Australian Match Cover Collectors Society. Promotional match book; current.

INDEX

This index is a combination of two listings:
1. Products and services tradenames.
2. Owners of products and services.

Swhiskette.
Australian Broom Co. Pty Ltd,
Melbourne; c.1952.

AAA cotton goods 21(j)
Abba 98(g)
Abbo-Liter medicine (36)n
Abbott, J. H. & Co. 131(a)
Abbott Laboratories 36(n)
Abo, paint 45(a); souvenirs 47(f)
Acme Beds Co. Ltd, The 150(b)
Acme butter 97(l)
Adam, A. S. Haik 148(b)
Adams, E. A. 48(f)
Adams, Herbert 104(f)
Adams, William & Co. Ltd 50(c)
Adams, W. T. 105(i)
Adder prickly pear destroyer 78(a)
Adelaide Brewery Co. Ltd, The 40(g)
Adelaide Milling Co. Ltd, The 111(b)
Adelaide on Wheels clothing 134(f)
Adelaide Tent & Verandah Blind Co. 94(h)
Admiral Peanuts 128(d)
Advance Australia alcoholic drinks 28(i)
Advance Australia, The 160(b)
Advance hosiery 29(b)
Advance Tasmania clothing 28(j)
Aerial, flour 111(a); cigarettes 161(d)
Aero agricultural chemicals 75(b)
Aeroplane, flour 112(i); jelly 123(e); records 157(g)
Agricultural Services Pty Ltd 23(ad)
Air Supply Packs Pty Ltd 43(h)
Aitcheson, H. 40(e)
A.J.C. clothing for animals 29(e)
Albert, Frank 157(a)
Albion Koala Cooker 149(f)
Alcock Bros. 21(j)
Alexander, A. & Co. 142(g)
Alexander, J. 32(b)
All Australian Graffiti Pty Ltd 58(l)
All the Rage jam 123(b)
Allans & Stark 57(b)
Allard, James 62(d)
Allcourt rubber footwear 48(i)
Allen, A. W. Ltd 127(e), 163(e)
Allen, Richard & Son (1919) Pty Ltd 23(s)
Allen, S. & Sons 112(f)
Alliance Temperance Ale 110(b)
Allied Food Industries 114(f)
Alpha Engineering Co. Ltd 23(v)
Alpha Laboratories 168(g)
Aluminium Pty Ltd 42(d)
Amalgamated Pharmacists Pty Ltd 168(k)
Amalgamated Wireless Australasia Ltd 157(i)
Amat-ice refrigeration 22(h)
American Cereal Co., The 174(c)
American Cream Soda 105(h)
American Traders (Adelaide) Ltd 36(x)
American Trading Co. of Australia 58(f)
Am-o-lin Laboratories 168(j)
Amor, W. A. 145(e)
Ampol Petroleum Ltd 89(c)
A.M.S. medicine 166(j)
A.N.A. Sewing Machine, The 149(b)
Anderson, A. W. 118(f)
Andrews & Son 112(d)
Angus, J. 80(a)
A.N.P. wood stains 64(b)
Ansell, E. N. & Sons 42(h)
Antibuzzbuzz fly preventive 70(a)
Anticary mouth wash 170(d)
Ant-I-Dope insecticide 36(h)
Anti-Football League 154(n)
Antiseptic cloths 22(a)
ANZAC joinery 31(a)
APL aluminium 42(d)
Apos Drug Co. 57(c)
Appy-Tiza foods 42(e)
Arbon 66(c)
Archer, W. H. 66(f)
Arendsen, H. & Sons Pty Ltd 26(m)
Ark, dried fruit 124(c); sporting goods 152(h)
Army & Navy Stores Ltd, The 32(f)
Arnott's biscuits 103(e)
Arsenical marking oil 70(h)
Artlay Mfg. Co. 152(c)
Asche, O. 149(e)
A.S.D. stock medicines and disinfectant 75(g)
Ashby, T. Cordial Factory 107(b)
Ashelford, N. & F. 36(b)
Aspro 163(b)
Associated Day Tours 53(g)
Atcherley & Dawson 40(c)
Atkins Quinine Tonic Wine 165(a)
Atlas apples 124(g)
Atlas Macaroni Mfg. Co. 115(j)
Atwell, B. A. 65(a)
Attracto clothing 23(s)
Auldana Ltd. 108(f)
Aulsebrook & Sons Ltd 104(a)
Ausette safety razors 26(m)
Auski Mfg. Co. 56(e)
Aussie, pianos and organs 19(a); –'s cigars 26(i); preserves 32(e); –Bear leather 53(c); –Roo leather 56(c); –Catchy-Foot fly paper 145(d)
Austin Motor Co. Ltd 175(c)
Austlpully pulleys 22(f)
Austral Canning Co. Pty Ltd, The 120(d)
Austral Ceylon Mutual Tea Co. Ltd, The 102(b)
Austral chemicals 26(c)
Austral Cycle Agency Ltd 26(a)
Austral Gut Co. 26(l)
Austral Matches Ltd 148(t)
Austral, milking machines 26(b); umbrellas and walking sticks 26(d); sewing machines 149(c)
Austral Otis Andebar Cannery Equipment Pty Ltd 84(i)
Austral Salt Producers Pty Ltd 117(d)
Australasian Breweries Ltd 109(b)
Australasian Films Ltd 158(h)
Australasian Fireman, The 160(a)
Australasian Hardware and Machinery 159(e)
Australasian Steel Split Pulleys Ltd 22(f)
Australasian United Paint Co. Ltd 85(f)
Australia and New Zealand Banking Group Ltd 92(k)
Australia Hotel Co. Ltd, The 23(r)
Australia matches 148(c)
Australian Agriculturist and Live Stock Journal, The 160(c)
Australian Anodisers 23(ac)
Australia Bitter Ale 109(e)
Australian Black carbon paint 47(a)
Australian Brewer's Journal, The 159(d)
Australian Chemical Products Co. 43(c)
Australian Cordial Maker, The 159(f)
Australian Cotton Co-op. Association Ltd, The 77(i)
Australian Egret butter 97(d)
Australian Explosives & Chemical Co. Ltd 81(d)
Australian Flag matches 148(k)
Australian Gold-Top Co. 49(b)
Australian Honey Producers Co-op. Society Ltd 123(j)
Australian Jam Co., The 123(c)
Australian Knitting Mills 23(q), 60(c)
Australian Labor Party 21(k)
Australian Life Agencies Ltd, The 79(a)
Australian Made symbol 27(d)
Australian Maid foods 44(e)
Australian Match, The 147(h)
Australian Match Cover Collectors Society 147(m)
Australian Match Works 148(k)(l)
Australian Mfg. & Importing Co. Ltd 65(g)
Australian Mining & White Lead Pty Ltd 94(f)
Australian Natural Products (Stains) Ltd 64(b)
Australian Pacific Traders Pty Ltd 113(c)
Australian Paint Co. 45(a), 85(g)
Australian Produce Co., The 74(h)
Australian Safety Matches 147(g)
Australian Sewing Machine, The 149(a)
Australian Souvenir Co., The 47(g)
Australian Sparkling Wines Ltd 108(d)
Australian Tack Mfg. Co. 23(x)
Australian Telephone Development Association 22(j)
Australian Vitamite Co., The 21(e)

Art.
James Sandy & Co.,
Sydney.
Artists' materials; 1907.

Index

Australians First, machinery 27(b); fruit 27(c)
Australino hats 26(f)
Australite, lamps 26(g); paint 52(d)
Austrawool shirts 26(e)
Austrella talking machines 26(k)
Austrola talking machines 26(j)
Auto, paints 85(b); bread 114(e); peanuts 128(g)
Automatic Bakeries Ltd 114(e)
Automatic Traders Pty Ltd 128(g)
Aut-O-Pie machinery 84(e)
Autophone Ltd 177(h)
Avondale Studios Pty Ltd 47(i)
AWA 157(i)
AWU farm chemicals 74(f)
Ayers Rock 25
Ay Kay M mills 23(q)

Babnaps nappies 135(c)
Bacal stock feed 77(i)
Bagley Sanoleo Chemical Co. 70(g)
Baily, F. J. 30(d)
Bain's white ant exterminator 48(b)
Ballarat Bertie 110(e)
Ballarat Brewing Co. 110(e)
Balloon flour 95(c)
Balmain Rugby League 156(a)
Baker, J. B. 53(d)
Baker Knitting Mills Pty Ltd, The 134(l)
Baker, W. Jno. 29(a)
Bambi Shmith 129(d)
Bang-er-oo toys 35(m)
Bank Bell clothing 134(d)
Bank of New South Wales 92(a)
Bankcard 92(t)
Banks Bell & Co. 134(d)
Banks Property Co. 70(b)
Banksia alcoholic drinks 66(g)
Bannister, Eli 55(e)
Banquet foods 116(b)
Bargain Shop, The 146(d)
Barnes & Co. Ltd 116(g)
Barnes, Crosby & Co. 28(c)
Barnes and Howard 36(k)
Barnet Glass Rubber Co. Ltd 48(i)
Barriereef Fashions 25(k)
Barter & Co. 114(b)
Bartleet Perry, J. E. 44(f)
Bayley Sims, A. W. 94(a)
BBB mattresses 150(k)
B.B. Company 41(f)
B.C. foods 23(p)
Bear, chemicals 52(b); hollow ware 53(e); confectionery 126(a)
Bears Rugby League team 156(g)
Beal, G. W. 50(d)
Beam batteries 86(f)
Beauchamp, W. H. & Co. Pty Ltd 124(g)
Beath, Schiess & Co. 29(b)
Beckers Pty Ltd 163(c)
Beech Forest Butter Factory Co. Ltd 98(a)
Bedford, Randolph 49(f)
Bedgood & Co. 131(b)
Bell, E. L. & C. Pty Ltd 148(j)(k)
Bell & Spence 34(e)
Bell's underwear 136(b)
Bellcraft Knitting Mills Pty Ltd 136(b)
Bellinger Central Co-op. Butter Co. Ltd 98(l)
Ben Trovato Wormecide 70(c)
Bendigo Digger Brand eucalyptus oil 166(f)
Bendigo & District Farmers & Fruitgrowers Co-op. Society Ltd, The 37(c)
Benjamin, A. L. 64(e)
Bennett, W. & J. McNeil 38(e)
Benson, E. & Co. 113(b)
Bent Glass Pty Ltd 43(k)
Bentley, Edward & Sons Pty Ltd 22(k), 152(i)
Berg silk ties 43(f)
Berger, L. & Sons 85(j)
Bergmann, F. A. 149(c)
Berts Soft Drinks 19(e)
Best's Continental Smallgoods 118(g)
Betjak flour 113(f)
Bevan, C. A. 41(c)
Bex 163(c)
B.H.P. 83(e), —Benzol 21(i)
Bickford, A. M. & Sons 60(a), 75(b), 101(h), 142(c), 165(e)
Big Fella soft drinks 107(j)
Big G. flour 112(e)
Bile Bean Mfg. Co., The 38(c)
Bill Brush paints 85(j)
Billabong windmills 70(k)
Billows Little Pty Ltd 116(d)
Billy Bluegum toys 35(h)
Billy Tea 100
Birt & Co. Ltd 60(b)
Black Boy Eczemacura 64(a)
Blackboy fruit 47(e)
Black Swan matches 148(p)
Blackham, W. H. 26(b), 63(i), 98(h)
Blakeys Boot Protectors Ltd 144(v)
Blake, W. A. Pty Ltd 37(h)
Blockli, W. 35(m)
Blo-Fli-Di 70(f)
Bloom, Leo 44(g)
Blossoms tobacco 64(e)
Blue Bird Hosiery Mills Pty Ltd 135(l)
Blue Gum oil 65(a)
Bluebell flour 111(h)
Bluee soap 35(c)
Blues Football team 154-155(a)
Blumenthal, B. 36(d)
Boars Head casings 93(d)
Bobby Dazzler clothing 38(d)
Bod-e-line clothing 35(a)
Boguslavsky, Alexander, Ltd 162(h)
Bombers Football team 154-155(c)
Bond, James 58(a)
Bond Street headwear 48(j)
Bond's Wear Pty Ltd 136(g)
Bonser saddlery 35(d)
Bonza Sheen brilliantine 33(b)
Boomaroo toys 152(c)
Bookallil, John and James Donovan 36(f)
Boomerang butter 97(e)
Boomerang Cigarette Papers Pty Ltd 48(k)
Biddell's Young Australia 127(o)
Boomerang, metal goods 48(a); explosives 48(c); foods 48(f); glass 48(g); stock licks and cures 48(h); —Harmonica, The 48(l); cream and butter 97(b); —Tonic 105(f); fly paper 145(e)
Boort Butter & Ice Co. Ltd 98(f)
Booth, Edgar 21(f)
Booth, J. A. & Co. 26(k), 102(e)
Borax Consolidated Ltd 177(a)
Boronia butter 98(l)
Bosisto's Parrot Brand eucalyptus oil 164(a)
Bosker rabbit poison 72(b)
Bowman Flag 28(a)
Boyshform Brassier Co., The 177(b)
Bradbury, R. A. & Co. 133(b)
Braddies confectionery 126(a)
Brandon, J. & L. M. 36(m)
Breakfast D. Light 115(c)
Brenco Products 170(f)
Brennan & Geragh 116(a)
Brewer, W. H. 28(d), 71(b)
Bridestowe Estate 141(f)
Bridge (Sydney Harbour), matches 148(o); cigarettes 162(c)
Briggs Bros. Pty Ltd 61(c)
Brighton Municipal Council 46(k)
Brisbane Chemical & General Supply Co. 43(g)
Brisbane Salt Co. 117(a)
Brisbane Soap Co. Ltd, The 139(k), 141(c)
Brisbon soap 43(g)
British-Australian Co. Pty Ltd, The 161(e)
British Australian Oil Co. Ltd, The 173(d)
British Australian Tobacco Co. Pty Ltd, The 34(g)
British Petroleum Company Ltd 88
British Xylonite Co. Ltd, The 176(c)
Broken Hill Pty Co. Ltd, The 21(i), 83(e)
Broken River Butter Factory 97(d)
Brooke, C. M. & Sons 102(h), 106(f)
Brooke's Oros Ltd 99(b)
Brockhoff, A. F. & Co. Pty Ltd 104(g)
Bronch-o-form medicine 168(d)
Brown, C. G. 22(c)
Brown & Dureau Ltd 34(f), 44(e)
Brownie Steel Products 84(b)
Brunton, John Pty Ltd 23(e)
Bryant & May Pty Ltd 50(i), 147(a), 148(h)(m)(r)
Bryta polish 20(d)
Buchanan's Cat paints 41(i)
Buckjumper hams and bacon 37(i)
Buckley & Nunn 133(l)
Budgeree for blowflies 47(b)
Budgerree Doll souvenirs 47(g)
Buesst & Bills Bros. Pty Ltd 150(k)
Bugs' Funeral Insecsterminator, The 146(d)
Bulldogs, Football team 154-155(e); —Rugby League team 156(b)
Bulletin (Sydney), The 159(a)
Bull, J. A. & Co. 101(g)
Bulls-Eye cereals 115(g)
Bull's Head 174(b)
Bunch of Dates, A, stationery 41(k)
Bungalow flour 96(d)
Bunge (Australia) Pty Ltd 96(k)
Bunni-Di-Brickette rabbit poison 72(g)
Bunnycide rabbit poison 72(i)
Bunyip, boot polish 143(d); embrocation 164(d)
Bunyip Soap Co. Ltd, The 63(h), 140(a)(f)
Burford, W. H. & Sons 139(a)
Burge's Bros. & Co. Ltd 150(m)
Burke & Wills foods 25(b)
Buring, Leo Pty Ltd 23(d)
Burnet, N. 66(d)
Burnside, W. K. Pty Ltd 144(w)
Bush, Albert 166(f)
Bushells Ltd 101(b)
Bushman, metal goods 37(b); butter 97(p); salt 117(a)
Butler, Edward & Son Ltd 35(d), 82(d)

Cafe flour 111(j)
Cahill, John & Co. 49(e)
Calendar flour 112(f)
Calfeteria feeding devices 36(u)
Calopedes lasts for shoes 82(g)
Cameron, R. W. & Co. 94(c)
Campbell Bros. Ltd 29(f), 139(c)
Campbell, James & Sons 84(c)
Campbell's Marguerite perfumery 141(c)
Canary butter 97(f)
Canberra cigars 25(e)
Cannot Be Exterminated clothing 73(a)
Can't Be Beat 43(c)
Canterbury-Bankstown Rugby League 156(b)
Canterbury Extra Stout 109(b)
Carbine Remedies 74(g)
Car-B-Que 36(v)
Carlton Brewery Ltd 109(i)
Carlton, First Prize Ale 109(c); —Ale 109(i)
Carlton Football Club 154-155(a)
Carlton & United Breweries Ltd 109(j)
Carlton & West End Breweries Ltd 109(c)

Coles & Garrard, Melbourne. Opticians; from an advertisement appearing 1927.

Index

E. J. Carroll. Films; 1920.

Carnegie, P. D. & Sons Ltd 177(c)
Carreras Ltd 162(g)(h)
Carter, A. 86(i)
Cartoon Filmads Co. 158(a)
Carwardine, W. H. 139(i)
Cascade Cordials Ltd 106(h)
Cash, W. E. 83(d)
Castle bacon and hams 118(c)
Castlemaine Brewery and Wood Bros. Co. Ltd, The 34(j)
Castlemaine Woollen Co. Ltd, The 56(w)
Castle Salt Co-op. Co. Ltd, The 117(b)
Castle, S. N. & Sons 85(k)
Catamaran Coal 42(f)
Cation & Hilton 118(b)
Cats Football team 154-155(f)
Caute, D. J. & Son 56(z)
Cave, F. & Co. Pty Ltd 57(e)
Central Spring Works 84(d)
Centralian foods 24(b)
Cereal Foods Pty Ltd 115(g)
Ceylon Tea Co., The 102(a)
Champion clothing 56(b)
Champion Gold-Top beverages 49(b)
Chandler, D. J. & W. H. 81(a)
Chandler, J. B. & Co. 150(d)
Charge Card Services Ltd 92(t)
Charlick, William Ltd 96(h)
Chavasse, A. L. 23(p)
Cheerio handkerchiefs 134(j)
Cheetham, J. H. 101(f)
Cheetham Salt Pty Ltd, The 117(c)
Cherry butter 97(g)
Chesty Bond 136(g)
Chickemite food 36(p)
Chief clothing 129(e)
Chimpanzees cigars 161(a)
Chipman, H. S. 87(a), 152(a)
Chiquita Banana 124(k)
Chloro Naptholeum disinfectant 139(d)
Choc-A-Bloc foods 36(c)
Chock-aroo chocolate 58(j)
Choke-A-Mouse mousetraps 36(k)
Choon, Sym & Co. 128(h)
Chows confectionery 126(a)
Christensen & Co. 132(b)
Chubb & Sons Lock & Safe Co. 175(g)
Chu-Chin-Chow stoves 149(e)
Church, J. 85(e)
Cicada manurial soil 77(f)
Cinema Motors Publicity Co. 158(e)
Cinesound Productions Limited 158(g)
Clare Mineral Waters Co. 105(k)
Clarence Mfg. Co. 36(y)
Clark & Fauset Ltd 62(h)
Clark, R. H. & Co. 85(i)
Clarke & Co. 37(d)
Clarke, D. H. Ltd. 22(b)
Clarke, I. P. & Co. 172(c)
Clarton Hodgson & Co. Ltd 37(g)
Clag 80(a)
Clavis Rheuma medicine 165(g)
Clipper Caravans 23(b)
Clean All Cleanser 139(l)
Clem's Cordials 56(ad)
Cloudform Dusts 71(f)
Coastal Farmers Co-op. Society Ltd, The 97(m)
Cockatoo, flour 59(b); cheese 63(i); jams and preserves 63(j); cigarettes 173(h)
Cockatoo Preserves Ltd 63(j)
Cockbill, J. 76(g)
Cockroach & Blackbeetle Extermination Co., The 146(c)
Cohen & Sons 20(h)
Cohen, S. Sons & Co. 149(h)
Cohn, A. S. 167(c)
Cohn, Julius 145(j)
Cole, C. R. 73(e)
Coles, G. J. & Coy Limited 136(e)
Collegian clothing 136(a)
Collingwood Football Club 154-155(b)
Collyns & Co. 172(a)
Colman, J. & J. 174(b)
Colonial Maid metal goods 44(f)
Colonial Sugar Refining Co. Ltd, The 94(e)
Columbia Graphophone Co. 175(f)
Commercial Bank of Australia Ltd, The 92(r)
Comica films 176(g)
Commonwealth Aircraft Corporation Ltd 83(g)
Commonwealth Bank of Australia 92(d)
Commonwealth Banking Corporation 92(e)
Commonwealth Fertilizers & Chemicals Ltd 75(f)
Commonwealth Games Australia (1982) Foundation Limited, The XII 54(f)
Commonwealth Laundry Journal, The 160(d)
Commonwealth Metallic Pty Ltd 36(q)
Commonwealth of Australia 29(i), 56 (ab)
Commonwealth of Australia Hall Mark Co., The 61(a)
Commonwealth Oil Corporation Ltd 55(d)
Commonwealth Oil Refineries Ltd 88(d)
Commonwealth, The, sanitary wares 172(d)
Commonwealth Trade Mark 30(c)
Commonwealth Umbrellarian, The 130(f)
Competition fruit cases 46(j)
Confederation of Australian Industry 27(d)
Connell, John & Co. Ltd 123(b)
Coo-ee Clothing Co. 34(h)
Coo-ee Mfg. Co. Ltd, The 106(d)
Coo-ee, produce (33)c; tobacco 34(a); tomato sauce 34(b); galvanized iron 34(c); alcoholic drinks 34(d); motor cycles 34(e); flour 34(f); cigarettes 34(g); –Kola 34(i); beverage 34(j), 106(d); wines 108(g), 172(a); matches 148(l)
Cookaburra, patty pans 61(c); musical instruments 157(b)
Cooke, Sidney Pty Ltd 81(c), 84(g)
Coomber, F. J. 161(i)
Coon Stick confectionery 50(e)
C.O.R. lubricants and fuels 88(d)
Cottee, A. J. 29(e)
Cottee, Spencer Milton 106(e)
Cotton, A. J. 46(j)
Cotton, T. W. Pty Ltd 35(b)
Corax fire extinguisher 84(a)
Corden, J. J. & Co. 118(e)
Corio Freezing Works 116(c)
Corowa Milling Co. Ltd 47(k), 113(a)(e)
Cosmopolitan Import Agency 82(f)
Country Freezing Co. Ltd 73(b)
Cox, F. D. and C. H. Parker 72(e)
Cox, H. W. 84(f)
Cox & Sons 136(c)
Coys Capitol Pickles 25(h)
Cozmon costumes 20(h)
Craddock, George & Co. 176(b)
Crafti, Edward 35(e)
Craig, Mostyn & Co. 37(i)
Crane, W. R. A. 122(e)
Crasho insecticide 145(f)
Cratchley Advertising Agency Pty Ltd 36(v)
Craven 'A' cigarettes 162(g)
Crem-Ogran cereals 115(d)
Creswell & Co. 28(b)
Creswick, A. R. 170(b)
Cricket Safety Matches, The 147(j)
Cronulla-Sutherland Rugby League 156(c)
Crosby Mann & Co. Ltd 66(a)
Crows Nest soft drinks 106(h)
Cunningham, Alex 131(d)
Cure-em-quick confectionery 163(e)
Curit medicine 41(c)
Curnow, Sylvia 169(c)
Curtis, T. Ltd 135(d)
Custalia custard 26(h)
Cutler cannery equipment 84(i)
Cycle flour 96(m)
Cyclo metal goods 87(k)
Cyclone Pty Ltd 83(h)

Daimler Co. Ltd 175(a)
Daimler Motoren Gesellschaft 174(f)
Dallison, F. H. 56(p)
Daly, H. 70(d)
Danks, John & Son Pty Ltd 70(k)
Danzer, H. 176(g)
Darkey soap 50(d)
Darling Downs Co-op. Bacon Co. Ltd 118(d)
Darling, John & Son Pty Ltd 113(f)(g)
Darveniza, T. 108(b)
Davey, E. & Sons 96(m)
Davies-Kitchen (Australia) Ltd 23(u)
Davies, W. 167(h)
Davis, A. J. 40(b)
Davis Bros. 63(d)
De Meric Ltd 80(b)
Dearden, Jonathan & Co. Ltd 173(a)
Deathdust farm chemicals 71(e)
Decoy-Em-All rabbit poison 72(e)
Defender snail killer 146(h)
Defiance blowfly oil 70(g)
De-Fly-Er vapourizer 145(l)
Delilah lingerie 134(l)
Demons Football team 154-155(h)
Denyer Bros. 74(d)
Department of Main Roads, New South Wales 24(f)
Department of Railways, New South Wales 64(j)
Department of Youth Sport and Recreation, Victoria 151(b)
Dependon cotton goods 32(a)
Depil-A-Tone 141(h)
Dethblo insecticide 145(j)
Dickson, T. A. 166(j)
Die Brücke publication 56(y)
Die Casters Pty Ltd 66(c)
Diggaburra tea 59(a)
Digger, fruits and nuts 31(c); –Junior toys 31(e); footwear 32(d); preserves 37(c); chemicals 75(d); flour 112(d); apples 124(j); –'Washo' soap 139(i)
Digger Tea Supply Co., The 59(a)
Diggers Commerce Agency, The 31(b)
Diminuentoe footwear 36(r)
Ding-Dong beverages 105(d)
Dingo, eucalyptus oil 58(a); alcoholic drinks 58(c); hardware 58(e); flour 93(a); –Taendstikker 148(g); matches 148(s)
Dinkum, Digger wool 31(d); tea 33(a); –Snowee beverages 106(f)
Disho soap 140(f)
Diviner medicine 167(b)
Dixon & Sons 34(a)
Doan's Dinner Pills 165(d)
Docker, William 85(c)
Dodge, L. W. & Co. 152(j)
Dodgshun, W. & Sons 27(a), 29(d), 57(g)
Dog Dynamite 71(a)
Dome clothing 22(d)
Dominion parachutes 56(a)
Don machinery 23(j)
Don, R. S. 23(i)
Don't Argue – Huttons is Best 119
Donaghy, M. & Sons 82(a)
Dorin, Marie 84(a)
Douglass, W. C. 115(c)
Doulton & Co. Ltd 172(d)
Dowd Associates Pty Ltd 23(f)

Index

Downer & Co. 63(c)
Downs & Sons Pty Ltd 21(a)
Downunda clothing 36(w)
Dr Blue Gum eucalyptus oil 52(a)
Dr Boxwell's Silent Pill 164(f)
Dragons Rugby League team 156(k)
Drever, W. M. F. 141(j)
Drinko treatment for alcoholism 35(l)
Drover foods 37(g)
Drug Houses of Australia 168(l)
Drummer Boy foods 41(e)
Duffield, J. E. & Co. 172(j)
Duff, T. & Bros. 82(e)
Dunlop, David 173(f)
Dunlop Rubber Co. of Australia Ltd, The 23(h)
Duraloid products 29(h)
Durham Chemicals (Australia) Pty Ltd 56(ac)
Durham, Joseph 143(c)
Duval Trading Co. 61(f)
Dux water heater 42(i)
Dyason & Son 62(c)
Dyson's Peninsular Motors Pty Ltd 23(aa)

Eagley Co. Pty Ltd, The 133(i)
Early Bird tobacco 161(e)
Early Kooka stoves 149(g)
Early Riser flour 20(i)
Easo furniture 35(e)
Eastern Suburbs Rugby League 156(d)
Easy to Play player pianos 157(d)
Eatmore fruit 99(a)
Eau de Queensland 141(a)
Eazoids for the throat 167(a)
Ebes Collection 31(f)
Ecco Lightning metal goods 23(n)
Echuca Co-op. Butter Factory 97(h)
Eckersley, John 46(c)
Ecks beer 106(b)
Eclipse Drench 70(b)
Edwards, F. W. 28(g)
Edwards, Urettra 41(h)
Eels Rugby League team 156(h)
Efftee Film Productions 158(f)
Eiffel Tower Blend of Tea 101(g)
Elastic Webbing (Australia) Pty Ltd 64(f)
Elco blankets 24(c)
Elder Smith & Co. Ltd 75(i)
Electra bicycles 87(d)
Electric Polish 142(a)
Elephant threads 22(k)
Elliott Bros. Ltd 72(b), 74(b)
Ellis & Kells Brewery (Darwin) Ltd 110(i)
Elliss & Sytton Pty Ltd 136(f)
Ellix, W. 145(d)
Embassy range of products 136(e)
Empire Beds 150(a)
Empire Motor & Cycle Co. 87(e)
Empire photographic papers 29(c)
Emu Bay Butter Factory Co., The 62(f)
Emu, beer 59(e); frame moulding 62(a); cordial sauce 62(c); pottery wares 62(d); butter and cheese 62(f); hardwoods 62(i); rope 62(j); —Grip for tyre repairs 87(h); —Factory butter 97(k); pale ale 109(f); salt 117(b); boot polish 143(f); stoves 149(d); corrugated iron 172(f); tool handles 172(j); —Twist tobacco 173(f)
Emu Brewery Co., The 59(e)
Encore Shoe 131(c)
Enright, Malcolm 33(d)
Equivita horse and cattle cure 75(e)
Ergon Brace & Leather Goods Mfg. Co. 133(j)
Erry, George Townsend 143(e)
Essendon Football Club 154-155(c)
Estee Trading Co. Pty Ltd 84(l)
Eta peanut butter 116(h)
Euclips confectionery 126(a)
Euky Bearub 164(g)
Eureka machinery 77(a)
Eurythmic films 158(d)
Even a man can do it 140(a)
Evans, H. D. 74(e)
Evans, H. J. 48(h)
Evenden's Spring Head nails 81(c)
Even Keel heels 132(j)
Everlite louvres 24(e)
Ever-Clear 23(ab)
Excello oranges 124(b)
Excelsior Vineyard 108(b)
Exhibit Boot 25(c)
Explorer bicycles 87(b)
Eye and Bee clothing 40(f)

Fair Dinkum Graphics, Arti Studio 33(d)
Fairisle clothing 19(c)
Falconer, F. S. 74(i)
Falls, E. G. 144(y)
Famous all over the States umbrellas 130(g)
Fantales 126(f)
Farbest Products Pty Ltd 107(f)
Farber, William Pty Ltd 113(d)
Farley, Alice 51(d)
Farmer & Co. 135(c)
Farmers & Settlers Co-op. Society Ltd 97(a)
Faulding, F. H. & Co. 62(e), 72(i), 170(e)
Faulkner, Ross Pty Ltd 153(f)
Favourite clothing 134(e)
Fay-mos clothing 41(f)
Featherweight flour 111(g)
Federal Cask Co. Pty Ltd 108(j)
Federal Flag foods 30(g)
Federal hop beer 109(h)
Federal Match Co., The 148(o)(q)
Federal Taendstikker 148(c)
Felsted, Theo & Good 32(a)
Felton Grimwade & Bickford Pty Ltd 164(g)
Ferguson, M. 81(b)
Fern beverages 66(h)
Fibrolite asbestos sheeting 83(c)
Fielder flour 112(c)
Filmads 158(a)
Findlay, R. B. 36(h)
Finucan, M. Bros. 49(c)
Fiorelli, Matteo 108(g)
Fire Brick & Pottery Works Pty Ltd 83(a)
Firmstone, W. T. 168(b)
Fischer, A. M. & G. 130(a)
Fischer, H. Ltd 153(j)
Fisher, Jaques & Co. 71(c)
Fisher, R. Pty Ltd 61(g)
Fisheries and Wildlife Division, Victoria 57(m)
Fitzroy Football Club 154-155(d)
Flag clothing 30(i)
Fleming, Hugh Duff 95(c)
Flit insecticides 145(k)
Florey, Joseph 131(c)
Fluenzol Pty Ltd, The 165(i)
Fly Cop insecticide 145(g)
Fly-Fire fire preventive 85(h)
Foley Bros. 97(o)
Football Punch 105(k)
Footers confectionery 126(a)
Footscray Football Club 154-155(e)
Forsyth, A. & Co. Ltd 60(g)
Forward Football Boot, The 153(b)
Foster Brewing Co. Ltd, The 109(d)
Foster-McLellan Co. 165(d)
Foulis, W. B. 56(q)
Fountain foods 28(g)
Four Sevens Mfg. Co., The 141(b)
Foureur, J. H. Ltd 42(a)
Fourex (XXXX), bitter ale 110(c); —Swan stout 110(h)
Fowler, D. & J. Ltd 24(b)
Fowlers Pty Ltd 44(h)
Fox, Thomas S. 120(g)
Foy & Gibson Pty Ltd 134(m)
Foys, Mark Ltd 150(h)
Frankston Springs Co. 105(h)
Frazer, S. 26(i)
Freddo Frog 127(c)
Freedman & Co. 134(e)
Freekic Football Boot, The 153(a)
Freney, Martin R. 75(h)
Freshcort rabbits 73(f)
Freshness Ltd 36(s)
Friedlander, M. 161(a)
Frieze Bros. Pty Ltd 19(c)
Fulford, C. E. 38(c)
Fumarat poison 146(j)
Furline cleaner 142(b)
Fuzzy Wuzzy foods 38(e)
Fysh, P.O. & Co. 24(c), 28(j)

Gadsden, Jabez 23(m)
Galaxy Drive-in 158(j)
Garden and Field 159(c)
Gardiner, W. H. 25(d)
Garrod & Roberts Ltd 141(d)
Gay Boy boot polish 144(x)
Gazeka, paints 51(d); boot polish 143(a)
Geelong Football Club 154-155(f)
Geelong Harbor Trust Commissioners, The 116(c)
Geisha dressed rice 40(d)
General Accessories Pty Ltd 87(k)
General Electric Co. 174(e)
General Motors Holden 86(j)
General Refrigerating Co. 22(h)
Giant macaroni 115(j)
Gibbs, Bright & Co. 71(f)
Gibson, A. B. & Sons Pty Ltd 36(j)
Gibsonia range of goods 134(m)
Gilbert, C. Ltd 134(a)
Gillard Gordon Ltd 53(a)
Gillespie Bros. & Co. 96(b)
Gillespie, J. 59(b)
Gillette Safety Razor Co. 174(h)
Gippsland and Northern Co-op. Ltd 77(h)
Given Away clothing 133(d)
Gladioli flour 113(a)
Gleeson, D. W. 163(a)
Glenford Clothing Co. Pty Ltd 36(w)
Glenora Seeds 77(j)
Gloag, M. W. & Son 173(g)
Globe tea 40(c)
Globe Tobacco Co., The 162(e)
Glo-White detergent 140(g)
Gloy Mfg. Co., The 176(d)
Gluca glue 21(c)
Glyco adhesives 80(d)
Glynn, C. M. Ltd 87(h)
Gnome candles and soap 138(h)
Goal Finder footballs 153(k)
Goanna Salve 167(e)
Golden Bee Honey 123(k)
Golden Crust Baking Co. 114(g)
Golden Fleece, soap 49(e); lubricants and fuels 89(a); baking powders 114(b); hosiery 133(f)
Golden Gum food 65(g)
Golden Nuggets confectionery 127(f)
Golden Strad strings 157(a)
Golden Wattle, elastic 64(f)
Golden Wattle Films Syndicate 158(b)
Golden West Swan flour 94(g)
Goldman, Mark 165(g)
Goldsmiths Alliance jewellery 54(b)
Gollin & Co. Pty Ltd 111(i)
Good Luck beverages 56(j)
Good Shot baking powder 114(a)

Kangaroo Gin.
T. H. Whitworth,
Melbourne; 1906.

Index

Halo.
Hales Ltd, Sydney.
Electric lamps; 1912.

Good-o confectionery 127(l)
Good-oh range of goods 47(h)
Goode, G. G. Ltd 162(h)
Go-Poof deodorants 36(s)
Gordon & Gotch 159(g)
Gotcher fishing gear 152(i)
Got-U fly paper 145(c)
Gould, S. G. 134(k)
Gowing Bros. 26(d)
Gowrie Dairy Supply 120(a)
G.P.O. flour 111(d)
Grafton Brewing Co. Ltd 110(j)
Graham Bros. 41(k)
Graham Chain Dairies 120(c)
Graham, G. & Co. 93(b)
Graham, R. F. 23(c)
Grain-O cereals 115(f)
Gramophone & Typewriter Ltd, The 174(i)
Gramp, G. & Sons Ltd 108(c)
Grant, H. A. & Co. 106(a)
Grant, J. H. 25(g), 72(c)
Granville, J. H. 80(d)
Gray, H. Augustus 125(a)
Gray, O. H. 24(e)
Gray, W. A. 166(g)
Grazcos Co-op. Ltd. 69(a)
Graziers' Meat Export Co. of New South Wales Ltd, The 46(e)
Great Southern Flour Mills Ltd, The 24(d), 93(a), 112(i)
Great Western Vineyard 108(a)
Greave, Harry 50(h)
Greenberg & Co. Ltd 43(f)
Gregory & Davidson Ltd 41(e)
Greyhound bicycles 87(c)
Griffith Co-op. Society Ltd, The 124(b)
Griffith, L. E. 78(a)
Griffith Sweets Pty Ltd 42(j), 127(j)
Griffiths' Signal tea 101(c)
Grippo pegs 35(i)
Gripwell, The driving belts 82(c)
Gum Leaf, shafts and poles 65(e), 87(g); disinfectants 65(h)
Gum-nut chocolates 65(j)
Gum Tree 65(d); metals 65(f); flour 66(a)
Gumlypta chemicals 53(a)
Gumrice cigarette papers 162(f)
Gunnersen, G. & Co. 60(e)
Gunyah tents 47(j)

Hagemann, John 145(a)
Half-Time drink 107(a)
Hallo, H. R. 99(a)
Hammond, A. T. & Co. 65(d)
Hancock's Golden Crust Pty Ltd 115(i)
Handy Ann soap 138(g)
Handy Jack soap 139(g)
Hanro (Australia) Bendigo Knitting Mills Pty Ltd 56(v)
Hansen & Co. 138(c)
Hansen Dairy Co. 46(h)
Happy Day milk 120(c)
Happy Family flour 112(h)
Happy Jack liver saline 168(g)
Hapytoz Pty Ltd 132(f)
Harcourt, A. 52(e)
Harcourt Fruit Supply Co. 124(d)
Hardie, James & Co. Pty Ltd 21(b), 83(c)
Hardite hardening compound 83(b)
Harold Shop Co. Pty Ltd, The 153(c)
Harp Tail Pheasant foods 63(a)
Harper, Robert & Co. Pty Ltd 25(b), 30(g)
Harrington & Co. Ltd 29(c)
Harris, W. 73(c)
Hart & Co. Pty Ltd 72(h)
Hat King, The 130(b)
Hattersley, A. H. 111(c), 114(c)
Hawkinsfilm Naturaltone Productions 158(i)
Hawks Football team 154-155(g)
Hawthorn Football Club 154-155(g)
Hawthorn, Rhodes & Co. 101(a)
Hayes, E. 73(g)
Hayward, Thomas & Son Ltd 111(g)
Haywood, C. D. 30(h)
H.C.P. Cola 53(h)
Healtheries Mfg. Co., The 20(d)
Hean, G. W. 166(h)
Heather Bell butter 97(c)
Heavy Duty trousers 135(e)
Hecla Electrics Pty Ltd 150(j)
Hedake Torpedo powders 167(h)
Hed-eez headache pills 167(i)
Heelsup Buckin for skin 167(g)
Heenzo mixture 166(h)
Heinz, H. J. & Co. 175(b)
Heknows flour 96(i)
Help us to Health you for fruit 124(d)
Help us to make Australia strong 31(f)
Henderson, R. C. Ltd 57(k)
Henderson, Scott & Co. 40(d)
Hendersons Federal Spring Works Pty Ltd 29(g)
Henn, Arnold V. & Co. 54(a)
Henty, James & Co. Mfg. Dept. Pty Ltd 138(e)
Hepburn, Malcolm & Co. 53(f)
Herald and Weekly Times Limited, The 154, 160(f)
Herald Clothing Co., The 135(f)
Herald Trading Co., The 135(g)
Herbert, B. 166(i)
Herbert, M. 87(j)
Hercules bicycles 87(a)
Heron butter 98(c)
Hertzberg, A. M. & Co. 46(i)
Heyman, P. W. 24(a), 52(i), 116(f)
Hibbard, A. R. 169(b)
Hi-Fi recording needles 23(y)
Hi-Lift flour 113(d)
Hilton, Emily 139(j)
Hindmarsh Morris, W. D. 167(g)
Hinds, H. H. Ltd 70(f)
His Master's Voice 174(i)
Hiv-Alu honey 123(i)
Hodge, M. F. & Sons Ltd 77(j)
Hoggite blow-fly cure 70(d)
Holland, Edwin 165(h)
Hollingsworth, W. & D. Thomson 164(e)
Holmes, R. & Co. Ltd 66(g)
Holmes, T. J. 41(d)
Hones-Tea 39(a)
Hooper, John & Co. 28(h)
Hopkins, A. V. 47(j)
Horn paints 177(i)
Horse and Sulky flour 113(e)
Howard, V. & J. T. 25(f)
Howe, S. Co. 77(a)
Hubbard, S. Ltd 177(g)
Hubbly Bubbly drinks 107(g)
Hudsons Eumenthol Chemical Co. 71(d)
Humoss Products 22(l)
Humphris & Sons Ltd 97(k), 105(f)
100's & 1000's confectionery 126(a)
Hunter Gate & Fence Co. Ltd, The 77(k)
Hunter, J. & Son Ltd 32(d), 153(a)(b)
Hunt, J. & L. 117(g)
Husbands, W. S. 40(a)
Hutchison, W. N. 47(b)
Hutton, J. C. 119
Ieraci Bros. 36(t)
Ilford Ltd 175(j)
I'm Powellised! 146(f)
Imperial Industries of Australia and New Zealand 58(k)
Independent accessories 19(b)
Inglis, James & Co. 100
Ingwersen, A. & R. 52(b)
International Harvester Co. of Australia Pty Ltd 173(j)
Intestone mixture 40(e)
Invigorating Cup tea, coffee, cocoa 102(e)
Ireland, Jessie 33(c)
Ironbark footwear 131(d)
Ironbark paper 65(c)
Irvine, H. W. H. 108(a)

Jackass building materials 60(e)
Jackett Bros. 96(f)
Jackie leather goods 61(d)
Jacko boot polish 144(w)
Jackson, J. & Son 35(h)
Jackson, T. C. 131(e)
Jaffa 126(d)
James, E. H. 82(h)
Jantzen Knitting Mills 175(l)
Jarke Pty Ltd 152(h)
Jarrett, S. F. 73(d)
Jelicious jelly crystals 36(y)
Jenkins, A. J. 26(c)
Jets Rugby League team 156(f)
Jewell Davis & Co. 37(b)
Jimmy the Granite cement 80(c)
Jinnie-Wash Clomobeal 137(b)
Joe the Koala travel goods 53(j)
John Bull cereals 115(e)
Johnson, F. R. 23(n)
Johnson, Richard & Nephew Ltd 177(j)
Johnston's Pty Ltd 150(c)
Jok-meg Dainties 125(b)
Jolly Niggerboys matches 50(i)
Jonchair furniture and upholstery 150(c)
Jones, J. P. 30(b)
Joshua's Boomerang brandy 48(d)
Juleff, J. & Sons 149(d)
Jules Bros. Pty Ltd 112(j)
Julies, A. 161(h)

Kagro scalp preparation 167(f)
Kaldo paints 20(e)
Kanga, paint 56(d); clothing 56(w)
Kangaratta footwear 131(b)
Kangaroo Coupon Tea Co., The 56(n)
Kangaroo Petroleum Co. Pty Ltd, The 89(d)
Kangarooster flour 58(i)
Kangaroo Table Salt Pty Ltd 117(e)
Kangaroo Valley Farmers & Settlers Co-op. Society Ltd 97(a)
Kangaroo, desiccated potatoes 54(d); velocipedes 54(e); matches 55(b), 148(b)(d)(f); fuels 55(d); paper 56(h); dry cells 56(i); gums and resins 56(k); oilstone 56(p); ropes 82(a); —Vineyards 108(e); salt 117(e); footballs 153(d); —s Football team 154-155(i); pills 168(f); draft hames 172(e); printing rollers 172(g); silk 172(h).
Kango Mfg. Pty Ltd 55(g)
Kangy toys 152(b)
Kan-Ka clothing 133(c)
Kan Kleen polish 142(l)
Karmel Bros. Pty Ltd 53(b)
Karroo Roo soap 55(a)
Katalo veterinary remedy 75(a)
Katoomba Thousand lottery 21(f)
Kay, B. 167(f)
Kay Chemical Co., The 142(l)
Keegan Bros. 80(g)
Keene Co., The 169(g)
Keep Australia Beautiful Council 30(j)
Kees, John & Sons Ltd 58(e)
Keillor, A. 143(h)
Ken the Kanga travel goods 55(j)

Index

Kenne, H. J. 168(c)
Kennedy, D. 143(f)
Kent Town Preserving Co. 62(g)
Kernel Cashew 128(b)
Kernot, W. C. 146(b)
Kevin Pappas 58(l)
Kicking Roo fruit 55(h)
Kift, T. & Son 85(l)
Kill Smell disinfectant 138(j)
Kimpton, W. S. & Sons 95(a)(d), 96(a)
Kinch, Mary Jane 170(a)
Kingaroy Kid peanuts 128(e)
King, B. V. Pty Ltd 169(e)
King, Stephen & Son 102(d)
King's Compo paint 49(d)
Kingfisher – 'Our Jack' 60(a)
Kingfisher shelving 61(g)
Kingsford-Smith, Sir Charles 30(e)
Kinkara tea 102(c)
Kinlyside & Winslow 33(a)
Kinnear, G. & Sons Pty Ltd 62(j)
Kiora corn ointment 169(b)
Kiss it and make it better 167(c)
Kitchen, E. W. 141(e)
Kitchen, J. & Sons 63(g), 88, 138(b)(h), 139(b)(h), 140(h)
Kiwi boot polish 144(a)
Kiz beverages 105(g)
Klar, J. H. 23(a)
Knight, E. R. 169(f)
Knight's Lal Lal fire bricks 83(a)
Knightwear cotton goods 177(e)
K9 hats 130(c)
Knowlman & Son 132(d)
Koala Mfg. Co. 52(h)
Koala, quilts 22(b); foods 52(f); stains 52(h); jelly crystals 52(j); jewellery 53(b); –Kola 53(d); scarves 135(m); boot polish 143(h)
Kolazone beverages 105(c)
Kolter & Co. 78(b)
Konfidence clothing 133(k)
Kon-Ka-Roo medicine 35(g)
Konkrete paint 22(i)
Kookaburra Cigarette Paper Tube Mfg. Co. 162(d)
Kookaburra, frozen meat 60(b); hosiery 60(c); sporting goods 60(d); –'Our Jacks' hats 60(f); bulbs and seeds 61(e); blind hollands 61(f); shoe laces 61(h); macaroni 115(i); matches 147(i)
Kooka Cooking Salt 117(k)
Kookooburra ropes 60(g)
Kool Mints 127(j)
Kooyana flour 95(j)
Korumburra Shire Council 60(h)
Kosciusko, foods 25(d); – Kakes 126(a)
Kraft Foods Ltd 44(b), 99(e)
Kraft Walker Cheese Co. Pty Ltd 36(e)
Kure-ettes medicine 41(d)
Kurrajong 66(e)
Kwick and Easie polish 142(i)
Kwik Heal chemicals 74(d)

La-By egg preservative 76(c)
Lactaloaf bread 114(f)
Lady Olive perfumery 141(e)
Lambs' Porto tobacco 161(c)
Landliner busline 23(aa)
Larnach, B. M. 43(j)
Larter's Common Sense Rat Exterminator 146(a)
Lascelles, Robert & Co. 54(e)
Lassetter, F. & Co. Ltd 70(a), 94(b)
Laundrena 139(m)
Laver Bros. & Co. 123(d)
Lawrence, E. & Co. 169(h)
Lazell, S. 166(d)
LBW beverages 107(d)
Leading Light glass 43(k)
Leakpruf cotton goods 77(g)
Ledger, W. J. 63(k), 168(f)
Lee, R. & Co. Ltd 64(h)
Lee, Robert 164(d)
Lee, Sam War 116(b)
Leech, R. 121(e)
Leeks Cockroach Expeller 146(e)
Leeming, William 132(a), 143(a)
Leggo, H. M. & Co. 122(g)
Lemos cordials 106(f)
Leslie, W. 115(d)
Le Souef, Lancelot 72(g), 146(j)
Letchfords Aussie Cola 107(c)
Let's Advance Australia 29(l)
Lever Bros. Ltd 138(a)(d)(g)(i), 139(e)(f), 142(e)
Leviathan Clothing Co. 133(k)
Lewer, W. E. 27(c)
Lewisco Mfg. Co. 134(j)
Lewis, William 82(g)
Leyshon, L. L. 38(d)
Liberty batteries 86(c)
Lichtner Ltd 20(i)
Life. Be In It 151(b)
Life. Be out of it 151(c)
Life-Boat foods 116(c)
Life Guard chemicals 166(k)
Lifeguard cigarettes 162(e)
Light Aircraft Pty Ltd 56(a)
Lilydale Aerated Water Co. Pty Ltd 66(h)
Limbless Soldiers' Association of Victoria 32(h)
Link-on-Fish 43(i)
Lions Football team 154-155(d)
Lion rope 21(a)
Liquid Sunshine beer 99(c)
Lismore Co-op. Dairy Co. Ltd., The 97(i)
Lister's Dingo Trail 58(b)
Lithgow Valley Colliery Company 51(b)
Little, Robert & Co. 95(f) to (i)
Local Government seals and shields 171
Login Corporation Pty Ltd 36(o)
Lohmann & Co. 56(k)
Lohn, Richard 51(c)
Long & Smith 50(e)
Long's Cream Cracker 103(f)
Longmore, Francis & Co. 122(d)
Love, Clifford & Co. 101(e), 139(m)
Love, J. R. & Co. 102(c)
£.s.d. manure 77(d)
L.S.D. medicine 77(m)
Lubra, chemicals 46(b); lubricants 88(i)
Lucky Cat Confectionery Co., The 127(n)
Lufft, E. & Son Pty Ltd 23(ab)
Lukes Ltd 19(b)
Luke Wright Marine Industries Pty Ltd 73(f)
Luna Park, Sydney 151(a)
Lu-Pol stock feeds 36(a)
Lush, L. J. 106(g)
Lustro Mfg. Co. 142(h)
Lyre Bird, wines and spirits 59(c), 63(c); smallgoods 63(d); tobacco 63(e); flour 96(c); matches 147(l); footballs 153(i)
Lyton, F. E. 79(b)

Maatschappij, Handel 96(d)
McAlpin, J. & Sons 111(e)
McCann Bros. 157(e)
McCarthy, F. A. & Co. 57(j)
McCorquodale Bros. 112(g)
McCracken's Brewery Ltd 109(e)
Macrae Knitting Mills Ltd 135(b)
McDonald's Family Restaurants 173(k)
McEvoy, Henry 142(b)
McEvoy, John & Sons 55(c), 133(e)
McKay, John 97(n)
McKeever & Co. 98(g)
Mackenzie, E. 165(c)
McKenzie, William & Co. 37(e)
Mackintosh, John Ltd 175(h)
McLaws, L. & S. 99(d)
McLean, W. & Co. 26(g)
McLeod, N. 102(g)
McLeod Paterson, A. 142(j)
McLintock & Co. Pty Ltd 166(k)
McMahon, H. & Co. 22(d)
McMicking, G. N. & Co. 86(b)
McNabs oatmeal 115(b)
MacRobertson confectionery 62(b), 127(a)
Macrow, A. & Sons Pty Ltd 149(a)
Mac's Cyder & Fruit Juices Pty Ltd 107(e)
Mac's Famous Big Boy hamburgers 99(d)
McWilliam, J. J. & Sons 108(e)
Made in Australia from Australian cloth by Australian workmen for Australian people 27(a)
Mae Vest inflatable vests 36(m)
Magician corn cure 169(c)
Magnetic rabbit poison 72(f)
Magpie, flour 59(d); soap 63(g)(h); ink 80(i); yacca gum 94(a); matches 148(m); –s Football team 154-155(b); –s Rugby League team 156(l); cigarettes 162(a)
Mag-Pies Supreme pie shop 43(l)
Maisie Chocolate Co., The 56(o)
Malcom, N. H. 124(f)
Malin, G. 65(j)
Mallee, eye drops 25(f); fruit 65(b)
Malleys Ltd 56(u)
Malvern Star bicycles 87(i)
Mandrake Salve 166(i)
Manly-Warringah Rugby League 156(e)
Mann, C. E. 57(l)
Manning, William 76(a)
Mannion, Thomas James 146(g)
Manu flour 112(j)
Marchant & Co. 105(b)
Marconi, J. C. 167(e)
Marcy, Frank Leo 115(h)
Margaret Mildara 108(h)
Marine salt 117(f)
Marko branding oils 75(c)
Marlow, Julius Pty Ltd 132(i)
Marlow, M. A. M. 146(i)
Marmite Food Extract Co. Ltd, The 44(a)
Marney, Jessey 167(e)
Marrickville Margarine Ltd 116(h)
Marsden, T. G. 168(h)
Marshall & Co. 133(c)
Marshall, W. C. & Co. 73(a)
Martin & Co. 164(f)
Martin, E. F. 61(d)
Martin, John & Co. Ltd 36(g)
Master Ladies Hairdressers Association of N.S.W., The 141(l)
Master Ladies Hairdressers & Cosmeticians Association of Victoria, The 141(m)
Master Pictures 158(h)
Masudaya & Co. 148(d)
Mat-A-door mats 43(j)
Match, The matches 41(b)
Matejka, Einrich 173(i)
Mather, A. W. 86(c)
Matthews, John 85(a)
Mauri Bros. & Thompson 34(i)
Maurice & Connell 55(f)
Max Milking Machine Co., The 176(f)
Maxwell, A. E. 75(e)
Medi-Chocs laxative 168(i)
Melbourne Cup matches 148(n)
Melbourne Football Club 154-155(h)
Mellor, F. R. 47(e)
Melrose Hop Ale 40(g)
Meltonian (Australia) Pty Ltd 143(i)

Merino.
Silk & Textile Printers
Ltd, Sydney.
Woolprints; 1947.

Index

Mildura Settlers Club, Vic.; 1929.

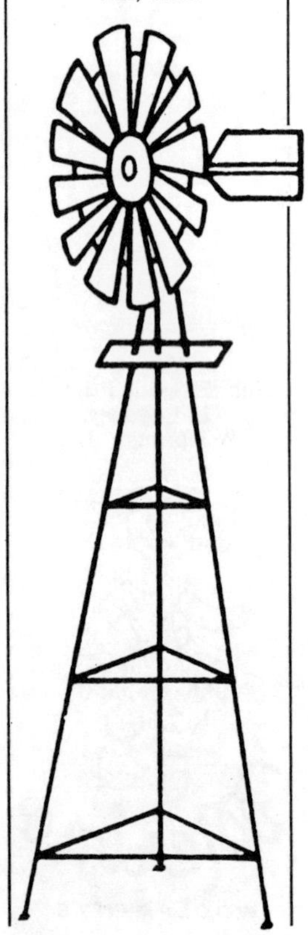

Mentho-Lyptus pastilles 66(i)
Menz, W. & Co. Ltd 38(b)
Mercedes 174(f)
Mermaid salt 117(c)
Merson's 'Wonder' cure for epilepsy 166(e)
Meters, Frank Samuel 133(d)
Metters Ltd 149(g)
Michelin Tyres 175(k)
Midson, J. J. 167(b)
Might Coote, J. & Co. 63(a)
Mia-mia 46(a)
M.I.A. wire products 84(j)
Mildura Fruit Preserving Co., The 65(b)
Mildura Winery Ltd 108(h)(i)
Milky Way polish 142(j)
Miller, C. & G. 152(g)
Miller's Feather Shop 50(a)
Mills Industries Ltd 21(c)
Millthorpe Butter & Bacon Co-op. Co. Ltd 98(i)
Milo 174(d)
Mincha butter 97(n)
Miniken, H. G. H. 105(j)
Minties 126(b)(c)
Miss Australia Club 23(f)
Mitchell & Co. Pty Ltd 77(e)
Mitchell, D. & Co. 114(a)
Mitchelson-Watson, J. A. 32(c)
Mitsui, Bussan, Kaisha Ltd 96(c), 111(h), 148(c)
M.L.A. Tube (tyres) 21(h)
Moa Sauce Co. 122(b)
Moffat, Hector 165(f)
Molasses Fodder 94(e)
Moline Plow Co. 176(l)
Monkey polish 142(e)
Montague de Ruisset, Alfred 143(d)
Montrose Wood Working Co. Pty Ltd 23(t)
Moo-Moon milk 120(e)
Moon clothing 133(e)
Moore, C. G. 85(d)
Moore, F. C. 77(m)
Moore, J. M. 34(c)
Moo-Vellous dairy products 36(x)
More Pork smallgoods 39(b)
Morlay Poultry Foods 76(b)
Morrows Ltd 52(f)
Mortein 145(a)
Moss, Mary Emily 74(a)
Motor Boat flour 96(f)
Motyer & Clement Pty Ltd 107(g)
Mrs B. Thrifty home bottling apparatus 44(h)
Mr Decay dental preparation 170(e)
Mr Peanut 128(i)
Muir, J. & T. 23(j)
Mulco 161(f)
Mulga butter and bacon 98(i)
Mulga Fred 129(a)
Mungo Scott Ltd 51(a), 112(h)
Municipal seals and shields 171
Muratti, B. Sons & Co. Ltd 176(a)
Murdochs in Park St. Pty Ltd 134(i)
Murphies confectionery 126(a)
Murphy, C. H. 21(h)
Murray Breweries Pty Ltd 106(b), 107(j)
Murray Bros. 133(a)
Murray, D. & W. Ltd 26(e), 60(f)
Murray, Thomas & Co. 133(f)
Murrumbidgee Co-op. Flour Milling Co. Ltd, The 112(b)
Mustdie insecticides 71(d)
Mutual, butter 98(h); tea 102(b)
Myatt, W. J. & Co. 177(d)
Myee butter 97(j)
Myer Emporium Ltd, The 25(k), 31(d), 36(r), 135(n), 141(i), 150(g), 170(c)
Myers Bros. & Ellis 36(c)
Myers & Co. 135(a)
Myers, F. E. & Bros. Co. 83(i)
Mylius Bros. – Eclipse Soap & Candle Co. 138(f)
Mylles, C. H. 36(p)
My, N. V. Handel 96(l)
Myon A Cigar Co. 25(e)

Nail-Pak 23(e)
Nance, Charles W. 46(a)
National Bank of Australasia Ltd, The 92(p)
National Cattle Food Co., The 77(b)
National Licorice Co. 50(j)
National Motor Car Mfg. Co. Ltd 61(b)
National Trustees Executors and Agency Co. of Australasia Ltd 19(a)
National Wire Products Pty Ltd 84(j)
Native Companions flour 51(a)
Native footballs 153(f)
Navy boot polish 143(e)
Neale, Constable & Co. Ltd 52(a)
Neptune barbed and fencing wire 77(c)
Neptune Oil Company 88(a)
Nestle, Henri 58(j), 174(d), 175(e)
Nettheim, K. S. & H. R. 134(h)
Neva-Rip clothing 135(f)
New South Wales Blinded Soldiers Tea Co., The 32(g)
New South Wales Rugby League 156(m)
New Zealand Pasture Implement Co. Pty Ltd 36(u)
New York Hamburger Gummi-Waarren Co. 177(f)
Newblades Ltd 127(m)
Newell, J. 97(l)
Newlands Bros. 150(a)
Newtown Rugby League 156(f)
Nicholas, Geo. R. & Co. 163(b)
Nicholls, F. C. 80(i)
Nicholson's Pty Ltd 157(h)
Nicoll, K. C. J. 23(y)
Nigger Boy licorice 50(j)
Nightingale, The Mop of Australia 42(g)
Niness, S. 132(e)
Nobbs, J. E. 84(e)
Nok-Out Mfg. Co. 145(h)
Nolyte eye shields 41(g)
Non-Tayr clothing 134(i)
Norco dairy produce 38(a)
North Coast Co-op. Co. Ltd, The 38(a), 97(j)
North Melbourne Football Club 154-155(i)
North Sydney Rugby League 156(g)
Notix sheep dip 70(j)
Novelta Textiles Pty Ltd 135(j)
Noveltie neckties 135(j)
Noxo Products Pty Ltd 71(g)
N.S.W. Aerated Water & Co. Ltd, The 105(c)
Nu Kik medicine 168(b)
Nubian Paint 50(c)
Nugget of the Southern Seas matches 148(i)
Nulla-nulla soap 47(c)
Num-Ba-Won toiletries 36(d)
Nursery condensed milk 120(a)
Nutting and Young 153(i)
Nutt & Jones 47(d)
Nuvarno Mfg. Co. 23(k)

Oakey Co-op. Dairy Co. Ltd 98(j)
O. B. clothing 134(h)
O'Brien, G. H. 39(a)
Occo soap 139(j)
Oceanic hose 23(h)
Oddy, W. 173(c)
Oertel, Charles 105(a)
Oh Boy flour 112(g)
Oil Sheep Dip Co., The 69(b), 75(c)
O.K., alcoholic drinks 20(c); jam 123(c)
O-Ke-Doke foods 36(e)
Old Everything timber 84(c)
Old Witch Salve Mfg. Co. 166(a)
Olitalia olive oil 36(t)
Olofone talking machines 21(d)
Olson, Olof Henry 21(d)
Olympic Tyre & Rubber Co. Pty Ltd 86(g)
Opossum fruit 57(e)
Orchardists' Chemical Works, The 57(i)
Orchard's clocks and watches 150(f)
Oriental Cigarette Co., The 161(b)
O'Riordan, M. & Sons 47(c)
Oriti, Vincenzo 56(aa)
Orlando Wines 108(c)
Orme, Keigwin & Co. 20(c)
Orna underwear 56(v)
Ornstien, Lewis 53(i)
Oros cordials 99(b)
O'Shea, J. A. 46(g)
O'Sullivan Bros. 116(j)
O.T. Limited 107(d)
Otway, A. E. 56(r)
Our Jack 165(e)
Our Wounded Hero foods 32(b)
Overell's Limited 153(k)
Overell, W. J. & Son Ltd 133(g)

Pabco Co. (Australia) Ltd 29(h)
Pacific Candy Co., The 128(a)
Pacific, footwear 20(a); boot polish 143(c)
Pacific Mfg. Co. Ltd 50(g), 65(h)
Pacific Tobacco Industries Australasia Ltd, The 162(b)(c)
Paddle footwear 132(c)
Palatine Mfg. Co. Pty Ltd, The 105(g)
Palmer's, Pink Powders 166(b); –Carrageen mixture 166(c)
Palmerston Dinner Ale 110(i)
Palm Ham 40(b)
Pals Pepmintum Chemical Co. 167(a)
Pannifex, H. C. & Co. 116(i)
Pannikin Blend tea 102(a)
Pansy butter 98(e)
Panthers Rugby League team 156(i)
Parisian Delicacies & Biscuit Co. 125(b)
Parkes & Gnosill Ltd 172(e)
Parramatta Rugby League 156(h)
Parramatta Tweed 133(a)
Parry & Co. 137(a)
Parson Bros. & Co. Pty Ltd 49(a), 115(a)(e)
Parsons' Starch 49(a)
Pasha coffee 101(e)
Pasho drink 36(b)
Passiona drink 106(e)
Patch rubber and gutta percha 82(h)
Patent Asphaltum Co. of N.S.W. 19(d)
Paterson & Co. Ltd 56(f), 66(b), 124(a)(h)
Paterson, Laing & Bruce Ltd 22(a), 56(b), 130(g)
Paterson, W. 64(a)
Pathfinder lubricants 88(h)
Payne's Ltd 66(i)
P. D. Magnetic Rabbit Poison Co., The 72(f)
Peach, H. 41(g)
Peanut Pete 128(b)
Peanut Twins 128(h)
Peapes & Co. Ltd 58(d)
Pearce, T. W. 31(a)
Pearladenta tooth paste 170(a)
Pears, A. & F. Ltd 174(j)
Pearson Soap Co. Pty Ltd 140(c)
Pear-Stroyer 78(b)
Peek, Frean & Co. Ltd 104(d)
Pegasus, veterinary remedies 74(b); oil 175(d)
Pelaco Ltd 129, 135(h)
Pelican tobacco 94(d)
Penguin Books 175(m)
Peninsula Co-op. Fruitgrowers Association Ltd 124(e)

Penrith Rugby League 156(i)
Pepmintum Chemical Co. 167(i)
Pep: the snappy little mag 160(h)
Peptomalt 114(d)
Perdriau Rubber Co. Ltd 52(g)
Pero Clothing Co. Pty Ltd 136(a)
Perry, J. 65(e), 87(g)
Pest-Ax insecticide 145(i)
Peter Panda insecticide 145(m)
Peter Pumpkin & Co. 123(h)
Peters Ice Cream 125(c)(h)
Phoebe Polish 142(c)
Phosphatum cattle medicine 74(h)
Pick-a-niny Freeze 125(a)
Piedagree footwear 36(g)
Piesse, F. & C. 115(f)
Pikedale Soldiers Settlement Co-op. Canning, Jam & Preserving Co. Ltd, The 32(e)
Pike, H. & Co. 107(a)
Pinke Zinke blockout 168(j)
Pinko eye powder 70(i)
Pioneer Handkerchief Co., The 134(c)
Pipe Hospital 161(i)
Pitt's poisoned wheat 146(b)
Planters Nut & Chocolate Co. 128(f)
Plant, W. & Co. Ltd 152(e)
Plasti Roo watch bands 36(l)
Platypus, floor cloth 57(g); eucalyptus oil 57(h); vermin destroyer 57(i); lubricants 57(j); foods 57(l); matches 147(k), 148(j)
Playford, H. 120(f)
Playing Cards flour 111(i)
Play-On football boots 153(c)
Plenty, G. J., Son & Co. 134(g)
Plonk insecticide 36(f)
Plymel 1914 Limited 47(a)
Polack Tyre & Rubber Co. Ltd, The 176(k)
Porcupine barbed wire 177(j)
Port Lincoln Fisheries Pty Ltd 43(i)
Porter, H. & Co. 130(h)
Possum, teats 42(h); alcoholic drinks 57(a); clothing and drapes 57(b); paper and stationery 57(d); paint 57(f)
Potmend cement 149(h)
Poultry Breeders Better Chick Association 76(d)
Poultry Humoss manure 22(l)
Powell, H. W. & C. Pty Ltd 146(f)
PPP Annihilator rabbit poison 72(a)
Puck combs 177(f)
Purabreth 170(f)
Pura Chemicals Pty Ltd 145(m)
Purcell, F. H. 77(l)
Pratt, E. M. 35(l)
Preservene candles and soap 138(e)
Preservol polish 56(z)
Preston Municipal Council 47(l)
Presto, rabbit poison 72(c); smallgoods 118(h)
Prettymiss frocks 136(f)
Price, A. S. & Co. 26(h)
Price Griffiths & Co. 34(d)
Prickly Pear Soap 78(c)
Prima Hosiery Pty Ltd 65(i)
Prince of WA ALES, The 43(a)
Pringle Stewart, A. 26(f)
Pritchard, R. R. 145(g)
Producers' Co-op. Distributing Society Ltd, The 76(f), 117(j)
Prosser, J. & Son 109(h)
Proud Bros. Pty Ltd 88(i)
Pyramid Girl footwear 132(d)
Pyramid Hill Butter & Cheese Factory 98(d)
Pyramints sweets 42(j)
Python, hooks and chains 82(d); machinery 84(f)

Qantas Airways 90
Quaker cereals 174(c)
Queensland Country Traders Ltd 123(l)
Queensland Preserves Ltd 41(l)
Quencher beverages 106(a)
Quick Lay stock feeds 36(i)
Quick Maid foods 44(g)
Qu-Rup salve 41(h)

Rabbit & Bacon Pie 73(d)
Rabbito rabbits 73(c)
Rabbitohs Rugby League team 156(j)
Rabbit, tea 41(j); flour 73(g)
Racer sporting goods 152(d)
Radam, W. 176(i)
Radio radiator cleanser 86(b)
Railroad flour 96(g)
Ram matches 148(a)
Ramsay, W. 144(a)
Ransom, P. L. 152(b)
Rat-Menu anti vermin 36(j)
Realest Pty Ltd 47(h)
Red Gum Pack apples 66(b)
Redheads matches 147(a)(e)
Reed Tobacco Co. 173(h)
Reel candles and soap 140(b)
Regan Palace Roller Flour Mills Ltd, The 112(c)
Reid, John 117(h)
Reid, Robert & Co. 25(a)
Remfry, F. 111(d)
René Henry 141(k)
Renmark Fruit Growers Co-op. Ltd, The 124(c)
Re-Nu rubber repair 87(j)
Repco Ltd 86(l)
Repin, Ivan 102(i)
Restinese furniture 150(g)
Resch's Waverley Brewery 99(c)
Returned Services League of Australia, The 32(i)
Revolver butter 98(k)
Rhino fertilizers 75(f)
Richards Bros. 59(d)
Richards, M. & Co. 34(b)
Richmond Football Club 154-155(j)
Rich, Pearl 82(b)
Rickards, C. A. Ltd 172(h)
Right-o confectionery 127(k)
Ringer machinery 37(a)
Rinso washing powder 138(i)
Ripa ripening systems 35(j)
River Murray Milling Co. Ltd, The 96(g)
Robertson, E. C. & Co. 36(a)
Robertson & Young Ltd 50(f)
Robur tea 101(a)
Rogerstone Supply Co. 25(i)
Romalo wines 108(d)
Ronatip oils 88(g)
Rondon shoes 132(h)
Roo Beauty apples 56(f)
Roo, Motors 56(q); boot polish 143(g)
Roofcool paint 85(e)
Rooide footwear 55(c)
Roope, H. M. 137(b)
Roosters Rugby League team 156(d)
Roseen cure 166(d)
Rosella Preserving Co. Ltd, The 64(g), 121
Rosenfeld & Co. 62(i)
Rowan, J. X. 148(n)
Royal Aero Club of N.S.W., The 90(a)
Royal Flush cisterns 43(d)
Rubber Adhesives Pty Ltd 80(e)
Rubbagrip adhesives 80(e)
Rubens, N. A. & Co. 157(b)
Rucker & Mackenzie 72(a)
Rumsey-Williams, W. 146(e)
Rundel & McMillan 37(a)
Russel Export Agency Pty Ltd 117(i)
Russell, G. J. & Son Pty Ltd 43(e)
Ryan, H. F. 168(d)
Ryland Bros. (Australia) Ltd 64(i)
Rypens, Gustave 20(b)

S.A. Black Boy Products Ltd 64(c)
Sackville, John Pty Ltd 35(a)
Sage, A. J. & Co. 56(i)
Saints Football team 154-155(k)
Salisbury Travel Goods Co. 53(j), 55(j)
Salkeld, H. W. & Co. 66(e)
Salpak Pty Ltd 117(k)
Saltau, H. & Sons 54(d)
Sambo foods 50(f)
Sanderson, John & Co. 74(f)
Sandford, Roy W. Ltd 86(a)
Sans Equa polish 56(x)
Santa Claus games and sporting articles 152(a)
S.A.P. rabbit poison 72(d)
Sargood Bros. 133(h), 134(b)
Sargood Gardiner Ltd 48(j)
Satanic perfumery 141(j)
Saturn soap 139(f)
Sausagina meat and preservatives 118(e)
Savaday washing machines 150(e)
Sayers, Allport Pty Ltd 71(e), 72(d)
Sayso biscuits 41(a)
Scales, N. G. 128(e)
Scammell, E. A. 71(a)
Scharff, Justus 94(d)
Schiesser, Jacques 176(e)
Schnapper foods 117(h)
Schoefield Preston & Co. Ltd 177(e)
Schramm & Co. Ltd 105(d)
Schroeder, F. P. H. 161(d)
Schuh, J. J. Tobacco Co. Pty Ltd 162(a)
Scientific Garden Utility Co., The 75(d)
Scotch oatmeal 115(a)
Scougall's 'Uwanta' cattle medicine 74(c)
Sea Eagles Rugby League team 156(e)
Senior Gut Mfg. Co. Ltd 152(f)
Sennitt's Ice Cream 125(e)
Shake-o salt 117(d)
Shampuna hair tonic 165(h)
Shand, Geo. F. 110(g)
Sharkol oil 117(j)
Sharks Rugby League team 156(c)
Sharpe Bros. 105(e)
Shearwool underwear 133(h)
Sheer perfumery 141(i)
Sheldon Drug Co. Ltd 141(g)
Shell butter 97(m)
Shell Transport & Trading Co., The 174(g)
Shepparton and District Co-op. Butter, Cheese and Ice Factory Co. Ltd, The 98(b)
Sherington Co., The 56(x)
Sherrin, T. W. 153(d)
Shirley, G. Ltd 77(d)
Shoe-R Cure liniment 42(c)
Shooboudge, S. E. 56(g)
Shrimpton, G. & Sons 130(c)
Shyne Mfg. Co. 144(x)
Sidney Brown & Co. Pty Ltd 122(i)
Silex Weed Destroyer 71(b)
Silver Eye flour 95(g)
Silvers, Eric 128(d)
Silver's Woorayl medicine 46(d)
Silver Wattle butter 64(d)
Simmons, Mick 23(w), 152(d)
Simons Leather Goods Co., The 36(l)
Simple Simon polish 142(g)
Simpson, A. A. 63(b)
Simpson, A. & Son 53(e)
Simpson Hain (1940) Pty Ltd 35(k)
Sims Bros. 97(f)
Sinclair Weaving Co. Ltd, The 23(o)
Singer Sewing Machines 174(a)

S.O.S.
T. E. Wade, Melbourne.
Chemicals for human use;
1918.

Index

Singleton Central Co-op. Dairy Co. Ltd 97(p)
Skillen & Walker 97(c)
Skipping Girl vinegar 122(f)
Slee, C. E. 95(b)
Sleigh, H. C. 89(a), 168(i)
Slick products 23(z), 142(k)
Slug-Em 146(i)
Slug-Go 146(g)
Small, Bruce Pty Ltd 87(i)
Smiling Feet 169(e)
Smokettes tobacco 35(f)
Smokogas rabbit poison 72(h)
Smith, F. E. 33(b)
Smith, Henry B. 168(a)
Smith, Mitchell & Co. 114(d)
Smith, Oliver 70(j)
Smith's Weekly 160(e)
S. N. Boot, The 132(e)
Snap tobacco 161(h)
Sniders & Abrahams Ltd 63(e)
Snowcap flour 96(j)
Snow Drop butter 97(q)
Sno-Man Serv-ice refrigerators 150(d)
Soap Works, The 55(a)
Soccer apples 124(a)
Solar Salt Ltd 117(f)
Solomon, David & Sons Ltd 135(e)
Solvento pesticide 146(c)
Solvol soap 139(h)
Sootha-Pain 168(h)
S.O.S. Chemical Co. 70(e)
Soren Skifter 177(k)
Southern Australian Portable Outfitting Co. 134(f)
Southern Cross, paints 30(a); woollen goods 30(d); information and press agency 30(f); matches 148(h); shearing machines 172(b)
Southern Cross Petroleum 89(f)
South Melbourne Football Club 154-155(l)
South Sydney Rugby League 156(j)
Sovereign Pictures 158(e)
Sparkling Wine boot polish 144(v)
Spark-o polish 22(g)
Spear Point tacks 23(x)
Specialised Heels Ltd 132(j)
Speed King bicycles 87(e)
Speede bathing and athletic costumes 135(b)
Spicer, James & Sons 56(h)
Spiderite consumption cure 164(e)
Spitfire blowlamps 84(l)
Spitzel, Aaron 54(b)
Spud's Potato Products 116(k)
Stanco (Australia) Pty Ltd 145(k)
Standard Double Stout 110(a)
Standard Oil Co. 175(d)
Standard Shoe & Leather Co., The 20(a)
Stang nerve pills 165(c)
Stanmare Mfg. Co. 139(g)
Starlight soap 138(a)
State Savings Bank of Victoria 92(h)
Stedman, James – Henderson's Sweets 126
Steam Rollers 127(g)
Steelbilt furniture 84(k)
Steele & Baker 95(j)
Steele, J. S. 145(f)
Stephens, R. 123(k)
Sterling Soap & Candle Co. Pty Ltd, The 35(c)
Stewart, C. A. 83(b)
St George Rugby League 156(k)
Stiffitis Ltd 167(d)
Stilbetta furniture and upholstery 150(i)
Stinton & Son 61(e)
St Kilda Football Club 154-155(k)
Stockman ointments 37(f)
Stockrider eucalyptus oil 37(d)
Stokes & Sons 48(e)
Stokvis, William 39(b)
Stormlight soaps 138(d)
Storpedo containers 43(h)
Stratton & Co. Pty Ltd 112(a)
Strauss, Levi & Co. 175(i)
Streemlyne side-car body 86(e)
Strength adhesive 80(b)
Strip Teasies sausage casings 36(o)
Stuart, Walker & Co. Ltd 93(d)
Stubbs, Walter 42(i)
Styx Malayan Mucilage 80(h)
Sullivan, J. J. Ltd 111(j)
Summers, George 56(j)
Summit battery 86(i)
Sun Chemical Corporation 177(i)
Sun News Pictorial, The 160(f)
Sun, powder for horses 74(i); paints 85(c); tea 102(d)
Sunbeams wool 20(b)
Sunbeem honey 123(j)
Sundowner jams 37(h)
Sunfed fruit 124(e)
Sunny Bill paints 85(i)
Sunnyvale Orchard 23(a)
Superior Dandelion Ale 109(a)
Super Speed 23(w)
Surefit clothing 55(f)
Sureflush Cistern Co. Ltd 43(d)
Surf 116(i)
Surfrider Suntan 168(k)
Surize baking powder 22(c)
Su-Tall soap 139(c)
Sutherland Smith, G. & Sons 59(c)
Swagman tents and ropes 37(e)
Swallow & Ariell 103(a), 104(e), 125(g)
Swamp corn cure 169(d)
Swan Brewery Co. Ltd, The 43(a), 110(h)
Swan, J. H. 70(h)
Swan white lead 94(f)
Swann disinfectants 21(g)
Swans Football club 154-155(l)
Swanton, G. H. & Co. Pty Ltd 96(j)
Swastic medicine 165(f)
Sweeter Song bird food 76(f)
Sweethearts Joy nuts 22(e)
Swift flour 111(c)
Syddo cloths 173(c)
Sydney Paper Mills Ltd, The 65(c)
Sydney Soap & Candle Co. Ltd, The 82(c)
Sydney Sports Stores 152(j)
(Sydney) Town Hall tapes 25(a)

TAA 91
Table butter and dripping 120(b)
Taffelshone Pty Ltd 57(f)
Tamar Valley Co-op. Ltd, The 58(g)
Tango 161(f)
Tank flour 112(a)
Taraxale Brewing Co. 107(h)
Taronga Zoo 51(e)
Tarzan's Grip cement 80(f)
Tasmanian Eucalyptus Oil Co. Ltd, The 57(h)
Tasmanian Jam & Preserved Fruit Co. 123(a)
Taubmans' 85(b)
Taxi flour 113(g)
Taylor, R. S. 26(j)
Taylors & Elliotts Ltd 141(a)
T.B.F. - The Baker's Friend yeast 114(c)
Tecnico Limited 150(l)
Teddy Bear biscuits 104(d)(e)
Teddy Beer 42(a)
Teds Peanuts 128(i)
Telephone flour 96(l)
Telephone Rentals Ltd 31(e)
Tenaxene 85(a)
Tenterfield Co-op. Butter Factory Co. Ltd 98(e)
Teslaconi 166(g)
Tex Turkey Farm 120(i)
The one star of the Southern Cross for footwear 132(b)
The straw without a flaw for hats 130(a)
The test of our shirts is in the wash tub 134(a)
Thomas, A. J. & Co. 57(d)
Thomas, F. W. 158(d)
Thomas, S. & Co. 111(a)
Thomas, W. & Co. (W.A.) Ltd 36(i)
Thompson, A. G. 60(d)
Thompson, J. R. & Co. 172(g)
Thompson, Thomas & Co. 120(b)
Thomson, Frederick 43(b)
Thomson, H. 106(i)
Thomson, M. & A. 35(i)
Thorn Brothers 30(a)
Thorp's Walnut Whipped Creams 42(b)
Three A's cigarettes 162(b)
3 Koalas records 53(i)
Thrills and Tingles confectionery 127(m)
Throaties 126(e)
Thurlstane (Australia) Pty Ltd 53(c), 56(c)
Tiefenbeck, J. I. 138(j)
Tiger Tim clothing 135(i)
Tigers Football club 154-155(j)
Tigers for the throat 168(c)
Tigers Rugby League team 156(a)
Tilley, A. 140(e)
Timid Joe dog soap 140(e)
Ti-Tree butter and cheese 66(f)
Tjap Semar flour 95(i)
Tolley, A. E. & S. 28(i)
Tom Piper canned foods 122(i)
Tommy Swallow 125(g)
Tootgarook Estate Pty Ltd, The 77(f)
Tooth & Co. Ltd 109(k)
Top Note Mixture canary seed 76(e)
Top tents, tarpaulins, blinds 94(h)
Toppy Toppa ice cream 125(f)
Torfol disinfectant 138(c)
Torpedo veterinary medicine 74(e)
Toucan flour 113(b)
Town Hall (Sydney) tapes 25(a)
Toyala toys 66(d)
Traders Ltd 123(e)
Tradesman clothing 135(g)
Trafalgar 161(g)
Trans-Australia Airlines 91
Trevena, Thomas 130(b)
Treybon tea 31(b)
Triggs, A. 41(a)
Triplets candles and soap 139(a)
Tropical Traders 55(h)
Trouchet, A. 169(a)
True Blue candles and soap 35(b)
T-Shoo paper 35(k)
Tucker Box Dog & Cat Food Co., The 25(j)
Tuff Tips for shoes 144(y)
Tug of War clothing 134(b)
Tui timber 82(i)
Tummies (Tum-Ease) 168(e)
Tuomy & Co. 57(a), 58(c)
Turf cigarettes 162(h)
Turner, F. A. 48(a)(g)
Turner & Henderson Ltd 63(f)
Twentieth Century tooth brushes 170(c)
20 Mule Team Brand 177(a)
Twin Elephants flour 96(k)
Twin Tie 135(a)

Ulladulla Refrigerating Butter Co. Ltd, The 97(e)
Umbrella foods 116(e)
Umbreakable Disc Records Ltd 157(g)
Uncle Osbro smallgoods 116(j)

Surfo Girl. Murdoch's in Park St. Pty Ltd, Sydney. Swimming costumes; 1928.

Union Bag & Paper Co., The 173(e)
Union foods 28(h)
Union Stores Ltd, The 23(l)
Union Theatres Ltd 158(c)
United Australian Blend tea 28(c)
United Australian Tea Co. 46(f)
United Distributing Companies Ltd 74(g), 139(d)
United Felt Hats Pty Ltd 130(d)
United Fruit Co. 124(k)
United Metal Industries Ltd 149(f)
United Service foods 32(c)
United paints 85(f)
United States of Australasia Mfg. Works 83(d)
United Vendors Pty Ltd 120(e)
U-no foot powder 169(f)
Ute wheelbarrows 36(q)

Vagg, George John 97(r)
Valentine's Restaurant 120(h)
Van Cooth & Co. 93(c)
Veall, A. J. Pty Ltd 150(e)
Vegemite 44(b), 99(e)
Velvet, soap 138(b); shaving stick 140(h)
Vere Le Roi Stokoe 35(f)
Verney, R. C. & Sons 122(a)
Vetch & Stokvis 118(a)
Veterinary Remedy Co., The 75(a)
Victor flour 47(k)
Victoria District Co-op. Flour Milling Ltd 112(e)
Victorian Central Citrus Association 56(t)
Victorian Football League, The 155(m)
Victorian Hardwood Milling & Seasoning Co. Pty Ltd, The 82(i)
Vincent's powders and tablets 163(d)
Vinegar Co. of Australia, The 122(f)
Virite Co. Ltd, The 23(g)
Vita Foods Supply Co. Pty Ltd 128(b)
Vital 'V' shirts 135(h)
Vitamite agricultural chemicals 21(e)
Vita-Seald 115(h)
V.O.A. Sound Productions Film House 55(i)
Voice of Australia, The 55(i)
Volkswagen Australia 172(k)
V & S tomato sauce 122(a)
Vulcan iron and steel 94(c)

W.A. Brushware Co. 56(m)
W.A. Match Co., The 148(p)
Wacker 38(f)
Wagga Lily flour 112(b)
Wagon-Lit mattresses 150(h)
Wagstaff, J. H. 75(g)
Waites, A. S. M. 168(e)
Walkabout footwear 132(g)
Walker, Fred & Co. 44(b), 116(e)
Walker, H. G. 142(a)
Wallaby eucalyptus oil 168(a)
Wallace, Hirst & Co. 30(i)
Wallaroo Phosphate Co. Ltd 74(j)
Walla Walla leather 54(c)
Waller, F. A. & Co. 96(e)
Wallworth & Co. 28(e)
Walters, Florence 145(c)
Walton, F. S. & Co. 135(i)
Walton, J. 127(k)
Wambidgee lime 25(g)
Waratah, preserves 64(g); paints and stains 64(h); wire netting and nails 64(i); –Motor Spirit 88(b)
Ward Bros. 20(f), 149(b)
Ward, C. G. 42(e)
Wardle, J. & Co. 65(f), 88(h)
Warren Tea Co. Ltd, The 41(j), 102(f)
Warrigal clothing 58(d)
Watson, A. E. 76(c)
Watson Co., The 176(h)
Watson, G. 145(i)
Wattle cigarettes 161(b)
Wattle Preserving Co. 122(c)
Wattle Tree tomato sauce 122(c)
Webb Bros. Pty Ltd 22(i)
Webb & Webb 20(j)
Webster, A. C. 139(l)
Webster & Co. 130(e)
Week-End foods 116(f)
Welcome Nugget tobacco 172(i)
Welcome to a good town for perfumery 141(g)
Welsbach Light Co. of Australia Ltd, The 176(j)
Wertheim, Hugo 27(b), 87(d), 157(f)
Westend Creamery Co-op. Co. Ltd, The 97(g)
Western Suburbs Rugby League 156(l)
Westral flour 24(d)
Westralia footballs 153(j)
Westralian Farmers Ltd, The 94(g)
Westwater Crayfish 117(i)
Whacco Pty Ltd 45(b)
Wheeler tyre compound 87(f)
Whiffen, C. F. 56(s)
While we live we'll grow 133(g)
White, A. F. & P. 143(g)
White Australia, pineapples 49(c); publications 49(f)
White Crow 122(d)
White Eyes confectionery 127(h)
White Frog fungicide 71(c)
White, George 35(g)
Whitehead, R. G. 80(f)
White, R. Pty Ltd 132(g)
White Way cleanser 47(d)
Whitmont, E. E. 129(e), 136(d)
Whoop-Whoop flour 96(h)
Whybrow & Co. 25(c)
Widdis Diamond Dry Cell Pty Ltd 86(f)
Wiggins, T. H. 37(f)
Wilkinson, L. T. 23(z), 142(k)
Wilks, E. F. & Co. Ltd 157(d)
Wiley, A. J. 47(f)
Wilga Productions Pty Ltd 135(k)
Williams, E. S. 28(f)
Williams, H. J. 141(h)
Williams, T. C. Co. 172(i)
Williams Trading Co. 140(b)
Williams, Z. E. 80(c), 169(d)
Williamson-Page 86(e)
Wills, George & Co. 93(e), 94(i)(j)
Wilmoth, John Victor 86(d)
Wilson, Arthur G. Ltd 77(g)
Wilson, James 70(c)
Wilson, W. 42(c)
Wiltshire's Pty Ltd 142(i)
Windmill flour 96(e)
Winkin & Blinkin clothing 53(f)
Wirth Laboratory 170(g)
Witch candles and soap 139(b)
Wolfe, R. B. 170(d)
Wolseley Sheep Shearing Machine Co. Ltd, The 172(b)
Wolverhampton Corrugated Iron Co. Ltd 172(f)
Wombat Boot Mfg. Co. Ltd, The 58(h)
Wombat, flour 58(f); fruit 58(g); –94(i)
Womerah 46(g)
Wonder insecticide 176(h)
Wonga butter 97(i)
Wonthaggi Butter Factory 98(c)
Wood & Co. 165(b)
Wood, G. Son & Co. 123(i)
Woods & Co. 46(b)
Woomera musical instruments 46(i)
Woo, Nam Sang 147(k)
WoolRuss clothing 43(e)
Wool Textile Manufacturers of Australia, The 22(m)
Wormald Bros. Pty Ltd 84(k)
Worregil rabbits and hares 73(b)
Wright's pianos 157(c)
Wright Varnish Co. 56(d)
Write to PA about it! for clothing 134(k)

XL Petroleum 88(j)
X-Press Tyre Services Pty Ltd 86(h)
XXXX (Fourex) Bitter Ale 110(c)

Yalooka butter 98(b)
Yankee Mfg. Co. 142(d)
Yarmouth oil clothing 133(b)
Yarraman tea 46(f)
Yates, Arthur & Co. 76(e)
Yet Ting Quoy, G. 22(e)
Yinnar Cream & Butter Factory 97(b)
York Flour Milling Co. Ltd 58(i)
Yorick bacon and hams 118(a)
YO-T tea 43(b)
You Cure 165(b)
Yonga oranges 124(f)
Young District Producers' Co-op. Association, The 31(c)
Young, R. B. 76(b)
Your Hat Sir! 130(d)
Yung, Shollenberger & Co. 54(c)

Zair, G. & J. 173(b)
Zam-Buk ointment, and soap 38(c)
Zanic 58(k)
Zebra coffee 102(f)
Zee-Nut 128(a)
Zenith paints 85(g)
Zig and Zag ice cream 125(h)
Zulu boot polish 50(g)

Westral.
The W.A. Traders
Co-op. Co.
Grocers; 1907.

THE SEARCH CONTINUES . . .

Our search for Australian trademarks has not ceased with the publication of this book. Not only are we still seeking additional information to upgrade any future editions of this volume, but work has commenced on a second volume to cover contemporary Australian designs from 1960 until the present. If you have commissioned or designed any kind of trademark, we would be pleased to hear from you. There are forms provided on page 192 for this purpose.
All material will be acknowledged and appreciated.

(a) The Film House Pty Ltd.
Film production, Melbourne.
Symbol by Alex Stitt; 1964.
(b) Baker Institute.
Medical research unit; Melbourne.
Logo by Garry Emery; 1967.
(c) (d) Dulux Australia Limited.
Domestic and industrial paints.
Logo by Huveneers Pty Ltd; 1970.
(e) Centrepoint.
Shopping centre, Sydney.
Symbol by Emery, Fowler-Brown, Sadgrove & Whaite Pty Ltd; 1971.
(f) Australian Conservation Foundation.
Symbol by Cato Hibberd Design Pty Ltd; 1972.
(g) Alvin Purple.
A feature film by Hexagon Productions.
Logo by Alex Stitt; 1972.
(h) Melbourne Chamber Orchestra, Paul Coppens, director.
Symbol by Con Aslanis; 1973.
(i) Collie & Co. Pty Ltd.
Printing inks.
Symbol by Cato Hibberd Design Pty Ltd; 1976.
(j) Australia Post.
Symbol by Huveneers Pty Ltd; 1976.
(k) Westside Film Society, Melbourne.
Symbol by Flett Henderson & Arnold; 1977.
(l) The Londoner Hotel, Melbourne.
Symbol by Alex Stitt; 1977.
(m) Landmark Builders Pty Ltd, Melbourne.
Symbol by Brian Sadgrove; 1978.

The Search Continues . . .

(a) Summer Wine. Commercial Bureau (Australia) Pty Ltd. Symbol by Brian Sadgrove; 1979.

(b) Cleanaway. Division of Brambles Holdings Ltd. Collection and disposal of industrial and domestic waste. Symbol by Huveneers Pty Ltd; 1979.

(c) Jam Factory. Shopping centre, Melbourne. Logo by Les Mason; 1979.

(d) The Queensberry Mint. Designers, casters and marketers of precious metal objects, Melbourne. Symbol by Flett Henderson & Arnold; 1980.

(e) Circus Oz. Alternate circus troupe. Logo by Bill Burrows, St John Lawrence Burrows; 1980.

(f) Upstairs at the Last Laugh. Cabaret owned and managed by J. Pinder and R. Evans, Melbourne. Logo by Steve Malpass, St John Lawrence Burrows; 1980.

(g) Owen King. Quality colour printer, Melbourne. Symbol by Garry Emery; 1980.

(h) Grendel. Animated feature film. Animation Australia Pty Ltd. Logo by Alex Stitt; 1980.

(i) Handcrafts of Australia. Alan and Barbara Marshall, Melbourne. Symbol by Alan Marshall; 1980.

(j) Victorian Arts Centre, Melbourne. Symbol by Cato Hibberd Design Pty Ltd; 1980.

(k) Kangarucci. Maarten Ustra Pty Ltd, casual clothing, Sydney. Logo by Tony Ward; 1980.

(l) Australian Design Award. Industrial Design Council of Australia. Symbol by Brian Sadgrove; 1973.

CALL FOR ENTRIES.

With the publication of this book our search for Australian trademarks has not ceased. Not only are we still seeking additional information to upgrade any future editions of this volume, but work has commenced on a second volume to cover contemporary Australian designs from 1960 until the present. If you have commissioned or designed a trademark, symbol, logo, emblem or complete corporate identity suitable for inclusion in such a volume we would be pleased to hear from you. All material will be acknowledged and appreciated.
Address all correspondence to:

The Search for
Australian Trademarks,
Mimmo Cozzolino,
PO Box 116 Coburg Vic. 3058.

THE SEARCH CONTINUES . . .

The Search for
Australian Trademarks,
Mimmo Cozzolino,
PO Box 116 Coburg Vic. 3058

Quality bromide (or clipping)
Do not mount; attach lightly with tape

Please type or print clearly

Trademark identification — Year in which mark was introduced

Name and address of sponsor of mark

Service or product for which mark was/is used

Name and address of designer/group

Name and signature of person submitting material

From *Symbols of Australia*, Mimmo Cozzolino. Simultaneously published by Penguin Books and Cozbook

THE SEARCH CONTINUES . . .

The Search for
Australian Trademarks,
Mimmo Cozzolino,
PO Box 116 Coburg Vic. 3058

Quality bromide (or clipping)
Do not mount; attach lightly with tape

Please type or print clearly

Trademark identification — Year in which mark was introduced

Name and address of sponsor of mark

Service or product for which mark was/is used

Name and address of designer/group

Name and signature of person submitting material

From *Symbols of Australia*, Mimmo Cozzolino. Simultaneously published by Penguin Books and Cozbook

PHOTOSTAT FOR EXTRA COPIES